# LEARNING TO CURSE

*Essays in
Early Modern
Culture*

## STEPHEN J. GREENBLATT

ROUTLEDGE
New York • London

To Martin Price and Alvin B. Kernan

First published in 1990

Paperback published in 1992 by

Routledge, an imprint of
Routledge, Chapman and Hall, Inc.
29 West 35th Street
New York, NY 10001

Published in Great Britain by

Routledge
11 New Fetter Lane
London EC4P 4EE

**Library of Congress Cataloging in Publication Data**

Greenblatt, Stephen Jay.
   Learning to curse : essays in early modern culture / Stephen
Greenblatt.
     p.  cm.
   Includes bibliographical references.
   ISBN 0-415-90173-1; ISBN 0-415-90174-X (pb)
   1. English literature—Early modern, 1500–1700—History and
criticism. 2. Great Britain—Civilization—16th century.
3. Renaissance. I. Title.
PR413.G74  1990
820.9′003—dc20

**British Library Cataloguing in Publication Data**

Greenblatt, Stephen J. (Stephen Jay)
   Learning to curse : essays in early modern culture.
   1. Culture
   I. Title
   306

   ISBN 0-415-90173-1
   ISBN 0-415-90174-X (pb)

# CONTENTS

# Acknowledgments

"Learning to Curse: Aspects of Linguistic Colonialism in the Sixteenth Century," in *First Images of America: The Impact of the New World on the Old*, ed. Fredi Chiappelli (Berkeley: University of California Press, 1976), pp. 561–580.

"Marlowe, Marx, and Anti-Semitism," in *Critical Inquiry* 5 (1978), pp. 291–307.

"Filthy Rites," in *Daedalus* 111 (1982), pp. 1–16.

"The Cultivation of Anxiety: King Lear and His Heirs," *Raritan* 2 (1982), pp. 92–124.

"Murdering Peasants: Status, Genre, and the Representation of Rebellion," in *Representations* 1 (1983), pp. 1–29.

"Psychoanalysis and Renaissance Culture," in *Literary Theory/Renaissance Texts*, ed. Patricia Parker and David Quint (Baltimore and London: Johns Hopkins University Press, 1986), pp. 210–224.

"Towards a Poetics of Culture," in *Southern Review* 20 (1987), pp. 3–15. A slightly different version of this essay appears as "Capitalist Culture and the Circulatory System," in *The Aims of Representation: Subject/Text/History*, ed. Murray Krieger (New York: Columbia University Press, 1987), pp. 257–73.

"Resonance and Wonder," in *Bulletin of the American Academy of Arts and Sciences* 43 (1990), pp. 11–34. Also in *Literary Theory Today*, ed. Peter Collier and Helga Geyer-Ryan (Cambridge: Polity Press, 1990), pp. 74–90.

Fulbright Scholar at Cambridge where, relieved from my undergraduate grade anxieties, I read and attended lectures in an omniverous but almost entirely undisciplined way. I had been struck by what seemed to me the uncanny modernity of Sir Walter Ralegh's poetry (which at that time meant that certain passages reminded me of "The Wasteland"), and I had been equally struck by what seemed to me the intellectual power and moral authority of one of my teachers, Raymond Williams. Marxist literary criticism had received short shrift in my undergraduate years at Yale. *Literary Criticism: A Short History*, by Wimsatt and Cleanth Brooks, devoted a grand total of 6 out of its 755 pages, to Marxist thought; "Marxism and the forms of social criticism more closely related to it," they wrote, "have never had any real concern with literature and literary problems." Small wonder then that the Marxist critic, "in all the severity of his logic, should have driven this method . . . to a conclusion that completely destroys the literary viewpoint." Marxism in short was not only historically uninterested in literature but programmatically incapable of understanding the concrete universal and hence of understanding art: "In the crudity both of its determinism and of its inconsistent propagandism, the socio-realistic tradition of literary criticism has on the whole contributed little to an understanding of the relation which universality bears to individuality in artistic expression."[1] I was not at all prepared then for the critical subtlety and theoretical intelligence of Raymond Williams. In Williams's lectures all that had been carefully excluded from the literary criticism in which I had been trained— who controlled access to the printing press, who owned the land and the factories, whose voices were being repressed as well as represented in literary texts, what social strategies were being served by the aesthetic values we constructed—came pressing back in upon the act of interpretation. Back in the United States I thought I could combine my fascination with Ralegh and the influence of Williams by undertaking a dissertation on the functions of writing in Ralegh's career.

I took my proposal to a very brilliant younger professor at Yale; he read it, looked up, and said, "If you want to do *that* kind of thing, why don't you do a scholarly edition of one of Ralegh's minor works?" I am certain that I was not mistaking the note of contempt I heard in that suggestion. It has taken the remarkable work of Stephen Orgel, Jerome McGann, and others during the past decade to enable me to see that what is at stake in editing texts is precisely the range of questions I most wished to ask. But at the time, I only heard dismissal—a sentence of exile to the hydroelectric plant in Ulan Bator. To my good fortune, I found someone else who was sufficiently interested in my project, and trusted me enough, to supervise the dissertation.

I recount this personal history precisely because it is not entirely personal—I was participating in a more general tendency, a shift away from a criticism centered on "verbal icons" toward a criticism centered on cultural artifacts. In my early years of teaching, I thought of this shift as a turn to Marxist aesthetics; more recently, in the wake of an interest in anthropology and post-structuralism, I have called what I do "cultural poetics" or "new historicism." The essays collected in this volume trace the uneven evolution of my critical methods and interests. But I am reluctant to confer upon any of these rubrics the air of doctrine or to claim that each marks out a quite distinct and well-bounded territory. To a considerable extent, in American universities critical affiliations like new historicism or deconstruction or now even Marxism are not linked to systematic thought. (They are like our political parties, confusing to Europeans because they are important but ideologically evasive and inconsistent.) It is possible in the United States to describe oneself and be perceived as a Marxist literary critic without believing in the class struggle as the principal motor force in history; without believing in the theory of surplus value; without believing in the determining power of economic base over ideological superstructure; without believing in the inevitability, let alone the imminence, of capitalism's collapse. Back in the 1970s, at a hotel in Morocco, a genial, gray-haired tourist from Hawaii offered me a shopping bag filled with marijuana that he didn't want to take across the border when he left the country the next morning. He was on his way, he said, to Mecca "to have a look around." When I expressed doubt that he, a non-Moslem, would be permitted to visit Mecca, he replied, "Hey man, we're all Moslems." Americans in general like porous borders; they think that access (at least for themselves) should be easy.

Does this mean that new historicism is a completely empty term, its relative success due entirely to the felicitous conjunction of two marketable signs: "new" and "ism"? I think not, though it will not do to exaggerate its coherence (nor am I overly sympathetic to calls for its systematization). For me it describes less a set of beliefs than the trajectory I have begun to sketch, a trajectory that led from American literary formalism through the political and theoretical ferment of the 1970s to a fascination with what one of the best new historicist critics calls "the historicity of texts and the textuality of history."[2] My own version of this trajectory was particularly shaped by Raymond Williams and by Michel Foucault, who taught regularly at Berkeley in the late 1970s and early 1980s. And there were other powerful intellectual encounters along the way with the work, for example, of Mikhail Bakhtin or Kenneth Burke or Michel de Certeau. But the intellectual course of which I speak points less to a doctrine, cobbled together out of a set of what an English publishing house calls "modern masters," than to a shared life experience.

When I arrived in Berkeley in 1969, the University of California was in turmoil which lasted throughout the year and into the next. National Guard troops and heavily armed squadrons of police battled massive student and faculty protests against the Viet Nam War; the campus was continually redolent of tear gas. Everything was in an uproar; all routines were disrupted; nothing could be taken for granted. Classes still met, at least sporadically, but the lecture platform would often be appropriated, with or without the professor's permission, by protesters, and seminar discussions would veer wildly from, say, Ben Jonson's metrics to the undeclared air war over Cambodia. Many students and at least some faculty were calling for the "reconstitution" of the university—though no one knew quite what "reconstitution" was—so that even ordinary classes had an air of provisionality. It was, in its way, sublime.

But despite the heady rhetoric and at least the partial reality of radical ferment, the internal intellectual structure of Berkeley remained for the most part at once stable and staunchly conservative. By "intellectual structure" I mean both the institutional organization that governs research and teaching and the informal network of discourse that determines who talks seriously to whom. On my first day on campus, I was taken to the English Department office housed in a large and imposing building with a grand neo-classical facade and an air of overwhelming respectability. (This building, incidentally, was revealed in recent years to be both contaminated with carcinogenic asbestos fibers and exceptionally vulnerable to earthquake danger.) My guide, the department chairman, told me with pride that virtually the entire building—the dozens of offices, the lounge, the library, the bulletin boards—was given over to English. When I saw the cramped quarters of several other departments, I understood the chairman's pleasure, but I also felt some dismay. For it was possible to spend one's days entirely in the company of other English professors, English graduate students, and English majors—one can imagine a worse fate, I suppose, but the arrangement played into the kind of intellectual isolationism and claustrophobia commonly confused in large American universities with responsible academic professionalism.

My own work was pulling me in other directions—I wanted in fact to erase all boundaries separating cultural studies into narrowly specialized compartments—and in the years that followed, I found people in other departments, at Berkeley and elsewhere, with whom to talk and exchange work. The essays in this collection are deeply indebted to these exchanges, but they also strike me as still written within the governing agenda of the particular discipline in which I had been trained. In part this is a mark of failure—my inability to carry out the utopian project of obliterating disciplinary boundaries altogether; in larger part it is a mark of my recognition that boundaries, provided they are permeable and negotiable, are useful things to think with.

## Story-telling

These essays reflect not only my desire to play with boundaries but my will to tell stories, critical stories or stories told as a form of criticism. In one of his last essays before his untimely death, Joel Fineman brilliantly explored the theoretical implications of new historicism's characteristic use of anecdotes. The anecdote, he writes, "determines the destiny of a specifically historiographic integration of event and context"; as "the narration of a singular event," it is "the literary form or genre that uniquely refers to the real." The anecdote has at once something of the literary and something that exceeds the literary, a narrative form and a pointed, referential access to what lies beyond or beneath that form. This conjunction of the literary and the referential, Fineman argues, functions in the writing of history not as the servant of a grand, integrated narrative of beginning, middle, and end but rather as what "introduces an opening" into that teleological narration: "The anecdote produces the effect of the real, the occurrence of contingency, by establishing an event as an event within and yet without the framing context of historical successivity, i.e., it does so only in so far as its narration both comprises and refracts the narration it reports."[3]

What is crucial for me in this account is the insistence on contingency, the sense if not of a break then at least of a swerve in the ordinary and well-understood succession of events. The historical anecdote functions less as explanatory illustration than as disturbance, that which requires explanation, contextualization, interpretation. Anecdotes are the equivalents in the register of the real of what drew me to the study of literature: the encounter with something that I could not stand not understanding, that I could not quite finish with or finish off, that I had to get out of my inner life where it had taken hold, that I could retell and contemplate and struggle with. The historical evidence—"mere anecdotes"—conventionally invoked in literary criticism to assist in the explication of a text seemed to me dead precisely because it was the enemy of wonder: it was brought in to lay contingency and disturbance to rest. I do not want history to enable me to escape the effect of the literary but to deepen it by making it touch the effect of the real, a touch that would reciprocally deepen and complicate history.

But I do not wish to pretend that these theoretical and programmatic considerations directly motivated the writing of these essays. It was first of all as a writer that I experienced the will to use stories, and I wished to do so less for reasons of hermeneutical method than for reasons bound up with my sense of myself, with my experience of identity. Trained to be sensitive to these "writerly" questions in the authors whom they analyze, literary critics are generally deaf to them in themselves: it is difficult for me even to think of myself as a "writer," the idea having, absurdly I suppose, something of the grandiose and romantic about it.

My earliest recollections of "having an identity" or "being a self" are bound up with story-telling—narrating my own life or having it narrated for me by my mother. I suppose that I usually used the personal pronoun "I" in telling my own stories and that my mother used my name, but the heart of the initial experience of selfhood lay in the stories, not in the unequivocal, unmediated possession of an identity. Indeed the stories need not have been directly about me for me to experience them as an expression of my identity: my mother was generously fond of telling me long stories I found amusing about someone named Terrible Stanley, a child whom I superficially resembled but who made a series of disastrous life decisions—running into traffic, playing with matches, going to the zoo without telling his mother, and so on. Stanley was the "other" with a vengeance, but he was also my double, and my sense of myself seemed bound up with the monitory tales of his tragicomic fate.

As I grew slightly older, this sense of identity as intertwined with narratives of the self and its doubles was confirmed by my father who also had a penchant for story-telling—stories not so gratifyingly focused on my small being as my mother's were, but compelling and wonderfully well-told stories of himself and of a cousin, a few years younger than he, by whom he was virtually obsessed. My father and his cousin came from almost identical backgrounds: first-generation Americans born in Boston to poor Jewish immigrants from Lithuania. Like my father, the cousin had become a lawyer, and here began the story. My father was named Harry J. Greenblatt; his cousin Joseph H. Greenblatt. But when the latter became a lawyer, he moved into the same building in which my father had his office, and he began to call himself J. Harry Greenblatt. He managed, or so my father thought, to siphon off some clients from my father's already established practice. By itself this would have been enough to cause considerable tension, but over the years J. Harry compounded the offense by apparently becoming richer than my father, Harry J.—wealth, as far as I can tell, being measured principally by the amount of money donated annually to local charities, the contributions printed annually in a small but well-perused booklet. There were, as I grew up, endless stories about J. Harry—chance encounters in the street, confusions of identity that always seemed to work to my father's disadvantage, tearful reconciliations that would quickly give way to renewed rancor. This went on for decades and would, I suppose, have become intolerably boring had my father not possessed considerable comic gifts, along with a vast repertory of other stories. But a few years before my father's death at 86, the rivalry and doubling took a strange twist: J. Harry Greenblatt was indicted on charges of embezzlement; the charges were prominently reported in the newspapers; and the newspapers mistakenly printed the name of the culprit as Harry J. Greenblatt. Busybodies phoned our house to offer their commiserations to my mother. The confusion was awkward, but it had at least one benefit: it enabled my father to tell a whole new set of stories about himself and his double. When you are in your 80s, new stories can be a precious commodity.

My father's narrative impulse, we can say, was a strategic way of turning disappointment, anger, rivalry, and a sense of menace into comic pleasure, a way of reestablishing the self on the site of its threatened loss. But there was an underside to this strategy that I have hinted at by calling his stories obsessive. For the stories in some sense *were* the loss of identity which they were meant to ward off— there was something compulsive about them, as if someone were standing outside of my father and insisting that he endlessly recite his tales. Near the end of his life, he would sometimes abandon the pretence of having a conversation, interrupt what was being said, and simply begin to tell one of his stories.

This sense of compulsiveness in the telling of stories is not simply a function of garrulous old age; it is, I think, a quality that attaches to narrative itself, a quality thematized in *The Arabian Nights* and *The Ancient Mariner*. In response to the compulsiveness there have arisen numerous social and aesthetic regulations—not only the rules that govern civil conversation but the rules that govern the production and reception of narrative in books, on screen, on the stage. And there have arisen too less evident but powerful psychic regulations that govern how much narrative you are meant to experience, as it were, within your identity.

One of the worst times I have ever been through in my life was a period—I cannot recall if it was a matter of days or weeks—when I could not rid my mind of the impulse to narrate my being. I was a student at Cambridge, trying to decide whether to return to America and go to law school or graduate school in English. "He's sitting at his desk, trying to decide what to do with his life," a voice—my voice, I suppose, but also not my voice—spoke within my head. "Now he's putting his head on his hand; now he is furrowing his brow; and now he is getting up to open the window." And on and on, with a slight tone of derision through it all. I was split off from myself, J. Harry to my Harry J. (or Terrible Stanley to my Stephen), in an unhappy reprise of my early sense of self as story. It was unhappy, I suppose, because by my early 20s my identity had been fashioned as a single being exactly corresponding to the personal pronoun "I," and the unpleasantly ironic "he" sounding inside my head felt like an internal violation of my internal space, an invasion of my privacy, an objectification of what I least wished to objectify. I experienced the compulsive and detached narrativizing voice as something that had seized me, that I could not throw off, for even my attempts to do so were immediately turned into narrative. It occurred to me that I might be going mad. When the voice left me, it did so suddenly, inexplicably, with the sound of something snapping.

If the experience I have just described intensified my interest in narrative, it made me quite literally wish to get the narratives outside myself. Hence perhaps the critical distance that I attempt to inscribe in and with the stories I tell, for the narrative impulse in my writing is yoked to the service of literary and cultural criticism; it pulls out and away from myself. Hence too perhaps my fascination with figures of estrangement: I could not endure the compulsive estrangement of my life, as if it belonged to someone else, but I could perhaps understand the uncanny otherness of my own voice, make it comprehensible and bring it under rational control by trying to understand the way in which all voices come to be woven out of strands of alien experience. I am committed to the project of making strange what has become familiar, of demonstrating that what seems an untroubling and untroubled part of ourselves (for example, Shakespeare) is actually part of something else, something different.

It is only now, I think, that I can even gesture toward a sense that the practice of writing is more than an act of self-expression. For it turns out that self-expression is always and inescapably the expression of something else, something different. A recognition and an understanding of the difference does not negate self-expression—I have been unpersuaded by arguments that the self has been radically deconstructed—but it does help one see more clearly where in the world one's identity comes from and what kinds of negotiation and conflict it entails. In my own case, I would have to analyze, for example, the presence in my father's stories (and speech rhythms and perceptions of the world) of the Yiddish humor of the stetl, adapted to very different American circumstances, as this humor is comparably adapted, say, in Woody Allen. I will not undertake this project, as it would be of interest principally to myself, but my work has attempted to undertake a comparable project at the broader level of the cultural identity fashioned in and by English literature.

## Literary Pleasure and Historical Understanding

Pleasure is an important part of my sense of literature—that is, part both of my own response (for pleasure and what I have called disturbance are often identical) and of what I most wish to understand. I am frequently baffled by the tendency especially in those explicitly concerned with historical or ideological functions of art to ignore the analysis of pleasure or, for that matter, of play. (Psychoanalytic critics have generally been far better at this, but too often at the cost of the suppression of history.) Literature may do important work in the world, but each sentence is not hard labor, and the effectiveness of this work depends upon the ability to delight. You certainly cannot hope to write convincingly about Shakespeare without coming to terms with what Prospero at the end of *The Tempest* claims was his whole "project": "to please." (The terrible line from *King Lear* echoes darkly as a condemnation of failed art: "better thou/Hadst not been born than not t'have pleas'd me better.")

But pleasure as a category is extremely elusive for historical understanding. We can marvel, as Marx did in the *Introduction to the Critique of Political Economy*, at its apparently transhistorical stability: the difficulty, Marx wrote, "does not lie in understanding that the Greek art and epos are bound up with certain forms of social development. It rather lies in understanding why they still afford us aesthetic enjoyment and in certain respects prevail as the standard and model beyond attainment." This stability poses a problem for any theory that insists in a strong way upon the historical embeddedness of literary texts (or cultural artifacts in general), insists, that is, upon the inseparability of their meaning from the circumstances of their making or reception. Few people would any longer credit Marx's own proposed solution, that the Greeks were the "historical childhood of humanity," and consequently that they possess for us an "eternal charm." Instead the supposed continuity of aesthetic response seems to lead most often to a notion of the inherence in the text itself of the power to produce aesthetic pleasure and to lead correspondingly to a notion that this pleasure is outside of history, disinterested and contemplative.

We can, however, argue that the transhistorical stability or continuity of literary pleasure is an illusion; we can suggest that there is little reason to believe that the pleasure generated by *The Tempest*, say, was the same for the Jacobean audience as it is for ourselves. The overt material sign of gratification—the applause for which Prospero asks at the close—is the same, but the actual nature of that gratification, the objects and sensations and meanings and practices by which it is provoked and to which it is attached, differs significantly. The monolithic and timeless character of pleasure would begin to crack apart: we would begin to question the validity of conflating theatrical pleasure with the "literary" (a category that did not exist in Shakespeare's time) or of conflating both with the "aesthetic"; we would ask if the pleasure experienced by the standing auditors in the pit was identical to that of the seated auditors in the galleries or if men and women were applauding for the same reasons; and we would certainly begin to wonder if the audience (at least half of them American tourists) delighting in a Royal Shakespeare Company production of *The Tempest* at Stratford is responding to the same signals to which playgoers in early-seventeenth-century London responded. The task then would be to historicize pleasure, to explore its shifts and changes, to understand its interests.

As will be clear to any reader of these essays, I am inclined toward this latter view, and I take heart from the remarkable recent studies that have been begun to give a history to sensations, states of being, and emotions that had seemed timeless: Delumeau on fear, Corbin on smell, Blumenberg on curiosity, and so forth. There is perhaps a comparable account to be given of theatrical pleasure. But I should note certain reservations. For there do seem to be long-term continuities in pleasure and in those things that trigger pleasure. Such continuities do not necessarily lead to theories of literary autonomy nor do they lead me to conclude that aesthetic pleasure is disinterested, but they should make us wary of exaggerating the psychological or moral distance that separates us from cultures temporally or geographically distant from our own. Moreover, it is extremely difficult to track historical differences in pleasure. Occasionally, there is a major institutional change that seems to signal a change in pleasure—for example, the shift in England from all-male to male-female playing companies—but even here the significance of the shift is extremely elusive. We can make some progress by looking closely at works that no longer give audiences pleasure and trying to deduce why they might have done so once, but it remains difficult to connect whatever we conclude with those works from the same period that still do produce pleasure. If we believe that aesthetic pleasure is unitary and fixed, we can at least trust our phenomenological or psychological analyses to help us gauge the experience of men and women in the past, but if pleasure is multiple, shifting, and time-bound, we have no assurance that there is any meaningful bridge between such analyses and historical study.

In these circumstances, I try to make a virtue of necessity and rethink the elusiveness that troubles me. That elusiveness is, I would argue, at once the sign and the consequence of the fact that neither the work of art nor the person experiencing the work of art nor the historical situation in which the work is produced or received fully *possesses* the pleasure that is art's principal reason for being and its ticket to survival. Virtually every form of aesthetic pleasure—and this is particularly true of theatrical pleasure—is located in an intermediate zone of social transaction, a betwixt and between. It is this mobility, a mobility that includes the power of ready mutation, rather than disinterestedness or stability, that enables the pleasures provoked by certain works of art to seem to endure unchanged for centuries.

### Fiction and Reality

Consider the following passage from Edmund Scott's *Exact Discourse of the Subtilties, Fashions, Pollicies, Religion, and Ceremonies of the East Indians* (1606). Scott was the principal Agent for the East India Company in Bantam, Java, in 1603–1605. They were years of commercial rivalry with the Dutch, fear of fire and theft, and growing hatred of both the Javanese and Chinese. He writes that the English caught a Chinese goldsmith who had, they believed, been involved in an attempt to rob them of their gold; the alleged culprit "would tell us nothing."

> Wherefore, because of his sullenness, I thought I would burn him now a little (for we were now in the heat of our anger). First I caused him to be burned under the nails of his thumbs, fingers, and toes with sharp hot iron, and the nails to be torn off. And because he never blemished [i.e. turned pale] at that, we thought that his hands and legs had been numbed with tying; wherefore we burned him in the arms, shoulders, and neck. But all was one with him. Then we burned him quite through the hands, and with rasps of iron tore out the flesh and sinews. After that, I caused them to knock the edges of his shin bones with hot searing irons. Then I caused cold screws or iron to be screwed into the bones of his arms and suddenly to be snatched out. After that all the bones of his fingers and toes to be broken with pincers. Yet for all this he never shed tear; no, nor once turned his

head aside, nor stirred hand or foot; but when we demanded any question, he would put his tongue between his teeth and strike his chin upon his knees to bite it off. When all the extremity we could use was but in vain, I caused him to be put fast in irons again; where the emmets [ants] (which do greatly abound there) got into his wounds and tormented him worse than we had done, as we might well see by his gesture. The [Javanese] king's officers desired me he might be shot to death. I told them that was too good a death for such a villain. . . . But they do hold it to be the cruellest and basest death that is. Wherefore, they being very importunate, in the evening we led him into the fields and made him fast to a stake. The first shot carried away a piece of his arm bone, and all the next shot struck him through the breast, up near to the shoulder. Then he, holding down his head, looked upon the wound. The third shot that was made, one of our men had cut a bullet in three parts, which struck upon his breast in a triangle; whereat he fell down as low as the stake would give him leave. But between our men and the Hollanders, they shot him almost all to pieces before they left him.[4]

What are we to do with such a passage? what is "history" to make of it? what kind of story do we want to tell about Scott and his victim—or not to tell about them? The Hakluyt Society editor, writing let us take note in 1943, makes no direct comment on this passage at all in his long introduction. Scott's narrative, he writes, "is an epic story of a grim struggle against disease and dangers of many descriptions, sustained by a dogged determination to keep the flag flying at all costs. Scott himself stands out, without any boasting or undue egotism, as a man of ability, who proved fully equal to all the calls made upon him. Calm and prudent, his constant vigilance frustrated many plots against the factory; and every emergency was faced with an energy and decision that soon brought a successful issue. . . . His proudest boast is that, small as were the numbers of resources of the English, they yet won and kept the good opinion of the Asiatics by whom they were surrounded, at the same time maintaining the honour of their sovereign and the good name of their country" (xxxix–lx).

The moral stupidity of this drivel obviously reflects the blind patriotism of a nation besieged, but it is also the expression of a more long-term historiographical project that extends at least to the Reverend Samuel Purchas who first published Scott's narrative in 1613 in his multi-volume commemoration of English voyages. This project is linked not only to a recording of the military exploits of the nation-state but to an analysis of broader institutional and social patterns of danger and well-being. The well-being in the case of Scott is succinctly summarized by Sir William Foster: "the final outcome" of the expedition, he writes, was "not unsatisfactory": "The investors had recovered not only their capital but a profit of ninety-five per cent" (xxx). Here too, of course, the passage I began by quoting simply disappears.

It is one of the virtues of traditional Marxist history that it could at least acknowledge—and not simply as an "aberration" or a sign of the barbarism of a "backward age"—the horror of Scott's account and attempt to understand it in terms of the nascent capitalist and imperialist venture in which it takes place. But this very understanding— and the theory of historical necessity to which it is wed—also runs the risk of losing the dark specificity of that account, the risk of absorbing the unspeakable but spoken rupture of human relatedness into an abstract, pre-packaged schema. The English boasted of the fact that, in contrast to continental practice, torture was, as Sir Edward Coke wrote, "directly against the common lawes of England."[6] But in fact between 1560 and 1620 torture was regularly used in the interrogation of Catholics accused of treason, and Scott is not unique in recording its use against racial as well as religious others. The link between capitalism and imperialism *does* manifest itself in Scott's writing and his actions, but we may doubt that this link is sufficient to explain either the writing or the actions or doubt that its history is the history that it most behooves us to tell when we read those terrible sentences.

But why do we read the sentences at all? Might we be better off quietly forgetting about them? Is it vulgar or lurid even to rehearse Scott's text? Scott is by our lights a sadist, but is it also sadistic to quote him? Is there not some hidden pleasure, some imaginative provocation, in this spectacle of torture? Is there something indecent about using such sentences to illustrate a point about historicism? The Chinese victim was uncannily, unimaginably, perhaps heroically silent; is it the historian's task, after all this time, finally to compel him to speak? But then if we are silent, if we turn our eyes away, are we not collaborating with Scott and with all the others like him?

A crime was committed—not the crime against property with which Scott was so concerned but the crime against humanity that he committed—and its textual trace has survived. Does it require a set of "implicit 'counterfactuals' " or "utopian postulates" to feel compelled to speak of this crime and to try to understand it? Does it require a "theory of history"? I don't think so; I think that all it initially requires is a hatred of cruelty and a capacity for wonder. But we cannot get very far without history. We have to know something about the East India Company, about the practice of torture in early modern Europe, about the behavior of the English in their own country and abroad, about prevailing conceptions of racial and religious difference. And we have to know something about texts.

What is the status of Scott's *Exact Discourse?* One of the principal achievements of post-structuralism has been to problematize the distinction between literary and non-literary texts, to challenge the stable difference between the fictive and the actual, to look at discourse not as a transparent glass through which we glimpse reality but as the creator of what Barthes called the "reality-effect." In more senses than one, the *Exact Discourse* is not an innocent text. Scott had shipped out on the voyage as a very minor figure; he had become the Agent at Bantam only after the death of two superiors. When he returned to London, he entered into a long dispute with the company over his remuneration, a dispute that was only resolved by arbitration in 1609, three years after the publication of his narrative. The *Exact Discourse* was almost certainly then part of Scott's campaign for a larger share of the profits, and every detail may well reflect his idea of what would most impress the Company's directors.

How can we be certain that what Scott reports in the passage I have quoted actually took place? The answer is that we cannot. There is, so far as I can tell, no corroborating testimony in the other documentary traces of the voyage, and at this distance even such testimony could not give us certainty. Moreover, in the fiction of the late sixteenth and early seventeenth century there are passages that are strikingly similar to Scott's; for example, Thomas Nashe's *The Unfortunate Traveller* (1593) has a description of an execution that fully rivals Scott's in its attention to detail, and, of course, Shakespeare's *King Lear* famously shows on stage the torture and blinding of the bound Earl of Gloucester. Scott's account is in the first-person, but that in itself is not enough to differentiate it from fiction, and there are no other formal features that enable us to secure such differentiation.

These considerations are unsettling, for they seem to threaten a loss of moral bearings, but they also force us to look again and more closely at the text, not to peer through it but to peer at it. If there is any value to what has become known as "new historicism," it must be here, in an intensified willingness to read all of the textual traces of the past with the attention traditionally conferred only on literary texts. What is unbearable about Scott's passage exists for us in the text, and not only in his complacent acceptance of his own acts. There is something about the sentences themselves that is horrible, something suggested by Elaine Scarry's remark, "Nowhere is the sadistic potential of a language built on agency so visible as in torture."[6] And it is in the context of this horribleness that the victim's silence—the torturer's inability to turn pain into a manifestation of his power, to extort so much as a scream that he could then record—takes on whatever meaning it has.

This is not the place to tease out the implications of Scott's text; I have only wanted to indicate the kinds of questions that it raises, for they are questions that are implicit in most of the essays. But I don't want to end without making explicit my conviction that the post-structuralist confounding of fiction and non-fiction is important but inadequate. It matters that *The Unfortunate Traveller* is marked out for us in a variety of ways as fiction and that Scott's *Exact Discourse* is not; it fundamentally alters our mode of reading the texts and changes our ethical position toward them. If we discovered that Scott's account was a fabrication, his text would thereby be revealed to be not a work of art but a lie. Our belief in language's capacity for reference is part of our contract with the world; the contract may be playfully suspended or broken altogether, but no abrogation is without consequences, and there are circumstances where the abrogation is unacceptable. The existence or absence of a real world, real body, real pain, makes a difference. The traditional paradigms for the uses of history and the interpretation of texts have all eroded—this is a time in which it will not do to invoke the same pathetically narrow repertoire of dogmatic explanations—but any history and any textual interpretation worth doing will have to speak to this difference.

## Notes

1. William K. Wimsatt, Jr. and Cleanth Brooks, *Literary Criticism: A Short History* (New York: Alfred A. Knopf, 1966), pp. 468–73.

2. Louis A. Montrose, "Professing the Renaissance: The Poetics and Politics of Culture," in *The New Historicism*, ed. H. Aram Veeser (New York & London: Routledge, 1989), pp. 15–36

3. Joel Fineman, "The History of the Anecdote: Fiction and Fiction," in *The New Historicism*, ed. H. Aram Veeser, pp. 49–76.

4. In *The Voyage of Sir Henry Middleton to the Moluccas, 1604–1606*, ed. Sir William Foster, C.I.E., Hakluyt Society Series 2, vol. 88 (London: Hakluyt Society, 1943), pp. 121–22. As Anne Barton has pointed out in a review of my book (*New York Review of Books* 38 [1991], p. 54), the Hakluyt Society editor omits from the opening sentence of this passage a phrase that emphasizes the "horrible symmetry" of the torture: "Wherefore, because of his sullennesse, *and that it was hee that fired us*, I thought I would burne him now a little. . ." (italics added).

5. *The Third Part of the Institutes of the Laws of England*, Chap. 2 (London: 1797), pp. 34–35. I owe this reference to "Torture and Truth in Renaissance England," an article by Elizabeth Hanson, forthcoming in *Representations*.

6. *The Body in Pain: The Making and Unmaking of the World* (New York: Oxford University Press, 1985), p. 27.

## 2

# Learning to Curse:
# Aspects of Linguistic
# Colonialism in the
# Sixteenth Century

At the close of *Musophilus*, Samuel Daniel's brooding philosophical poem of 1599, the poet's spokesman, anxious and uncertain through much of the dialogue in the face of his opponent's skepticism, at last rises to a ringing defense of eloquence, and particularly English eloquence, culminating in a vision of its future possibilities:

> And who in time knowes whither we may vent
> The treasure of our tongue, to what strange shores
> This gaine of our best glorie shal be sent,
> T'inrich vnknowing Nations with our stores?
> What worlds in th'yet vnformed Occident
> May come refin'd with th'accents that are ours?[1]

For Daniel, the New World is a vast, rich field for the plantation of the English language. Deftly he reverses the conventional image and imagines argosies freighted with a cargo of priceless words, sailing west "T'inrich vnknowing Nations with our stores." There is another reversal of sorts here: the "best glorie" that the English voyagers will carry with them is not "the treasure of our faith" but "the treasure of our tongue." It is as if in place of the evangelical spirit, which in the early English voyages is but a small flame compared to the blazing mission of the Spanish friars, Daniel would substitute a linguistic mission, the propagation of English speech.

Linguistic colonialism is mentioned by continental writers as well but usually as a small part of the larger enterprise of conquest, conversion, and settlement. Thus Peter Martyr writes to Pope Leo X of the "large landes and many regyons whiche shal hereafter receaue owre nations, tounges, and maners: and therwith embrase owre relygion."[2] Occasionally, more substantial claims are made. In 1492, in the introduction to his *Gramática*, the first grammar of a modern European

16

tongue, Antonio de Nebrija writes that language has always been the partner ("compañera") of empire. And in the ceremonial presentation of the volume to Queen Isabella, the bishop of Avila, speaking on the scholar's behalf, claimed a still more central role for language. When the queen asked flatly, "What is it for?" the bishop replied, "Your Majesty, language is the perfect instrument of empire."[3] But for Daniel, English is neither partner nor instrument; its expansion is virtually the goal of the whole enterprise.

Daniel does not consider the spread of English a conquest but rather a gift of inestimable value. He hasn't the slightest sense that the natives might be reluctant to abandon their own tongue; for him, the Occident is "yet unformed," its nations "unknowing." Or, as Peter Martyr puts it, the natives are a *tabula rasa* ready to take the imprint of European civilization: "For lyke as rased or vnpaynted tables, are apte to receaue what formes soo euer are fyrst drawen theron by the hande of the paynter, euen soo these naked and simple people, doo soone receaue the customes of owre Religion, and by conuersation with owre men, shake of theyr fierce and natiue barbarousnes."[4] The mention of the nakedness of the Indians is typical; to a ruling class obsessed with the symbolism of dress, the Indians' physical appearance was a token of a cultural void. In the eyes of the Europeans, the Indians were culturally naked.

This illusion that the inhabitants of the New World are essentially without a culture of their own is both early and remarkably persistent, even in the face of overwhelming contradictory evidence. In his journal entry for the day of days, 12 October 1492, Columbus expresses the thought that the Indians ought to make good servants, "for I see that they repeat very quickly whatever was said to them." He thinks, too, that they would easily be converted to Christianity, "because it seemed to me that they belonged to no religion." And he continues: "I, please Our Lord, will carry off six of them at my departure to Your Highnesses, that they may learn to speak." The first of the endless series of kidnappings, then, was plotted in order to secure interpreters; the primal crime in the New World was committed in the interest of language. But the actual phrase of the journal merits close attention: "that they may learn to speak" (*para que aprendan a hablar*).[5] We are dealing, of course, with an idiom: Columbus must have known, even in that first encounter, that the Indians could speak, and he argued from the beginning that they were rational human beings. But the idiom has a life of its own; it implies that the Indians had no language at all.

This is, in part, an aspect of that linguistic colonialism we have already encountered in *Musophilus:* to speak is to speak one's own language, or at least a language with which one is familiar. "A man would be more cheerful with his dog for company," writes Saint Augustine, "than with a foreigner."[6] The unfamiliarity of their speech is a recurrent motif in the early accounts of the New World's inhabitants, and it is paraded forth in the company of all their other strange and often repellent qualities. The chronicler Robert Fabian writes of three savages presented to Henry VII that they "were clothed in beasts skins, & did eate raw flesh, and spake such speach that no man could understand them, and in their demeanour like to bruite beastes." Roy Harvey Pearce cites this as an example of the typical English view of the Indians as animals, but Fabian is far more ambiguous, for he continues: "Of the which upon two yeeres after, I saw two apparelled after the maner of Englishmen in Westminster pallace, which that time I could not discerne from Englishmen, til I was learned what they were, but as for speach, I heard none of them utter one word."[7] When he sees the natives again, are they still savages, now masked by their dress, or was his first impression misleading? And the seal of the ambiguity is the fact that he did not hear them utter a word, as if the real test of their conversion to civilization would be whether they had been able to master a language that "men" could understand.

In the 1570s the strangeness of Indian language can still be used in precisely the same way. In his first voyage to "Meta Incognita," as George Best reports, Frobisher captured a savage to take home with him as ". . . a sufficient witnesse of the captaines farre and tedious travell towards the unknowen parts of the world, as did well appeare by this strange infidell, whose like was never seene, read, nor heard of before, and whose language was neither knowen nor understood of any. . . ."[8] For Gregorio García, whose massive study of the origins of the Indians was published in 1607, there was something diabolical about the difficulty and variety of languages in the New World: Satan had helped the Indians to invent new tongues, thus impeding the labors of Christian missionaries.[9] And even the young John Milton, attacking the legal jargon of his time, can say in rhetorical outrage, "our speech is, I know not what, American, I suppose, or not even human!"[10]

Of course, there were many early attempts to treat Indian speech as something men could come to understand. According to John H. Parry, "All the early friars endeavoured to master Indian languages, usually Nahuatl, though some acquired other languages; the learned Andrés de Olmos, an early companion of Zumárraga, was credited with ten."[11] Traders and settlers also had an obvious interest in learning at least a few Indian words, and there are numerous word lists in the early accounts, facilitated as Peter Martyr points out by the fortuitous circumstance that "the languages of all the nations of these Ilandes, maye well be written with our Latine letters."[12] Such lists even suggested to one observer, Marc Lescarbot, the fact the Indian languages could change in time, just as French had changed from the age of Charlemagne. This, he explains, is why Cartier's dictionary of Indian words, compiled in the 1530s, is no longer of much use in the early seventeenth century.[13]

Indian languages even found some influential European admirers. In a famous passage, Montaigne approvingly quotes in translation several Indian songs, noting of one that "the invention hath no barbarism at all in it, but is altogether Anacreontic." In his judgment, "Their language is a kind of pleasant speech, and hath a pleasing sound and some affinity with the Greek terminations."[14] Ralegh, likewise, finds that the Tivitivas of Guiana have "the most manlie speech and most deliberate that euer I heard of what nation soeuer,"[15] while, in the next century, William Penn judges Indian speech "lofty" and full of words "of more sweetness or greatness" than most European tongues.[16] And the great Bartolomé de Las Casas, as he so often does, turns the tables on the Europeans:

> A man is apt to be called barbarous, in comparison with another, because he is strange in his manner of speech and mispronounces the language of the other. . . . According to Strabo, Book XIV, this was the chief reason the Greeks called other peoples barbarous, that is, because they were mispronouncing the Greek language. But from this point of view, there is no man or race which is not barbarous with respect to some other man or race. . . . Thus, just as we esteemed these peoples of these Indies barbarous, so they considered us, because of not understanding us.[17]

Simple and obvious as this point seems to us, it does not appear to have taken firm hold in the early years of conquest and settlement. Something of its spirit may be found in Oviedo's observation of an Indian interpreter failing to communicate with the members of another tribe: "[he] did not understand them better than a Biscayan talking Basque could make himself intelligible to a person speaking German or Arabic, or any other strange language."[18] But the view that Indian speech was close to gibberish remained current in intellectual as well as popular circles at least into the seventeenth century.[19] Indeed it is precisely in educated, and particularly humanist, circles that the view proved most tenacious and extreme. The rough, illiterate sea dog, bartering for gold trinkets on a faraway beach, was far more likely than the scholar to understand that the natives had their own tongue. The captains or lieutenants whose accounts we read had stood on the same beach, but when they sat down to record their experiences, powerful cultural presuppositions asserted themselves almost irresistibly.

For long before men without the full command of language, which is to say without eloquence, were thought to have been discovered in the New World, Renaissance humanists *knew* that such men existed, rather as modern scientists knew from the periodic table of the necessary existence of elements yet undiscovered. Virtually every Renaissance schoolboy read in Cicero's *De oratore* that only eloquence had been powerful enough "to gather scattered mankind together in one place, to transplant human beings from a barbarous life in the wilderness to a civilized social system, to establish organized communities, to equip them with laws and judicial safeguards and civic rights."[20] These lines, and similar passages from Isocrates and Quintilian, are echoed again and again in the fifteenth and sixteenth centuries as the proudest boast of the *stadium humanitatis*. Eloquence, wrote Andrea Ugo of Siena in 1421, led wandering humanity from a savage, bestial existence to civilized culture. Likewise, Andrea Brenta of Padua declared in 1480 that primitive men had led brutish and lawless lives in the fields until eloquence brought them together and converted barbaric violence into humanity and culture.[21] And more than a hundred years later, Puttenham can make the same claim, in the same terms, on behalf of poetry:

> Poesie was th'originall cause and occasion of their first assemblies, when before the people remained in the woods and mountains, vagarant and dispersed like the wild beasts, lawlesse and naked, or verie ill clad, and of all good and necessarie prouision for harbour or sustenance vtterly vnfurnished: so as they litle diffred for their maner of life, from the very brute beasts of the field.[22]

Curiously enough, a few pages later Puttenham cites the peoples of the New World as proof that poetry is more ancient than prose:

> This is proued by certificate of marchants & trauellers, who by late nauigations haue surueyed the whole world, and discouered large countries and strange peoples wild and sauage, affirming that the American, the Perusine & the very Canniball, do sing and also say, their highest and holiest matters in certaine riming versicles and not in prose.[23]

But it was more reasonable and logically consistent to conclude, as others did, that the savages of America were without eloquence or even without language. To validate one of their major tenets, humanists needed to reach such a conclusion, and they clung to it, in the face of all the evidence, with corresponding tenacity.

Moreover, both intellectual and popular culture in the Renaissance had kept alive the medieval figure of the Wild Man, one of whose common characteristics is the absence of speech. Thus when Spenser's Salvage Man, in Book VI of the *Faerie Queene*, wishes to express his compassion for a distressed damsel, he kisses his hands and crouches low to the ground,

> For other language had he none, nor speach,
> But a soft murmure, and confused sound
> Of senselesse words, which Nature did him teach.[24]

To be sure, the Wild Man of medieval and Renaissance literature often turns out to be of gentle blood, having been lost, as an infant, in the woods; his language problem, then, is a consequence of his condition, rather than, as in Cicero, its prime cause. But this view accorded perfectly with the various speculations about the origins of the Indians, whether they were seen as lost descendants of the Trojans, Hebrews, Carthaginians, or Chinese. Indian speech, that speech no man could understand, could be viewed as the tattered remnants of a lost language.[25]

It is only a slight exaggeration, I think, to suggest that Europeans had, for centuries, rehearsed their encounter with the peoples of the New World, acting out, in their response to the legendary Wild Man, their mingled attraction and revulsion, longing and hatred. In the Christian Middle Ages, according to a recent account, "the Wild Man is the distillation of the specific anxieties underlying the three securities supposedly provided by the specifically Christian institutions of civilized life: the securities of *sex* (as organized by the institution of the family), *sustenance* (as provided by the political, social, and economic institutions), and *salvation* (as provided by the Church)."[26] These are precisely the areas in which the Indians most disturb their early observers. They appear to some to have no stable family life and are given instead to wantonness and perversion.[27] Nor, according to others, are they capable of political organization or settled social life. Against the campaign to free the enslaved Indians, it was argued that once given their liberty, they would return to their old ways: "For being idle and slothfull, they wander vp & downe, and returne to their olde rites and ceremonies, and foule and mischieuous actes."[28] And everywhere we hear of their worship of idols which, in the eyes of the Europeans, strikingly resemble the images of devils in Christian art.[29]

Certainly the Indians were again and again identified as Wild Men, as wild, in the words of Francis Pretty, "as ever was a bucke or any other wilde beast."[30] "These men may very well and truely be called Wilde," writes Jacques Cartier, at once confirming and qualifying the popular name, "because there is no poorer people in the world."[31] Peter Martyr records tales of Wild Men in the New World, but he distinguishes them from the majority of the inhabitants:

> They say there are certeyne wyld men whiche lyue in the caues and dennes of the montaynes, contented onely with wilde fruites. These men neuer vsed the companye of any other: nor wyll by any meanes becoome tame. They lyue without any certaine dwellynge places, and with owte tyllage or culturynge of the grounde, as wee reade of them whiche in oulde tyme lyued in the golden age. They say also that these men are withowte any certaine language. They are sumtymes seene. But owre men haue yet layde handes on none of them.[32]

As Martyr's description suggests, Wild Men live beyond the pale of civilized life, outside all institutions, untouched by the long, slow development of human culture. If their existence is rude and repugnant, it also has, as Martyr's curious mention of the Golden Age suggests, a disturbing allure. The figure of the Wild Man, and the Indians identified as Wild Men, serve as a screen onto which Renaissance Europeans, bound by their institutions, project their darkest and yet most compelling fantasies. In the words of the earliest English tract on America:

> the people of this lande haue no kynge nor lorde nor theyr god. But all thinges is comune/this people goeth all naked. . . . These folke lyuen lyke bestes without any resonablenes and the wymen be also as comon. And the men hath conuersacyon with the wymen/who that they ben or who they fyrst mete/is she his syster/his mother/his daughter/or any other kyndred. And the wymen be very hoote and dysposed to lecherdnes. And they ete also on[e] a nother. The man etethe his wyfe his chylderne. . . . And that lande is ryght full of folke/ for they lyue commonly, iii. C. [300] yere and more as with sykenesse they dye nat.[33]

This bizarre description is, of course, an almost embarrasingly clinical delineation of the Freudian id. And the id, according to Freud, is without language.

At the furthest extreme, the Wild Man shades into the animal—one possible source of the medieval legend being European observation of the great apes.[34] Language is, after all, one of the crucial ways of distinguishing between men and beasts: "The one special advantage we enjoy over animals," writes Cicero, "is our power to speak with one another, to express our thoughts in words."[35] Not surprisingly, then, there was some early speculation that the Indians were subhuman and thus, among other things, incapable of receiving the true faith. One of the early advocates on their behalf, Bernadino de Minaya, recalls that, on his return to Spain from the New World,

> I went on foot, begging, to Valladolid, where I visited the cardinal and informed him that Friar Domingo [de Betanzos, an exponent of the theory that the Indians were beasts] knew neither the Indians' language nor their true nature. I told him of their ability and the right they had to become Christians. He replied that I was much deceived, for he understood that the Indians were no more than parrots, and he believed that Friar Domingo spoke with prophetic spirit. . . .[36]

The debate was dampened but by no means extinguished by Pope Paul III's condemnation, in the bull *Sublimis Deus* (1537), of the opinion that the Indians are "dumb brutes created for our service" and "incapable of receiving the Catholic faith."[37] Friar Domingo conceded in 1544 that the Indians had language but argued against training them for the clergy on the grounds that their language was defective, lacking the character and copiousness necessary to explain Christian doctrine without introducing great improprieties which could easily lead to great errors.[38] Similarly, Pierre Massée observes that the Brazilian Indians lack the letters F, L, and R, which they could only receive by divine inspiration, insofar as they have neither "Foy, Loy, ne Roy."[39] Ironically, it is here, in these virtual slanders, that we find some of the fullest acknowledgment of the enormous cultural gap between Europeans and Indians, and of the near impossibility of translating concepts like conversion, Incarnation, or the Trinity into native speech.[40]

Perhaps the profoundest literary exploration of these themes in the Renaissance is to be found in Shakespeare. In *The Tempest* the startling encounter between a lettered and an unlettered culture is heightened, almost parodied, in the relationship between a European whose entire source of power is his library and a savage who had no speech at all before the European's arrival. "Remember / First to possess his books," Caliban warns the lower-class and presumably illiterate Stephano and Trinculo,

> for without them
> He's but a sot, as I am, nor hath not
> One spirit to command: they all do hate him
> As rootedly as I. Burn but his books.[41]

This idea may well have had some historical analogue in the early years of conquest. In his *Thresor de l'histoire des langves de cest univers* (1607), Claude Duret reports that the Indians, fearing that their secrets would be recorded and revealed, would not approach certain trees whose leaves the Spanish used for paper, and Father Chaumonot writes in 1640 that the Hurons "were convinced that we were sorcerers, imposters come to take possession of their country, after having made them perish by our spells, which were shut up in our inkstands, in our books, etc.,—inasmuch that we dared not, without hiding ourselves, open a book or write anything."[42]

The link between *The Tempest* and the New World has often been noted, as, for example, by Terence Hawkes who suggests, in his book *Shakespeare's Talking Animals*, that in creating Prospero, the playwright's imagination was fired by the resemblance he perceived between himself and a colonist. "A colonist," writes Hawkes,

> acts essentially as a dramatist. He imposes the 'shape' of his own culture, *embodied in his speech*, on the new world, and makes that world recognizable, habitable, 'natural,' able to speak his language.[43]

Conversely,

> the dramatist is metaphorically a colonist. His art penetrates new areas of experience, his language expands the boundaries of our culture, and makes the new territory over in its own image. His 'raids on the inarticulate' open up new worlds for the imagination. (212)[44]

The problem for critics has been to accommodate this perceived resemblance between dramatist and colonist with a revulsion that reaches from the political critiques of colonialism in our own century back to the moral outrage of Las Casas and Montaigne. Moreover, there are many aspects of the play itself that make colonialism a problematical model for the theatrical imagination: if *The Tempest* holds up a mirror to empire, Shakespeare would appear deeply ambivalent about using the reflected image as a representation of his own practice.

Caliban enters in Act I, cursing Prospero and protesting bitterly: "This island's mine, by Sycorax my mother, / Which thou tak'st from me" (I. ii. 333–34). When he first arrived, Prospero made much of Caliban, and Caliban, in turn, showed Prospero "all the qualities o'th'isle." But now, Caliban complains, "I am all the subjects that you have, / Which first was mine own King." Prospero replies angrily that he had treated Caliban "with human care" until he tried to rape Miranda, a charge Caliban does not deny. At this point, Miranda herself chimes in, with a speech Dryden and others have found disturbingly indelicate:

> Abhorred slave,
> Which any print of goodness wilt not take,
> Being capable of all ill! I pitied thee,
> Took pains to make thee speak, taught thee each hour
> One thing or other: when thou didst not, savage,
> Know thine own meaning, but wouldst gabble like
> A thing most brutish, I endow'd thy purposes
> With words that made them known. But thy vile race,
> Though thou didst learn, had that in't which good natures
> Could not abide to be with; therefore wast thou
> Deservedly confin'd into this rock,
> Who hadst deserv'd more than a prison.[45]

To this, Caliban replies:

> You taught me language; and my profit on't
> Is, I know how to curse. The red plague rid you
> For learning me your language!
>
> (I. ii. 353–67)

Caliban's retort might be taken as self-indictment: even with the gift of language, his nature is so debased that he can only learn to curse. But the lines refuse to mean this; what we experience instead is a sense of their devastating justness. Ugly, rude, savage, Caliban nevertheless achieves for an instant an absolute if intolerably bitter moral victory. There is no reply; only Prospero's command: "Hagseed, hence! / Fetch us in fuel," coupled with an ugly threat:

> If thou neglect'st, or dost unwillingly
> What I command, I'll rack thee with old cramps,
> Fill all thy bones with aches, make thee roar,
> That beasts shall tremble at thy din.
>
> (I. ii. 370–73)

What makes this exchange so powerful, I think, is that Caliban is anything but a Noble Savage. Shakespeare does not shrink from the darkest European fantasies about the Wild Man; indeed he exaggerates them: Caliban is deformed, lecherous, evil-smelling, idle, treacherous, naive, drunken, rebellious, violent, and devil-worshipping.[46] According to Prospero, he is not even human: a "born devil," "got by the devil himself / Upon thy wicked dam" (I. ii. 321–22). *The Tempest* utterly rejects the uniformitarian view of the human race, the view that would later triumph in the Enlightenment and prevail in the West to this day. All men, the play seems to suggest, are *not* alike; strip away the adornments of culture and you will *not* reach a single human essence. If anything, *The Tempest* seems closer in spirit to the attitude of the present-day inhabitants of Java who, according to Clifford Geertz, quite flatly say, "To be human is to be Javanese."[47]

And yet out of the midst of this attitude Caliban wins a momentary victory that is, quite simply, an assertion of inconsolable human pain and bitterness. And out of the midst of this attitude Prospero comes, at the end of the play, to say of Caliban, "this thing of darkness I / Acknowledge mine" (V. i. 275–76). Like Caliban's earlier reply, Prospero's words are ambiguous; they might be taken as a bare statement that the strange "demi-devil" is one of Prospero's party as opposed to Alonso's, or even that Caliban is Prospero's slave. But again the lines refuse to mean this: they acknowledge a deep, if entirely unsentimental, bond. By no means is Caliban accepted into the family of man; rather, he is claimed as Philoctetes might claim his own festering wound. Perhaps, too, the word "acknowledge" implies some moral responsibility, as when the Lord, in the King James translation of Jeremiah, exhorts men to "acknowledge thine iniquity, that thou hast transgressed against the Lord thy God" (3:13). Certainly the Caliban of Act V is in a very real sense Prospero's creature, and the bitter justness of his retort early in the play still casts a shadow at its close. With Prospero restored to his dukedom, the match of Ferdinand and Miranda blessed, Ariel freed to the elements, and even the wind and tides of the return voyage settled, Shakespeare leaves Caliban's fate naggingly unclear. Prospero has acknowledged a bond; that is all.

Arrogant, blindly obstinate, and destructive as was the belief that the Indians had no language at all, the opposite conviction—that there was no significant language barrier between Europeans and savages— may have had consequences as bad or worse. Superficially, this latter view is the more sympathetic and seductive, in that it never needs to be stated. It is hard, after all, to resist the story of the *caciques* of the

Cenú Indians who are reported by the Spanish captain to have rebutted the official claim to their land thus:

> what I said about the Pope being the Lord of all the universe in the place of God, and that he had given the land of the Indies to the King of Castille, the Pope must have been drunk when he did it, for he gave what was not his; also . . . the King, who asked for, or received, this gift, must be some madman, for that he asked to have that given him which belonged to others.[48]

It is considerably less hard to resist the account of the *caciques* of new Granada who declared in a memorial sent to the pope in 1553 that "if by chance Your Holiness has been told that we are bestial, you are to understand that this is true inasmuch as we follow devilish rites and ceremonies."[49] The principle in both cases is the same: whatever the natives may have actually thought and said has been altered out of recognition by being cast in European diction and syntax.

Again and again in the early accounts, Europeans and Indians, after looking on each other's faces for the first time, converse without the slightest difficulty; indeed the Indians often speak with as great a facility in English or Spanish as the Renaissance gentlemen themselves. There were interpreters, to be sure, but these are frequently credited with linguistic feats that challenge belief. Thus Las Casas indignantly objects to the pretense that complex negotiations were conducted through the mediation of interpreters who, in actual fact, "communicate with a few phrases like 'Gimme bread,' 'Gimme food,' 'Take this, gimme that,' and otherwise carry on with gestures."[50] He argues that the narratives are intentionally falsified, to make the *conquistadores'* actions appear fairer and more deliberative than they actually were. There may have been such willful falsification, but there also seems to have been a great deal of what we may call "filling in the blanks." The Europeans and the interpreters themselves translated such fragments as they understood or thought they understood into a coherent story, and they came to believe quite easily that the story was what they had actually heard. There could be, and apparently were, murderous results.[51]

The savages in the early accounts of the New World may occasionally make strange noises—"Oh ho" or "bow-wow"[52]—but, once credited with intelligible speech, they employ our accents and are comfortable in our modes of thought. Thus the amorous daughter of a cruel *cacique*, we learn in *The Florida of the Inca*, saved the young Spanish captive with the following words:

> Lest you lose faith in me and despair of your life or doubt that I will
> do everything in my power to save you . . . I will assist you to escape
> and find refuge if you are a man and have the courage to flee. For
> tonight, if you will come at a certain hour to a certain place, you will
> find an Indian in whom I shall entrust both your welfare and mine.[53]

It may be objected that this is narrative convention: as in adventure
movies, the natives look exotic but speak our language. But such
conventions are almost never mere technical conveniences. If it was
immensely difficult in sixteenth-century narratives to represent a language barrier, it is because embedded in the narrative convention of
the period was a powerful, unspoken belief in the isomorphic relationship between language and reality. The denial of Indian language or
of the language barrier grew out of the same soil that, in the mid-
seventeenth century, would bring forth the search for a universal
language. Many sixteenth-century observers of the Indians seem to
have assumed that language—their language—represented the true,
rational order of things in the world. Accordingly, Indians were frequently either found defective in speech, and hence pushed toward
the zone of wild things, or granted essentially the same speech as the
Europeans. Linguists in the seventeenth century brought the underlying assumption to the surface, not, of course, to claim that English,
or Latin, or even Hebrew expressed the shape of reality, but to advo-
cate the discovery or fashioning of a universal language that would
do so.

Behind this project, and behind the narrative convention that fore-
shadowed it, lay the conviction that reality was one and universal,
constituted identically for all men at all times and in all places. The
ultimate grounds for this faith were theological and were many times
explicitly voiced, as here by Ralegh in his *History of the World:*

> The same just God who liueth and gouerneth all thinges for euer,
> doeth in these our times giue victorie, courage, and discourage, raise,
> and throw downe Kinges, Estates, Cities, and Nations, for the same
> offenses which were committed of old, and are committed in the
> present.[54]

There is a single faith, a single text, a single reality.

This complex of convictions may illuminate that most startling
document, the *Requerimiento*, which was drawn up in 1513 and put
into effect the next year. The *Requerimiento* was to be read aloud
to newly encountered peoples in the New World; it demands both
obedience to the king and queen of Spain as rulers of the Indies by

virtue of the donation of the pope, and permission for the religious fathers to preach the true faith. If these demands are promptly met, many benefits are promised, but if there should be refusal or malicious delay, the consequences are made perfectly clear:

> We shall take you and your wives and your children, and shall make slaves of them, and as such shall sell and dispose of them as their Highnesses may command; and we shall take away your goods, and shall do you all the mischief and damage that we can, as to vassals who do not obey, and refuse to receive their lord, and resist and contradict him; and we protest that the deaths and losses which shall accrue from this are your fault, and not that of their Highnesses, or ours, nor of these cavaliers who come with us. And that we have said this to you and made this Requisition, we request the notary here present to give us his testimony in writing, and we ask the rest who are present that they should be witnesses of this Requisition.[55]

Las Casas writes that he doesn't know "whether to laugh or cry at the absurdity" of the *Requerimiento*, an absurdity born out in the stories of its actual use.[56] In our times, Madariaga calls it "quaint and naive," but neither adjective seems to me appropriate for what is a diabolical and, in its way, sophisticated document.[57]

A strange blend of ritual, cynicism, legal fiction, and perverse idealism, the *Requerimiento* contains at its core the conviction that there is no serious language barrier between the Indians and the Europeans. To be sure, there are one or two hints of uneasiness, but they are not allowed to disrupt the illusion of scrupulous and meaningful communication established from the beginning:

> On the part of the King, Don Fernando, and of Doña Juana, his daughter, Queen of Castile and Leon, subduers of the barbarous nations, we their servants notify and make known to you, as best we can, that the Lord our God, Living and Eternal, created the Heaven and the Earth, and one man and one woman, of whom you and we, and all the men of the world, were and are descendants, and all those who come after us.[58]

The proclamation that all men are brothers may seem an odd way to begin a document that ends with threats of enslavement and a denial of responsibility for all ensuing deaths and losses, but it is precisely this opening that justifies the close. That all human beings are descended from "one man and one woman" proves that there is a single human essence, a single reality. As such, all problems of communication are merely accidental. Indeed, the *Requerimiento* conveniently passes over in silence the biblical account of the variety of languages and the scattering of mankind. In Genesis 11, we are told that "the whole earth was of one language, and of one speech," until men began to build the tower of Babel:

> And the Lord said, Behold, the people is one, and they have all one language; and this they begin to do: and now nothing will be restrained from them, which they have imagined to do. Go to, let us go down, and there confound their language, that they may not understand one another's speech. So the Lord scattered them abroad from thence upon the face of all the earth: and they left off to build the city. (Gen. 11:6–8)

In place of this, the *Requerimiento* offers a demographic account of the dispersion of the human race:

> on account of the multitude which has sprung from this man and woman in the five thousand years since the world was created, it was necessary that some men should go one way and some another, and that they should be divided into many kingdoms and provinces, for in one alone they could not be sustained[59]

The Babel story has to be omitted, for to acknowledge it here would be to undermine the basic linguistic premise of the whole document.

The *Requerimiento*, then, forces us to confront the dangers inherent in what most of us would consider the central liberal tenet, namely the basic unity of mankind. The belief that a shared essence lies beneath our particular customs, stories, and language turns out to be the cornerstone of the document's self-righteousness and arrogance. It certainly did not cause the horrors of the Conquest, but it made those horrors easier for those at home to live with. After all, the Indians had been warned. The king and queen had promised "joyfully and benignantly" to receive them as vassals. The *Requerimiento* even offered to let them see the "certain writings" wherein the pope made his donation of the Indies. If, after all this, the Indians obstinately refused to comply, they themselves would have to bear responsibility for the inevitable consequences.

The two beliefs that I have discussed in this paper—that Indian language was deficient or non-existent and that there was no serious language barrier—are not, of course, the only sixteenth-century attitudes toward American speech. I have already mentioned some of the Europeans, missionaries, and laymen who took native tongues seriously. There are, moreover, numerous practical acknowledgments of the language problem which do not simply reduce the native speech to gibberish. Thus René de Laudonnière reports that the Indians "every houre made us a 1000 discourses, being merveilous sory that we could not understand them." Instead of simply throwing up his hands, he proceeds to ask the Indian names for various objects and comes gradually to understand a part of what they are saying.[60]

But the theoretical positions on Indian speech that we have considered press in from either side on the Old World's experience of the New. Though they seem to be opposite extremes, both positions reflect a fundamental inability to sustain the simultaneous perception of likeness and difference, the very special perception we give to metaphor. Instead they either push the Indians toward utter difference—and thus silence—or toward utter likeness—and thus the collapse of their own, unique identity. Shakespeare, in *The Tempest*, experiments with an extreme version of this problem, placing Caliban at the outer limits of difference only to insist upon a mysterious measure of resemblance. It is as if he were testing our capacity to sustain metaphor. And in this instance only, the audience achieves a fullness of understanding before Prospero does, an understanding that Prospero is only groping toward at the play's close. In the poisoned relationship between master and slave, Caliban can only curse; but we know that Caliban's consciousness is not simply a warped negation of Prospero's:

> I prithee, let me bring thee where crabs grow;
> And I with my long nails will dig thee pig-nuts;
> Show thee a jay's nest, and instruct thee how
> To snare the nimble mamoset; I'll bring thee
> To clustering filberts, and sometimes I'll get thee
> Young scamels from the rock.
>
> (II. ii. 167–72)

The rich, irreducible concreteness of the verse compels us to acknowledge the independence and integrity of Caliban's construction of reality. We do not sentimentalize this construction—indeed the play insists that we judge it and that we prefer another—but we cannot make it vanish into silence. Caliban's world has what we may call *opacity*, and the perfect emblem of that opacity is the fact that we do not to this day know the meaning of the word "scamel."

But it is not until Vico's *New Science* (1725) that we find a genuine theoretical breakthrough, a radical shift from the philosophical assumptions that helped to determine European response to alien languages and cultures. Vico refuses to accept the position by then widely held that "in the vulgar languages meanings were fixed by convention," that "articulate human words have arbitrary significations." On the contrary, he insists, "because of their natural origins, they must have had natural significations."[61] Up to this point, he seems simply to be reverting to the old search for a universal character. But then he makes a momentous leap:

> There remains, however, the very great difficulty: How is it that there are as many different vulgar tongues as there are peoples? To solve it, we must here establish this great truth: that, as the people have certainly by diversity of climates acquired different natures, from which have sprung as many different customs, so from their different natures and customs as many different languages have arisen. (p. 133)

For Vico, the key to the diversity of languages is not the arbitrary character of signs but the variety of human natures. Each language reflects and substantiates the specific character of the culture out of which it springs.

Vico, however, is far away from the first impact of the New World upon the Old, and, in truth, his insights have scarcely been fully explored in our own times. Europeans in the sixteenth century, like ourselves, find it difficult to credit another language with opacity. In other words, they render Indian language transparent, either by limiting or denying its existence or by dismissing its significance as an obstacle to communication between peoples. And as opacity is denied to native speech, so, by the same token, is it denied to native culture. For a specific language and a specific culture are not here, nor are they ever, entirely separable. To divorce them is to turn from the messy, confusing welter of details that characterize a particular society at a particular time to the cool realm of abstract principles. It is precisely to validate such high-sounding principles—"Eloquence brought men from barbarism to civility" or "All men are descended from one man and one woman"—that the Indian languages are peeled away and discarded like rubbish by so many of the early writers. But as we are now beginning fully to understand, reality for each society is constructed to a significant degree out of the *specific* qualities of its language and symbols. Discard the particular words and you have discarded the particular men. And so most of the people of the New World will never speak to us. That communication, with all that we might have learned, is lost to us forever.

### Notes

1. Samuel Daniel, *Poems and a Defence of Ryme*, ed. Arthur Colby Sprague (Cambridge 1930) 11, 957–962.

2. Peter Martyr, *The Decades of the Newe Worlde (De orbe novo)*, trans. Richard Eden, Decade 3, Book 9, in *The First Three English Books on America*, ed. Edward Arber (Birmingham 1885) 177.

3. Antonio de Nebrija, *Gramática de la lengua castellana*, ed. Ig. González-Llubera (Oxford 1926) 3; Lewis Hanke, *Aristotle and the American Indians: A Study in Race Prejudice in the Modern World* (Chicago and London 1959) 8.

4. Martyr (n. 2 above) Decade 2, Book 1, p. 106

5. Christopher Columbus, *Journals and Other Documents on the Life and Voyages of Christopher Columbus*, trans. and ed. Samuel Eliot Morison (New York 1963) 65. For the Spanish, see Cristoforo Colombo, *Diario de Colón, libro de la primera navegación y descubrimiento de la Indias*, ed. Carlos Sanz López [facsimile of the original transcript] (Madrid 1962) fol. 9b. There has been considerable debate about Columbus' journal, which survived only in Las Casas' transcription. But Las Casas indicates that he is quoting Columbus here, and the words are revealing, no matter who penned them.

6. Augustine, *Concerning The City of God against the Pagans*, trans. Henry Bettenson, ed. David Knowles (Harmondsworth 1972) Book 19, Ch. 7, p. 861. The whole passage, with its reference to Roman linguistic colonialism, is interesting in this context:

> . . . the diversity of languages separates man from man. For if two men meet, and are forced by some compelling reason not to pass on but to stay in company, then if neither knows the other's language, it is easier for dumb animals, even of different kinds, to associate together than these men, although both are human beings. For when men cannot communicate their thoughts to each other, simply because of difference of language, all the similarity of their common human nature is of no avail to unite them in fellowship. So true is this that a man would be more cheerful with his dog for company than with a foreigner. I shall be told that the Imperial City has been at pains to impose on conquered peoples not only her yoke but her language also, as a bond of peace and fellowship, so that there should be no lack of interpreters but even a profusion of them. True; but think of the cost of this achievement! Consider the scale of those wars, with all that slaughter of human beings, all the human blood that was shed!

For a variation of the theme of linguistic isolation, see Shakespeare, *Richard II*, ed. Peter Ure (Cambridge, Mass. 1956) I. iii. 159–173.

7. Robert Fabian, in Richard Hakluyt, *The Principal Navigations, Voyages, Traffiques, and Discoveries of the English Nation . . .* (12 vols. Glasgow 1903–05) 7. 155. Roy Harvey Pearce, "Primitivistic Ideas in the *Faerie Queene.*" *Journal of English and Germanic Philology* 44 (1945) 149.

8. In Hakluyt (n. 7 above) 7. 282.

9. See Lee Eldridge Huddleston, *Origins of the American Indians; European Concepts, 1492–1729*, Latin American Monographs 11 (Austin, Tex. 1967) 66.

10. Milton, *Prolusiones*, ed. Donald Leman Clark, trans. Bromley Smith, in *Works*, ed. Frank Allen Peterson (18 vols. New York 1931–38) 12. 277.

11. John H. Parry, *The Spanish Seaborne Empire* (London and New York 1966) 163. Cf. France V. Scholes and Ralph L. Roys: "Although some of the friars, notably Fray Luis de Villalpando and Fray Diego de Landa, learned to speak and write Maya and gave instruction to the others, it is doubtful whether more than half of the clergy became proficient in the language." Quoted in *Landa's relación de las cosas de Yucatán*, trans. Alfred M. Tozzer, *Papers of the Peabody Museum of American Archaeology and Ethnology* 18 (1941) 70 n. 313.

12. Martyr (n. 2 above) Decade 1, Book 1, p. 67. See, in the same volume, Sebastian Münster, p. 29, and Martyr, Decade 2, Book 1, p. 138. For examples of word lists, see Martyr, Decade 3, Book 1, p. 45; Francisco López de Gómara, *The Pleasant Historie of the Conquest of the Weast India, now called New Spayne*, trans. T. N. (London 1578) 370 ff.; John Davis, in Hakluyt (n. 7 above) 7. 398–399; Sir Robert Dudley, in Hakluyt, 10. 211–212; William Strachey, *The Historie of Travell into Virginia Britania (1612)*, ed. Louis B. Wright and Virginia Freund, Hakluyt Society, Ser. 2, 103 (London 1953) 174–207; James Rosier, "Extracts of a Virginian Voyage made An. 1605. by Captaine George Waymouth," in Samuel Purchas, *Hakluytus Posthumus, or Purchas his Pilgrimes*, Hakluyt Society, Extra series (20 vols. Glasgow 1905–07; rpt. of 1625 ed.) 18. 359. The most delightful of the lists is Roger Williams, *A Key into the Language of America* (London 1643; rpt. Providence, R.I. 1936). There are also sample conversations in Indian languages; see Williams, *Key;* Jean de Léry, *Navigatio in Brasiliam Americae*, Ch. 19, in Theodor de Bry, *Americae tertia pars* (Frankfort 1592) 250 ff.; Martyr (n. 2 above) Decade 3, Book 8, p. 170.

13. Lescarbot, in Claude Duret, *Thresor de l'histoire des langues de cest univers* (Cologny 1613) 954–955. I am indebted for this reference and for many useful suggestions to Professor Natalie Zemon Davis.

14. Montaigne, *Selected Essays*, trans. John Florio, ed. Walter Kaiser (Boston 1964) 79. The possibility that Indian language has traces of Greek is explored by Sarmiento de Gamboa and Gregorio García (see Huddleston [n. 9 above] 30, 73), and by Thomas Morton, *New English Canaan*, in *Tracts and Other Papers Relating Principally to the Origin, Settlement, and Progress of the Colonies in North America*, comp. Peter Force (4 vols. Washington [c. 1836–47]; rpt. New York 1947 and Gloucester, Mass. 1963) 2. 15–18.

15. Raleigh, *The Discoverie of the large and bewtiful Empire of Guiana*, ed. V. T. Harlow (London 1928) 38.

16. Quoted in Gary B. Nash, "The Image of the Indian in the Southern Colonial Mind," in *The Wild Man Within: An Image in Western Thought from the Renaissance to Romanticism*, ed. Edward Dudley and Maximillian E. Novak (Pittsburgh 1972) 72. See, likewise, Cornelius J. Jaenen, "Amerindian Views of French Culture in the Seventeenth Century," *Canadian Historical Review* 55 (1974) 276–277.

17. Bartolomé de Las Casas, *A Selection of his Writings*, trans. and ed. George Sanderlin (New York 1971) 144. Thomas More makes the same point in the early sixteenth century to defend English: "For as for that our tong is called barbarous, is but a fantasye. For so is, as euery lerned man knoweth, euery strange language to other." (*Dialogue concerning Heresies*, quoted in J. L. Moore, *Tudor-Stuart Views on the Growth, Status, and Destiny of the English Language*, Studien zur Englischen Philologie 41 (Halle 1920) 19.

18. Oviedo, quoted in Sir Arthur Helps, *The Spanish Conquest of America and its Relation to the History of Slavery and to the Government of Colonies*, ed. M. Oppenheim (4 vols. London 1900–04; rpt. New York 1966) 1. 269.

19. For a nineteenth-century variation, see Daniel Webster's remark in a letter to Ticknor, 1 March 1826: "I ought to say that I am a total unbeliever in the new doctrines about the Indian languages. I believe them to be the rudest forms of speech; and I believe there is as little in the languages of the tribes as in their laws, manners, and customs, worth studying or worth knowing. All this is heresy, I know, but so I think"; see George Ticknor Curtis, *Life of Daniel Webster* (2 vols. New York 1872) 1. 260. By 1826, it should be noted, Webster is on the defensive. I owe this reference to Professor Larzer Ziff.

20. Cicero, *De oratore* I. viii. 33, in *On the Good Life*, trans. Michael Grant (Harmondsworth 1971) 247.

21. Andrea Ugo and Andrea Brenta, in Karl Müllner, *Reden und Briefe Italienischer Humanisten* (Vienna 1899) 110–111, 75–76. See, likewise, in the same volume, the orations of Lapo de Castiglionchio, Andrea Giuliano of Venice, Francesco Filelfo, Antonio da Rho, Tiphernas (Gregorio da Città di Castello), and Giovanni Toscanella.

22. George(?) Puttenham, *The Arte of English Poesie* (London 1589; Scolar Press facs. ed. Menston 1968) 3–4. The myth that Orpheus tamed wild bests by his music is intended to show, according to Puttenham, "how by his discreete and wholesome lessons vttered in harmonie and with melodious instruments, he brought the rude and sauage people to a more ciuill and orderly life, nothing, as it seemeth, more preuailing or fit to redresse and edifie the cruell and sturdie courage of man then it" (4). Without speech, according to Hobbes, "there had been amongst men, neither commonwealth, nor society, nor contract, nor peace, no more than amongst lions, bears, and wolves," *Leviathan*, ed. Michael Oakeshott (Oxford 1960) 18.

23. Puttenham (n. 22 above) 7. See also Sir Philip Sidney, *An Apologie for Poetrie*, in *English Literary Criticism: The Renaissance*, ed. O. B. Hardison, Jr. (New York 1963): "Euen among the most barbarous and simple Indians where no writing is, yet haue they their Poets, who make and sing songs, which they call *Areytos*, both of theyr Auncestors deedes and praises of theyr Gods: a sufficient probabilitie that if euer learning come among them, it must be by hauing theyr hard dull wits softned and sharpened with the sweete delights of Poetrie. For vntill they find a pleasure in the exercises of the minde, great promises of much knowledge will little perswade them that knowe not the fruites of knowledge" (102). On the Indian *Areytos*, see Martyr (n. 2 above) Decade 3, Book 7, pp. 166–167; likewise, Las Casas, *History of the Indies*, trans. and ed. Andrée Collard (New York 1971) 279–280. For a comparable phenomenon in the British Isles, see J. E. C. Hill, "Puritans and The Dark Corners of the Land,'" *Royal Historical Society Transactions*, Ser. 5, 13 (1963) 82: "On Sundays and holy days, we are told of North Wales about 1600, 'the multitude of all sorts of men, women and children' used to meet to hear 'their harpers and crowthers sing them songs of the doings of their ancestors.'"

24. *The Faerie Queene*, VI. iv. 11, in *The Works of Edmund Spenser. A Variorum Edition*, ed. Edwin Greenlaw *et al.* (9 vols. Baltimore 1932–49). On Spenser's Wild Man, see Pearce (n. 7 above) and Donald Cheney, *Spenser's Image of Nature: Wild Man and Shepherd in "The Faerie Queene"* (New Haven 1966). On the figure of the Wild Man, see Dudley and Novak (n. 16 above); Richard Bernheimer, *Wild Men in the Middle Ages: A Study in Art, Sentiment, and Demonology* (Cambridge, Mass. 1952).

25. On the comparison of Indian and Old World words, see Huddleston (n. 9 above) esp. 23, 30, 37, 44, 91–92. The Indians were described by Cotton Mather as "the veriest *ruines of mankind*, which [were] to be found any where upon the face of the earth": quoted in Roy Harvey Pearce, *Savagism and Civilization: A Study of the Indian and the American Mind* (Baltimore 1965; rpt. 1967) 29.

26. Hayden White, "The Forms of Wildness: Archaeology of an Idea," in Dudley and Novak (n. 16 above) 21.

27. "Thei vse no lawful coniunction of mariage, but euery one hath as many women as him listeth, and leaueth them agayn at his pleasure," Sebastian Münster, *A Treatyse of the Newe 'India,'* trans. Richard Eden, in Arber (n. 2 above) 37. See, likewise, Martyr (n. 2 above) Decade 3, Book 1, p. 138; Martyr, trans. Michael Lok, in *A Selection of Curious, Rare, and Early Voyages and Histories of Interesting Discoveries chiefly published by Hakluyt* . . . (London 1812) Decade 8, Ch. 8, p. 673; Laudonnière, in Hakluyt (n. 7 above) 8. 453; Henry Hawks, in Hakluyt (n. 7 above) 9. 386; Bernal Diaz del Castillo, *The Conquest of New Spain*, trans. J. M. Cohen (Baltimore 1963) 19, 122, 124. On one of Frobisher's voyages, a native man and woman, captured separately, are brought together before the silent and eagerly expectant sailors. The observers are astonished at the

"shamefastnes and chastity of those Savage captives" (in Hakluyt [n. 7 above] 7. 306).

28. Martyr, trans. Lok (n. 27 above) Decade 7, Ch. 4, p. 627. "Wandering up and down" seems almost as much of an offense as idolatry. There is a trace of this disapproval and anxiety in the description of Othello as an "erring barbarian," an "extravagant and wheeling stranger."

29. See for example, Martyr, trans. Lok (n. 27 above) Decade 4, Ch. 9, p. 539: "with such a countenance, as we use to paint hobgoblings or spirites which walke by night."

30. In Hakluyt (n. 7 above) 11.297. Note that Spenser uses the same metaphor for his Wild Man: "For he was swift as any bucke in chace" (*FQ*, VI. iv. 8).

31. In Hakluyt (n. 7 above) 8. 201–202.

32. Martyr, ed. Arber (n. 2 above) Decade 3, Book 8, p. 173

33. *Of the newe landes*, in Arber (n. 2 above) p. xxvii; cf. Wilberforce Eames, "Description of a Wood Engraving Illustrating the South American Indians (1505)," *Bulletin of the New York Public Library* 26 (1922) 755–760.

34. See Horst Woldemar Janson, *Apes and Ape Lore in the Middle Ages and the Renaissance* (London 1952).

35. Cicero, *De oratore* I. viii. 32, in *On the Good Life* (n. 20 above) 247.

36. Quoted in Lewis Hanke, "Pope Paul III and the American Indians," *Harvard Theological Review* 30 (1937) 84.

37. Quoted in Hanke (n. 36 above) 72; likewise in Hanke (n. 3 above) 19.

38. Quoted in Hanke (n. 36 above) 102. On his death-bed, Domingo de Betanzos recanted his denigration of the Indians.

39. Massée, in Duret (n. 13 above) 945.

40. For a more sympathetic grasp of the problem of translating religious concepts, see Las Casas (n. 23 above) 238–239; Marc Lescarbot, *History of New France*, trans. W. L. Grant (3 vols. Toronto 1907–14) 2. 179–180; José de Acosta, *The Natural and Moral History of the Indies*, trans. Edward Grimston [1604], ed. Clements R. Markham, Hakluyt Society 60–61 (2 vols. London 1880) 2. 301–302. Cornelius Jaenen (n. 16 above) suggests that the difficulty was more cultural than linguistic: "The natives saw some danger in divulging their religious vocabulary to the evangelists of the new religion, therefore they refused to cooperate extensively in the linguistic task of compiling dictionaries and grammars, and of translating religious books" (277).

41. *The Tempest*, ed. Frank Kermode (Cambridge, Mass. 1954) III. ii. 90–93.

42. Duret (n. 13 above) 935; Chaumonot, quoted in Jaenen (n. 16 above) 275–276.

43. Terence Hawkes, *Shakespeare's Talking Animals* (London 1973) 211. For another appraisal of colonialism in *The Tempest*, see Dominique O. Man-

noni, *Prospero and Caliban: The Psychology of Colonization*, trans. Pamela Powesland (New York 1956) 97–109.

44. "Raids on the inarticulate"—the quotation is from T. S. Eliot's *Four Quartets* and, as Hawkes uses it, eerily invokes the sixteenth-century fantasy that the Indians were without speech.

45. The lines are sometimes attributed, without any textual authority, to Prospero. "Which any print of goodness wilt not take," it might be noted, plays on the *tabula rasa* theme.

46. Shakespeare even appeals to early seventeenth-century class fears by having Caliban form an alliance with the lower-class Stephano and Trinculo to overthrow the noble Prospero. On class-consciousness in the period, see Christopher Hill, "The Many-Headed Monster in Late Tudor and Early Stuart Political Thinking," in *From the Renaissance to the Counter-Reformation. Essays in Honor of Garrett Mattingly*, ed. Charles H. Carter (New York 1965) 296–324.

47. Clifford Geertz, "The Impact of the Concept of Culture on the Concept of Man," in his selected essays, *The Interpretation of Cultures* (New York 1973) 52. I am indebted throughout to this suggestive essay.

48. Enciso, *Suma de geographia*, quoted in Helps (n. 18 above) 1. 279–280.

49. Quoted in Hanke (n. 36 above) 95. It is not impossible that the *caciques* said something vaguely similar; see Las Casas (n. 23 above) 82: "what could we expect from these gentle and unprotected Indians suffering such torments, servitude and decimation but immense pusillanimity, profound discouragement and annihilation of their inner selves, to the point of doubting whether they were men or mere cats?"

50. Las Casas (n. 23 above) 241

51. *Ibid.*, 50–52, 130–131.

52. Both are in James Rosier (n. 12 above) 18. 342, 344.

53. Garcilaso de la Vega, *The Florida of the Inca*, trans. and ed. John Grier Varner and Jeannette Johnson Varner (Austin, Tex. 1951) 69–70; quoted by Howard Mumford Jones, *O Strange New World, American Culture: The Formative Years* (New York 1964; Viking paperback ed. 1967) 25–26.

54. Sir Walter Ralegh, *The History of the World* (London 1614) II. xix. 3, pp. 508–509.

55. In Helps (n. 18 above) 1. 266–267.

56. Las Casas (n. 23 above) 196. "For the actual use of the *Requerimiento*, see Lewis Hanke, *The Spanish Struggle for Justice in the Conquest of America* (Philadelphia 1949; rpt. Boston 1965) 34.

57. Salvador de Madariaga, *The Rise of the Spanish American Empire* (New York 1947) 12.

58. In Helps (n. 18 above) 1. 264.

59. *Ibid.*

60. In Hakluyt (n. 7 above) 8. 466.

61. Giambattista Vico, *The New Science,* trans. Thomas G. Bergin and Max H. Fisch (Ithaca 1948) 132.

# 3

# Marlowe, Marx, and
# Anti-Semitism

A fantasy: Barabas, the Jew of Malta, had two children. The eldest, Abigail, sickened by the revelation that her father had murdered her Christian suitor, converted and entered a nunnery. The other child, a son, likewise apostatized; indeed he wrote a violently anti-Semitic pamphlet denouncing the essence of his father's religion as huckstering, its basis self-interest, its jealous god money. The pamphlet concluded with a call for the emancipation of mankind from Judaism, but, curiously, the son did not convert to Christianity and try to assimilate. On the contrary, he insisted that his father's hated religion was simply the practical essence of Christianity, the thing itself stripped of its spiritual mystifications. The Christians who prided themselves on their superiority to Jews were themselves practicing Judaism in their daily lives, worshipping money, serving egoistic need, buying and selling men as commodities, as so many pounds of flesh. The son's name, of course, was Karl Marx.

The purpose of this paper is to read Marlowe's *The Jew of Malta* in the light of Marx's "On the Jewish Question."[1] Fantasy aside, this is neither an obvious nor a particularly promising enterprise. There was no "Jewish Question" in Marlowe's England; there were scarcely any Jews.[2] Civil society, the rights of man, the political state, the concept of citizenship—Marx's basic terms—would have been quite incomprehensible to an Elizabethan. Marx's central theme, that political emancipation is not the same as human emancipation, would likewise have been incomprehensible in an age in which there was scarcely a conception of politics, in the modern sense, let alone a dream that man might some day be emancipated from both state and religion. Marx's discourse is informed by the Enlightenment, the American and French Revolutions, Feuerbach's analysis of religion, and the growth of capitalism; its occasion, a critique of Bruno Bauer's *Die Judenfrage* and "Die Fähigkeit der heutigen Juden und Christen, frei zu werden," depends upon the particular, historically determined situation of the Ashkenazic Jews of nineteenth-century Germany; its rhetoric is colored both by the virulent modern strain of popular anti-Semitism and by the author's own troubled relationship to the religion of his fathers.[3]

Nevertheless, Marx's essay has a profound bearing upon *The Jew of Malta;* their conjunction enriches our understanding of the authors' relation to ideology and, more generally, raises fruitful questions about a Marxist reading of literature. The fact that both works use the figure of the perfidious Jew provides a powerful interpretive link between Renaissance and modern thought, for despite the great differences to which I have just pointed, this shared reference is not an accident or a mirage. "On the Jewish Question" represents the nineteenth-century development of a late sixteenth-century idea or, more accurately, a late sixteenth-century trope. Marlowe and Marx seize upon the Jew as a kind of powerful rhetorical device, a way of marshaling deep popular hatred and clarifying its object. The Jew is charged not with racial deviance or religious impiety but with economic and social crime, crime that is committed not only *against* the dominant Christian society but, in less "pure" form, by that society. Both writers hope to focus attention upon activity that is seen as at once alien and yet central to the life of the community and to direct against the activity the anti-Semitic feeling of the audience. The Jews themselves in their real historical situation are finally incidental in these works, Marx's as well as Marlowe's, except insofar as they excite the fear and loathing of the great mass of Christians. It is this privileged access to mass psychology by means of a semimythical figure linked in the popular imagination with usury, sharp dealing, and ruthless cunning that attracts both the sixteenth-century playwright and the nineteenth-century polemicist.[4]

Twentieth-century history has demonstrated with numbing force how tragically misguided this rhetorical strategy was, how utterly it underestimated the irrationality, the fixation upon its object, and the persistence of anti-Semitism. The Christian hatred of the Jew, nurtured by popular superstition, middle-class *ressentiment*, the frequent complicity of Church and state, the place of the Jews in the European economy, and the complex religious and cultural barriers, would not be so easily turned against a particular structure of economic or social relations or a cast of mind that crossed racial and religious boundaries but would light with murderous force upon the whole Jewish community. It is folly to attempt to use a people as a rhetorical device or to exploit popular prejudice as a force for constructive change, let alone moral enlightenment. Even granting that historical hindsight gives us an unearned wisdom, even granting all of the mitigating intentions with which the authors evidently used the figure of the Jew, we are obliged to acknowledge that there is something unsavory, inexcusable, about both works. Their nature is subdued to what it works in, like the dyer's hand; they are, I would insist, defiled by the dark forces they are trying to exploit, used by what they are trying to use. But this acknowledgement, necessary if we are to keep our moral bearings and look unflinchingly at the horrors of our history, is not identical with understanding. The latter will come only by patiently exploring what I have called the shared rhetorical strategy of *The Jew of Malta* and "On the Jewish Question."

I will begin by looking briefly at a famous use of the Jewish stereotype that contrasts sharply with Marlowe's and Marx's. *The Merchant of Venice* is built around a series of decisive structural conflicts—Old Law vs. New Law, Justice vs. Mercy, Revenge vs. Love, Calculation vs. Recklessness, Thrift vs. Prodigality—all of which are focused upon the central dramatic conflict of Jew and Gentile or, more precisely, of Jewish fiscalism and Gentile mercantilism.[5] The great economic utility of Shylock—and of the Jew in this period—is his possession of liquid assets, assets which he is committed, for his very existence, to employ actively.[6] In general, in the northern Italian city-states, when the Christian merchants were weaker, the Jewish moneylenders were stronger; in Venice, as Brian Pullan has shown, there was a vigorous attempt by the merchant class to undermine the power of Jewish moneylenders through the establishment of the Monte di Caritá, Christian lending institutions that would disrupt the Jews' "bargains" by providing interest-free loans.[7] All of this seems to be reflected in the hatred Shylock and Antonio have for each other, hatred Antonio attributes to the fact that he has "oft deliver'd from his forfeitures / Many that have at times made moan to me" (3.3.22–23).[8]

If Shylock is set against Antonio on grounds of fiscalism vs. mercantilism, he is set against Portia on grounds equally based upon the economic position of Jews in early modern Europe. As Jacob Katz observes, the constant application of capital, to which the Jews were committed, precluded investment in immovable property. The law did not permit the Jew to acquire land, and the Jew, for his part, did not attempt to secure such permission:

> Landed property attracted the ordinary burgher who attained wealth because of the feeling of stability and economic security it gave him and the social prestige involved. But in his peculiar situation, the Jew would set no great store by either. He could not hope to perpetuate his wealth in that locality, nor did he seek a niche in the dominant social

and economic hierarchy. The economic nexus linking the Jew with his environment was purely instrumental.[9]

In Shakespeare's play this economic nexus is suggested above all by Shylock's usury, but it is also symbolized by his nonparticipation in Venetian society, his cold, empty house, and such subtle indicators of value as his hostility to masquing–"the vile squealing of the wry-neck'd fife" (2.5.30). All of this is in sharp contrast to Portia, who has plenty of liquid assets; she can offer at a moment's notice enough gold to pay Antonio's 3000-ducat debt "twenty times over" (3.2.306). But her special values in the play are bound up with her house at Belmont and all it represents: its starlit garden, enchanting music, hospitality, social prestige. That is, the economic nexus linking Portia with her environment is precisely *not* instrumental; her world is not a field in which she operates for profit, but a living web of noble values and moral orderliness.

Shylock is the antithesis of this world, as he is of the Christian mercantilism of Venice. He is the "alien," the "stranger cur," "a kind of devil," in short, the "faithless Jew." Even the language he shares with the Christian Venetians does not provide a bridge between them; he may use the same words, but he uses them in a wholly different sense:

> *Shylock:* Antonio is a good man.
> *Bassanio:* Have you heard any imputation to the contrary?
> *Shylock:* Ho no, no, no, no: my meaning in saying he is a good
> man, is to have you understand that he is sufficient.
> [1.3.10–15]

Shylock needs to explain his use of the apparently innocuous "good man," as he will later be pressed to explain why he insists, against all reason and self-interest, upon his bond: linguistically, psychologically, ethically, as well as religiously, he is different. To be sure, he appeals at moments to his sameness–"Hath not a Jew eyes?"—and this sameness runs like a dark current through the play, intimating secret bonds that no one, not even the audience, can fully acknowledge. For if Shakespeare subtly suggests obscure links between Jew and Gentile, he compels the audience to transform its disturbing perception of sameness into a reassuring perception of difference. Indeed the Jew seems to embody the abstract principle of *difference* itself, the principle to which he appeals when the Duke demands an explanation for his malice:

Some men there are love not a gaping pig!
Some that are mad if they behold a cat!
And others when the bagpipe sings i'th'nose,
Cannot contain their urine. . . .

[4.1.46–49]

The examples would be whimsical—evoking a motive no grander than allegory—were they not spoken by Shylock, knife in hand; instead, they bespeak impulses utterly inaccessible to reason and persuasion; they embody what the rational mind, intent upon establishing an absolute category of difference, terms *madness*.

*The Jew of Malta* opens with an apparent gesture toward the same principle of differentiation that governs *The Merchant of Venice*. Marlowe's Jew is introduced in the prologue by Macheuill as one "Who smiles to see how full is bags are cramb'd"; he enters, then, already trailing clouds if ignominy, already a "marked case." But while never relinquishing the anti-Semitic stereotype, Marlowe quickly suggests that the Jew is not the exception to but rather the true representative of his society. Though he begins with a paean to liquid assets, Barabas is not primarily a usurer, set off by his hated occupation from the rest of the community, but a great merchant, sending his argosies around the world exactly as Shakespeare's much-loved Antonio does. His pursuit of wealth does not mark him out but rather establishes him— if anything, rather respectably—in the midst of all the other forces in the play: the Turks exacting tribute from the Christians; the Christians expropriating money from the Jews; the convent profiting from these expropriations; religious orders competing for wealthy converts; the prostitute plying her trade and the blackmailer his. When the governor of Malta asks the Turkish "Bashaw," "What wind drives you thus into *Malta* rhode?" the latter replies with perfect frankness, "The wind that bloweth all the world besides, / Desire of gold" (3.1421–23). Barabas' own desire of gold, so eloquently voiced at the start and vividly enacted in the scene in which he hugs his money bags, is the glowing core of that passion which fires all the characters. To be sure, other values are expressed—love, faith, and honor—but as private values, these are revealed to be hopelessly fragile, while as public values, they are revealed to be mere screens for powerful economic forces. Thus, on the one hand, Abigail, Don Mathias, and the nuns are killed off with remarkable ease and, in effect, with the complicity of the laughing audience. (The audience of the Royal Shakespeare Company's brilliant 1964 production roared with delight when the poisoned nuns came tumbling out of the house.)[10] On the other hand, the public invocation of Christian ethics or knightly honor is always linked by Marlowe to baser motives. The knights concern themselves with Barabas' "inherent sinne" only at the moment when they are about to preach him out of his possessions, while the decision to resist the "barbarous mis-beleeuing *Turkes*" facilitates all too easily the sale into slavery of a shipload of Turkish captives. The religious and political ideology that seems at first to govern Christian attitudes toward infidels in fact does nothing of the sort; this ideology is clearly subordinated to considerations of profit. In Marx's terms, both religion and the political state are shown to rest upon the foundation of civil society which is entirely governed by the relentless pursuit of money.

Because of the primacy of money, Barabas, for all the contempt heaped upon him, is seen as the dominant spirit of the play, its most energetic and inventive force. A victim at the level of religion and political power, he is, in effect, emancipated at the level of civil society, emancipated in Marx's contemptuous use of the word:

> The Jew has emancipated himself in a Jewish manner, not only by acquiring the power of money, but also because *money* had become, through him and also apart from him, a world power, while the practical Jewish spirit has become the practical spirit of the Christian nations. The Jews have emancipated themselves in so far as the Christians have become Jews. [P. 35]

Barabas' avarice, egotism, duplicity, and murderous cunning do not signal his exclusion from the world of Malta but rather his central place within it. His "Judaism" is, again in Marx's words, "a universal *antisocial* element of the *present time*" (p. 34).

For neither Marlowe nor Marx does this recognition signal a turning away from Jew-baiting; if anything, Jew-baiting is intensified even as the hostility it excites is directed as well against Christian society. Thus Marlowe never discredits anti-Semitism, but he does discredit early in the play a "Christian" social concern that might otherwise have been used to counter a specifically Jewish antisocial element. When the governor of Malta seizes the wealth of the Jews on the grounds that it is "better one want for a common good, / Then many perish for a priuate man" (1.331–32), an audience at all familiar with the New Testament will hear in these words echoes not of Christ but of Caiaphas and, a few lines further on, of Pilate.[11] There are, to be sure, moments of social solidarity—as when the Jews gather around Barabas to comfort him or when Ferneze and Katherine together mourn the death of their sons—but they are brief and ineffectual. The true emblem of the society of the play is the slave market where

"Euery ones price is written on his backe" (2.764).[12] Here in the market-place men are literally turned, in Marx's phrase, "into *alienable*, sale-able objects, in thrall to egoistic need and huckstering" (p. 39). And at this level of society, the religious and political barriers fall away: the Jew buys a Turk at the Christian slave market. Such is the triumph of civil society.

For Marlowe as for Marx, the dominant mode of perceiving the world, in a society hagridden by the power of money and given over to the slave market, is *contempt*, contempt aroused in the beholders of such a society and, as important, governing the behavior of those who bring it into being and function within it. This is Barabas' con-stant attitude, virtually his signature; his withering scorn lights not only on the Christian rulers of Malta ("thus slaues will learne," he sneers, when the defeated governor is forced into submission [5.2150]), but on his daughter's suitor ("the slaue looks like a hogs cheek new sindg'd" [2.803]), his daughter ("An *Hebrew* borne, and would become a Christian. / *Cazzo, diabolo*" [4.1527–28]), his slave Ithamore ("Thus euery villaine ambles after wealth / Although he ne're be richer then in hope" [3.1354–55]), the Turks ("How the slaue jeeres at him," ob-serves the governor of Barabas greeting Calymath [5.2339]), the pimp, Pilia-Borza ("a shaggy, totter'd staring slaue" [4.1858]), his fellow Jews ("See the simplicitie of these base slaues" [1.448]), and even, when he has blundered by making the poison too weak, himself ("What a damn'd slaue was I" [5.2025]). Barabas' frequent asides assure us that he is feeling contempt even when he is not openly expressing it, and the reiteration of the derogatory epithet "slaue" firmly anchors this contempt in the structure of relations that governs the play. Barabas's liberality in bestowing this epithet—from the governor to the pimp—reflects the extraordinary unity of the structure, its intri-cate series of mirror images: Pilia-Borza's extortion racket is repeated at the "national" level in the extortion of the Jewish community's wealth and at the international level in the Turkish extortion of the Christian tribute. It is as if the play were anticipating the historian Frederic Lane's notion of Renaissance international relations as a kind of glorified gangsterism, a vast "protection" racket.[13]

At all levels of society in Marlowe's play and behind each version of the racket (and making it possible) is violence or the threat of violence, and so here too Barabas' murderousness is presented both as a characteristic of his accursed tribe and as the expression of a universal phenomenon. This expression, to be sure, is extravagant—he is responsible, directly or indirectly, for the deaths of Mathias, Lodowick, Abigail, Pila-Borza, Bellamira, Ithamore, Frair Jacamo, Friar Barnadine, and innumerable poisoned nuns and massacred soldiers—but then everything about Barabas is extravagant: he is more contemptuous than anyone else, more resourceful, cynical, egotistical, and avaricious. The difference, however, in each of these cases is of degree rather than of kind; Barabas expresses in extreme, unmediated form the motives that have been partially disguised by the spiritual humbug of Christianity. Barabas cannot *in the last analysis* be assimilated to his world—Marlowe ultimately veers away from so entirely sociological a conception—but it is important to grasp the great extent to which the Jew is *brought into being* by the Christian society around him. His extraordinary energy does not alter the fact of his passivity throughout the play; his actions are always *responses* to the initiatives of others. Not only is the plot of the whole play set in motion by the governor's expropriation of Barabas' wealth, but each of Barabas' particular plots is a reaction to what he perceives as a provocation or a threat. Only his final stratagem—the betrayal of the Turks—seems an exception, since the Jew is for once in power, but even this fatal blunder is a response to his perfectly sound perception that *"Malta hates me, and in hating me / My life's in danger"* (5.2131–32).

Barabas' passivity sits strangely with his entire domination of the spirit of the play, and, once again, we may turn to Marx for an explication:

> Judaism could not create a new world. It could only bring the new creations and conditions of the world within its own sphere of activity, because practical need, the spirit of which is self-interest, is always passive, cannot expand at will, but *finds* itself extended as a result of the continued development of society. [P. 38]

Though the Jew is identified here with the spirit of egotism and selfish need, his success is credited to the triumph of Christianity which "objectifies" and hence alienates all national, natural, moral, and theoretical relationships, dissolving "the human world into a world of atomistic, antagonistic individuals" (p. 39). The concrete emblem of this alienation in Marlowe's play is the slave market: its ideological expression is the religious chauvinism that sees Jews as inherently sinful, Turks as barbarous misbelievers.

*The Jew of Malta* ends on a powerfully ironic note of this "spiritual egoism" (to use Marx's phrase) when the governor celebrates the treacherous destruction of Barabas and the Turks by giving due praise "Neither to Fate nor Fortune, but to Heauen" (5.2410). (Once again, the National Theater's audience guffawed at this bit of hypocritical sententiousness.) But we do not have to wait until the closing moments of the play to witness the Christian practice of alienation. It is, as I have suggested, present throughout and nowhere more powerfully than in the figure of Barabas himself. For not only are Barabas' actions called forth by Christian actions, but his identity itself is to a great extent the product of the Christian conception of a Jew's identity. This is not entirely the case: Marlowe invokes an "indigenous" Judaism in the wicked parody of the materialism of Job and in Barabas' repeated invocation of Hebraic exclusivism ("These swine-eating Christians," etc.). Nevertheless, Barabas' sense of himself, his characteristic response to the world, and his self-presentation are very largely constructed out of the materials of the dominant, Christian culture. This is nowhere more evident than in his speech which is virtually composed of hard little aphorisms, cynical adages, worldly maxims—all the neatly packaged nastiness of his society. Where Shylock, as we have seen, is differentiated from the Christians even in his use of the common language, Barabas is inscribed at the center of the society of the play, a society whose speech is a tissue of aphorisms. Whole speeches are little more than strings of sayings: maxims are exchanged, inverted, employed as weapons; the characters enact and even deliberately "stage" proverbs (with all of the manic energy of Breughel's "Netherlandish Proverbs"). When Barabas, intent upon poisoning the nuns, calls for the pot of rice porridge, Ithamore carries it to him along with a ladle, explaining that since "the prouerb saies, he that eats with the deuil had need for a long spoone, I haue brought you a Ladle" (3.1360–62).[14] And when Barabas and Ithamore together strangle Friar Barnadine, to whom Abigail has revealed their crimes in confession, the Jew explains, "Blame not vs but the prouerb, Confes & be hang'd" (4.1655).

Proverbs in *The Jew of Malta* are a kind of currency, the compressed ideological wealth of the society. Their terseness corresponds to that concentration of material wealth that Barabas celebrates: "Infinite riches in a little roome." Barabas' own store of these ideological riches comprises the most cynical and self-serving portion:

> Who is honour'd now but for his wealth?
> [1.151]

> *Ego mihimet sum semper proximus.*
> [1.228]

> A reaching thought will search his deepest wits,
> And cast with cunning for the time to come.
> [1.455–56]

> . . . in extremitie
> We ought to make barre of no policie.
> [1.507–8]

> . . . Religion
> Hides many mischiefes from suspition.
> [1.519–20]

> Now will I shew my selfe to haue more of the Serpent
> Then the Doue; that is, more knaue than foole.
> [2.797–98]

> Faith is not to be held with Heretickes.
> [2.1076]

> For he that liueth in Authority,
> And neither gets him friends, nor fils his bags,
> Liues like the Asse that *Æsope* speaketh of,
> That labours with a load of bread and wine,
> And leaues if off to snap on Thistle tops.
> [5.2139–43]

> For so I liue, perish may all the world.
> [5.2292]

This is not the exotic language of the Jews but the product of the whole society, indeed its most familiar and ordinary face. And as the essence of proverbs is their anonymity, the effect of their recurrent use by Barabas is to render him more and more typical, to *de-individualize* him. This is, of course, the opposite of the usual process. Most dramatic characters—Shylock is the appropriate example—accumulate identity in the course of their play; Barabas loses it. He is never again as distinct and unique an individual as he is in the first moments:

> Goe tell 'em the Iew of *Malta* sent thee, man:
> Tush, who amongst 'em knowes not *Barabas?*
> [1.102–3]

Even his account of his past—killing sick people or poisoning wells—tends to make him more vague and unreal, accommodating him to an abstract, anti-Semitic fantasy of a Jew's past. The shift that critics have noted in Barabas' language, from the resonant eloquence of the opening to the terse irony of the close, is part of Marlowe's rhetorical design. It is one of the ways in which he reveals Barabas as the alienated essence of Christian society.

Even the Jew's exclusion from political power does not mark him off decisively from Christian society; rather it enacts, as Marx puts it, "the contradiction between politics and the power of money." The relationship between Barabas and the world of the play is almost perfectly expressed by Marx's own aphorisms:

> The Jew, who occupies a distinctive place in civil society, only manifests in a distinctive way the Judaism of civil society.
>
> Judaism has been preserved, not in spite of history, but by history.
>
> It is from its own entrails that civil society ceaselessly engenders the Jew. [P. 36]

With these aphorisms we are close to the heart of *The Jew of Malta*, as close, in any case, as Marx's "On the Jewish Question" will take us. But precisely at this point we should, I think, feel a certain uneasiness, for where Marx would collapse the Jew into "the Judaism of civil society," Marlowe insists upon elements of Barabas' character which do sharply and qualitatively distinguish him even from the world that has engendered him and whose spirit he expresses. For his own part, Barabas insistently excludes himself from all groups, Turks, Christians, *and* Jews:

> Nay, let 'em combat, conquer, and kill all,
> So they spare me, my daughter, and my wealth.
> [1.191–92]

By itself this sentiment is not surprising; it is simply the expression of that ruthless egotism fostered by the whole society. But Barabas does seem set apart from everyone in the play, especially in his cold clarity of vision, his apparent freedom from all ideology. "A counterfet profession is better / Then vnseene hypocrisie" (1.531–32), he tells his daughter. In the long run, the play challenges this conviction, at least from the point of view of survival; the governor, who is the very embodiment of "vnseene hypocrisie," eventually triumphs over the Jew's "counterfet profession." But Marlowe uses the distinction to direct the audience's allegiance toward Barabas; to lie and to know that one is lying seems more attractive, more moral even, than to lie and believe that one is telling the truth.

The ethical basis of such a discrimination does not bear scrutiny; what matters is that the audience becomes Barabas' accomplice. And the pact is affirmed over and over again in Barabas' frequent, malevolently comic asides:

> *Lodowick:* Good *Barabas* glance not at our holy Nuns
> *Barabas:* No, but I doe it through a burning zeale,
>   *Hoping ere long to set the house a fire.* (Aside)
>      [2.849–51]

Years ago, in Naples, I watched a deft pickpocket lift a camera from a tourist's shoulder bag and replace it instantaneously with a rock of equal weight. The thief spotted me watching but did not run away—instead he winked, and I was frozen in mute complicity. In *The Jew of Malta*, the audience's conventional silence becomes the silence of the passive accomplice, winked at by his fellow criminal. Such a relationship is, of course, itself conventional. The Jew has, for the audience, something of the attractiveness of the wily, misused slave in Roman comedy who is always on the brink of disaster, always revealed to have a trick or two up his sleeve. The mythic core of this character's endless resourcefulness is comic resurrection, and, though Barabas is destined for a darker end, he is granted at least one such moment: thrown over the city walls and left for dead, he springs up full of scheming energy. At this moment, as elsewhere in the play, the audience waits expectantly for Barabas' recovery, *wills* his continued existence, and hence identifies with him.[15]

Along with this identification, the audience grants Barabas certain traditional rights by allowing him the privileged status of unmasker or satirist. Where in Marx's "On the Jewish Question" there is an unvoiced but essential boundary between the author, who stands free of the social structure he excoriates, and the Jew, who is the quintessential product of that social structure, in Marlowe's play the boundary is blurred and the Jew linked in subtle ways with the playwright. The result is that even as the audience perceives Barabas as the alienated essence of Christian society, it identifies with Barabas as the scourge of that society.

The most striking indication of a subtle link between Marlowe and his hero, a link that distinguishes the Jew from the world around him and justifies the audience's identification with him, is Barabas' unique capacity for what one must call aesthetic experience. In his opening soliloquy this is manifested as an eloquent appreciation of his wealth:

> Bags of fiery *Opals, Saphires, Amatists,*
> *Iacints,* hard *Topas,* grasse-greene *Emeraulds,*
> Beauteous *Rubyes,* sparkling *Diamonds,*
> And seildsene costly stones. . . .
>      [1.60–63]

Though the passion for wealth is widely shared, no one else in the play is capable of such a response. And it becomes clear that it is not only wealth that excites Barabas' energy, eloquence, and delight; money is not finally the jealous god of the Jew of Malta. To be sure, Barabas does speak to the end of turning a profit, but wealth is gradually displaced as the *exclusive* object of his concern; his main object through the latter half of the play seems to be revenge, at any cost, upon the Christians. Then, with his attempt to destroy the Turks and restore the Christians to power, it becomes evident that even revenge is not Barabas' exclusive object. At the end he seems to be pursuing deception virtually for its own sake:

> why, is not this
> A kingly kinde of trade to purchase Townes
> By treachery, and sell 'em by deceit?
> Now tell me, worldlings, vnderneath the sunne
> If greater falsehood euer has bin done.
> [5.2329–33]

As Barabas, hammer in hand, constructs the machinery for this climactic falsehood, it is difficult not to equate him with the playwright himself, constructing the plot, and Marlowe appears consciously to encourage this perception: "Leaue nothing loose, all leueld to my mind," Barabas instructs his carpenters, "Why now I see that you haue Art indeed" (5.2285–86). Deception here takes on something of the status of literary art, and we might recall that Plato's rival Gorgias held that deception—*apate*—is the very essence of the creative imagination: the tragic artist's special power is the power to deceive. Such a conception of art does not preclude its claim to strip away fraud since tragedy "with its myths and emotions has created a deception such that its successful practitioner is nearer to reality than the unsuccessful, and the man who lets himself be deceived is wiser than he who does not." This paradox in Gorgias depends upon an epistemology and ontology summed up in his proposition that "Nothing whatever exists." And, as I have argued elsewhere, it is precisely this dark vision, this denial of Being, that haunts all of Marlowe's plays.[16]

Barabas devises falsehoods so eagerly because he is himself a falsehood, a fiction composed of the sleaziest materials in his culture. At times he seems almost aware of himself as such: "we are villaines both" (5.979), he announces to Ithamore after they have run through a catalog of outrageous, blatantly fictional misdeeds. In celebrating deception, he is celebrating himself—not simply his cunning, his power to impose himself on others, his inventiveness, but his very distance from ontological fullness. Barabas is the Jewish Knight of Non-Being. From this perspective, the language shift, to which I alluded earlier, is a deliberate assault upon that immediacy, that sense of presence, evoked at the beginning in Barabas's rich poetry with its confident sense of realized identity. "Infinite riches in a little roome" is speech dreaming its plenitude, its *possession* of being.[17] Without that opening soliloquy, so unlike anything Barabas speaks thereafter, we would have no norm by which to measure his *effacement;* he exists subsequently in the failure of the opening rhetoric to return, in the spaces between his words, in his lack of substance. He is a thing of nothing.

This is why the particular objects Barabas sets for himself and passionately pursues seem nonetheless curiously unreal: nothing can desire nothing. But if there is no substance, within or without, there remains in Barabas an intense, playful energy. Marlowe's hero is not defined finally by the particular object he pursues but by the eerie playfulness with which he pursues it. This playfulness manifests itself as cruel humor, murderous practical jokes, a penchant for the outlandish and the absurd, delight in role-playing, entire absorption in the game at hand and consequent indifference to what lies outside the boundaries of the game, radical insensitivity to human complexity and suffering, extreme but disciplined aggression, hostility to transcendence and indeed to the whole metaphysics of presence. There is some evidence for a similar dark playfulness in Marlowe's own career, with the comic (and extremely dangerous) blasphemies, the nearly overt (and equally dangerous) homosexuality, the mysterious stint as double agent, and, of course the cruel, aggressive plays themselves. The will to play flaunts society's cherished orthodoxies, embraces what the culture finds loathsome or frightening, transforms the serious into the joke and then unsettles the category of the joke by taking it seriously. For Barabas, as for Marlowe himself, this is play on the brink of an abyss, *absolute* play.

Nothing could be further from Marx. To be sure, Marx dreamed of play as the very center of social existence but only in a society transformed by communism. The essential quality of this revolutionary playfulness is the return of man's powers to himself through the abolition of the division of labor and hence a liberated polymorphousness:

> As soon as the distribution of labour comes into being, each man has a particular, exclusive sphere of activity, which is forced upon him and from which he cannot escape. He is a hunter, a fisherman, a shepherd, or a critical critic, and must remain so if he does not want

to lose his means of livelihood; while in communist society, where nobody has one exclusive sphere of activity but each can become accomplished in any branch he wishes, society regulates the general production and thus makes it possible for me to do one thing today and another tomorrow, to hunt in the morning, fish in the afternoon, rear cattle in the evening, criticise after dinner, just as I have a mind, without ever becoming hunter, fisherman, shepherd or critic.[18]

This is, in effect, a hypostatization of the experience of writing or reading literature, a realization at the level of the body in time and space of what we now only imaginatively experience. Marx then reserves, in the ideal scheme of things, an extraordinarily privileged place for what we think of as the play of art. But precisely by locating this experience in an historical or, if you will, posthistorical moment, Marx cuts literature off from absolute play, from its essence as Marlowe conceives it. Before its concrete, material realization in a truly communist society, play can never be in and for itself; it is rather a way station, a form of planning, a mode at once of criticism and of prophecy. The vision of the revolutionary society for Marx, like the apocalyptic vision in Christianity, undermines the autonomy of play and renders it a critical reflection upon everything that exists or a model of nonalienated labor.[19] As the former, play may keep man from being locked in the reified structures of his particular society; as the latter, it may keep alive in a dark time certain vital human possibilities. But it is not emancipation itself which must always be pursued beyond the particular moments of liberated artistic play.[20]

It is this passionate, relentless pursuit of emancipation that governs Marx's rhetorical strategy in "On the Jewish Question," and it is this rhetorical strategy—the quest for a world without "Jews" or "Judaism"—that is ultimately blocked in The Jew of Malta by Marlowe's absolute play, that is, by his buried identification with Barabas. This identification should not be overstated: Barabas is not, after all, an artist; the trap door and cauldron are not a playwright's plot but a Machiavelli's. The connection between the artist and the Jew is only strong enough to complicate the conclusion, based on our use of Marx's essay, that Barabas is the alienated essence of Christian society. To shore up this conclusion, we could argue that Barabas' passion for deceptive play does not exist for its own sake but rather to serve his instinct for survival: "For so I liue, perish may all the world" (5.2292). Such an argument would serve to reintegrate Barabas into the now familiar world of rapacious egotism. Yet beneath this egotism, so zestfully proclaimed in his asides, lies a dark, indeed scarcely visible, but potent self-destructiveness.

This self-destructiveness certainly does not exist at the level of conscious motivation, and with a character who manifests as little interiority as Barabas, it is difficult and quite possibly pointless to talk of unconscious motivation. The self-destructiveness rather is built into the very structure of Barabas' identity. He is determined, he says, to survive, determined not to be "a senseless lumpe of clay / That will with euery water wash to dirt" (1.450–51), determined not to "vanish ore the earth in ayre, / And leaue no memory that e're I was" (1.499–500). Yet the play as a whole depicts Barabas' own commitment to just such erosion of himself as a complex, integrated subject. Having cut himself off from everyone and everything, neither persecuted outsider nor accepted insider, he is a far more shadowy figure at the close than he was at the start. That he dies in his own trap is no accident, nor is it solely the result of the governor's superior cunning: his career is in its very essence suicidal. He proclaims that he always wants to serve his own self-interest: *"Ego mihimet sum semper proximus"* (1.228); but where exactly is the self whose interests he serves? Even the Latin tag betrays an ominous self-distance: "I am always my own neighbor," or even, "I am always *next* to myself." Beneath the noisy protestations of self-interest, his career is a steady, stealthy dispossession of himself, an extended vanishing, an assault upon the subject.

Once again we might attempt to reintegrate Barabas into his world and find in his self-destructiveness the supreme expression of that "human self-estrangement" Marx saw embodied in the Jew. But we are prevented from doing so by the uncanny sense that we have an unmistakable complicity in Barbaras' whole career, that Marlowe would have us admire Barabas' progress toward the boiling cauldron as he would have us admire the Jew's cynical clarity of vision and his playfulness. Where Marx depicts human self-estrangement in order to turn his readers toward pursuit of human emancipation, Marlowe depicts something very similar in order to disabuse his audience of certain illusions. And the greatest of these illusions is that human emancipation can be achieved.

Marx can finally envisage the liberation of mankind from what he inexcusably calls "Judaism." Marlowe cannot. In fact, Marlowe celebrates his Jew for being clearer, smarter, and more self-destructive than the Christians whose underlying values Barabas travesties and transcends. Self-destructiveness in the play, as elsewhere in Marlowe's work, is a much-admired virtue, for it is the sign that the hero has divested himself of hope and committed himself instead to the anarchic, playful discharge of his energy. Nothing stands in the way of this discharge, not even survival, and certainly not that imaginary construction, that collection of social scraps and offal, that is Barabas' identity. This identity—everything that marks him as at once his society's most-hated enemy and its most characteristic product—is in the last analysis subordinate to his radical will to play, the will that is inseparable from the process that destroys him.

*The Jew of Malta* diverges most crucially from Marx at the point at which the latter invokes, in effect, what Ernst Bloch calls *Das Prinzip Hoffnung*, the principle of hope. In Marx there is the principle of hope without the will to play; in Marlowe, the will to play without the principle of hope.

## Notes

1. All citations to Marlowe's *The Jew of Malta (Complete Works*, ed., C. F. Tucker Brooke [Oxford, 1910]) and Marx's "On the Jewish Question" *(Early Writings*, trans. and ed. T. B. Bottomore [New York, 1963]) will appear in the text.

2. On Jews in Renaissance England, see Cecil Roth, *A History of the Jews in England* (Oxford, 1964); Salo W. Baron, *A Social and Religious History of the Jews*, 2ed., vol. 2, *Citizen or Alien Conjurer* (New York, 1967); and C. J. Sisson, "A Colony of Jews in Shakespeare's London," *Essays and Studies* 22 (1937): 38–51.

3. On Marx's essay, see Shlomo Avinieri, *The Social and Political Thought of Karl Marx* (Cambridge, 1968), pp. 43–46; Isaiah Berlin, *Karl Marx: His Life and Environment*, 3d ed. (London, 1963), pp. 27, 99–100; Jean-Yves Calvez, *La Pensée de Karl Marx*, 6th ed. (Paris, 1956), pp. 64–78; Franz Mehring, *Karl Marx: The Story of His Life*, trans. Edward Fitzgerald (Ann Arbor, Mich., 1962), pp. 68–73; Robert C. Tucker, *Philosophy and Myth in Karl Marx* (Cambridge, 1961), pp. 111–13; and Istvan Meszaros, *Marx's Theory of Alienation* (London, 1970), pp. 28–31, 71–74.

4. Anti-Semitism, it should be emphasized, is never merely a trope to be adopted or discarded by an author as he might choose to employ zeugma or eschew personification. It is charged from the start with irrationality and bad faith and only partly rationalized as a rhetorical strategy. Marlowe depicts his Jew with the compulsive cruelty that characterizes virtually all of his work, while Marx's essay obviously has elements of a sharp, even hysterical, denial of his religious background. It is particularly tempting to reduce the latter work to a dark chapter in its author's personal history. The links I am attempting to establish with Marlowe or the more direct link with Feuerbach, however, locate the essay in a far wider context. Still, the extreme violence of the latter half of Marx's work and his utter separation of himself from the people he excoriates undoubtedly owe much to his personal situation. It is interesting that the tone of the attack on the Jews rises to an almost ecstatic disgust at the moment when Marx seems to be locating the Jews most clearly as a

product of bourgeois culture; it is as if Marx were eager to prove that he is in no way excusing or forgiving the Jews.

5. All citations to *The Merchant of Venice*, ed. John Russell Brown (Cambridge, Mass., 1955), will appear in the text. There is a useful summary of the voluminous criticism of the play by Norman Rabkin, "Meaning and Shakespeare," in *Shakespeare 1971*, ed. Clifford Leech and J. M. R. Margeson, Proceedings of the World Shakespeare Congress, Vancouver, 1971 (Toronto, 1972, pp. 89–106. Of particular importance are C. L. Barber's chapter on the play in *Shakespeare's Festive Comedy* (Princeton, N.J., 1959) and Barbara Lewalski's "Biblical Allusion and Allegory in *The Merchant of Venice*," *Shakespeare Quarterly* 13 (1962): 327–43. On usury and Shakespeare's play, see John W. Draper, "Usury in *The Merchant of Venice*," *Modern Philology* 33 (1935): 37–47; E. C. Pettet, "*The Merchant of Venice* and the Problem of Usury," *Essays and Studies* 31 (1946): 19–33; and Benjamin Nelson, *The Idea of Usury: From Tribal Brotherhood to Universal Otherhood* (Princeton, N.J., 1949). On fiscalism and mercantilism, see Immanuel Wallerstein, *The Modern World-System: Capitalist Agriculture and the Origins of the European World-Economy in the Sixteenth Century* (New York, 1974), pp. 147–51.

6. See Jacob Katz, *Tradition and Crisis: Jewish Society at the End of the Middle Ages* (1st ed., 1958; New York, 1971), pp. 46–47; see also Anthony Molho, "A Note on Jewish Moneylenders in Tuscany in the Late Trecento and Early Quattrocento," in *Renaissance Studies in Honor of Hans Baron*, ed. Anthony Molho and John A. Tedeschi (Florence, 1971), pp. 101–17.

7. See Brian Pullan, *Rich and Poor in Renaissance Venice: The Social Institutions of a Catholic State, to 1620* (Oxford, 1971).

8. Shylock seems, in part at least, to confirm this notion at 3.1.46 ff.

9. Katz, *Tradition and Crisis*, pp. 47–48.

10. This was the invention of the director, Clifford Williams; in Marlowe's text only the dying Abigail appears. There is a discussion of this and other productions of Marlowe's play in James L. Smith's "*The Jew of Malta* in the Theatre," in *Christopher Marlowe*, ed. Brian Morris, Mermaid Critical Commentaries (London, 1968), pp. 1–23.

11. See G. K. Hunter, "The Theology of Marlowe's *The Jew of Malta*," *Journal of the Warburg and Courtauld Institutes* 27 (1964): 236.

12. Shylock attempts to make this a similarly central issue in the trial scene, but, as we might expect, the attempt fails (4.1.90–100).

13. Frederic C. Lane, *Venice and History* (Baltimore, 1966).

14. For the Jew as devil, see Joshua Trachtenberg, *The Devil and the Jews: The Medieval Conception of the Jew and Its Relation to Modern Antisemitism* (New Haven, Conn., 1943).

15. See my "The False Ending in *Volpone*," *JEGP* 75 (1976): 93.

16. For Gorgias, see Mario Untersteiner, *The Sophists*, trans. Kathleen Freeman (Oxford, 1954), p. 113; Thomas G. Rosenmeyer, "Gorgias, Aeschylus,

and *Apate*," *American Journal of Philology* 76 (1955): 255–60. For Marlowe's "Gorgian" aesthetic, see my "Marlowe and Renaissance Self-Fashioning," in *Two Renaissance Mythmakers*, ed. Alvin B. Kernan, Selected Papers from the English Institute 1975–76 (Baltimore, 1977).

17. For an illuminating discussion of this concept of presence in Western ontotheology, see Jacques Derrida, *Of Grammatology*, trans. Gayatri Chakravorty Spivak (Baltimore, 1974), pp. 27–73.

18. Marx, *The German Ideology*, pt. 1, in *The Marx-Engels Reader*, ed. Robert C. Tucker (New York, 1972), p. 124.

19. On the problematical status of play in Marx's thought, see Francis Hearn, "Toward a Critical Theory of Play," *Telos* 30 (1976–77): 145–60; on art as a model of nonalienated labor, see Hans Robert Jauss, "The Idealist Embarrassment: Observations on Marxist Aesthetics," *New Literary History* 7 (1975): 191–208.

20. The most searching exploration in Marxist thought of these "moments" of emancipation is by Jürgen Habermas; see esp. "Toward a Theory of Communicative Competence," *Recent Sociology*, no. 2, ed. Hans Peter Dreitzel (New York, 1970), pp. 115–48; and *Knowledge and Human Interests*, trans. Jeremy J. Shapiro (Boston, 1971). For an ambitious exploration of the opposition of play and seriousness in Renaissance culture, see Richard A. Lanham, *The Motives of Eloquence: Literary Rhetoric in the Renaissance* (New Haven, Conn., 1976).

# 4

# Filthy Rites

*On the evening of November 17, 1881, during my stay in the village of Zuñi, New Mexico, the Nebue-Cue, one of the secret orders of the Zuñis, sent word to Mr. Frank H. Cushing, whose guest I was, that they would do us the unusual honor of coming to our house to give us one of their characteristic dances, which, Cushing said, was unprecedented.*[1]

So writes Captain John G. Bourke, Third Cavalry, U.S. Army, Indian fighter and amateur ethnographer, author of *An Apache Campaign* and *Snake Dance of the Moquis of Arizona, Mackenzie's Last Fight with the Cheyennes* and *Notes on the Theogony and Cosmogony of the Mojaves.* The ceremonies began auspiciously enough with a ritual cleansing of the long living room, but when, at nightfall, the dance began, the honored guest found himself strangely unsettled. Some of the dancers were arrayed, with appropriate picturesqueness, in breech-cloths and wild turkey feathers, but others were dressed in cast-off American army uniforms, and one, clad in a long india-rubber gossamer robe, and with a pair of goggles, painted white, over his eyes, appeared to be got up in imitation of a Catholic Priest.

Captain Bourke had seated himself at one side of the dark room, behind a table on which was a small coal-oil lamp. The feeble light of the lamp cast a faint glow behind his head, and it is to this halo that he attributes the performance that followed: "The dancers suddenly wheeled into line, threw themselves on their knees before my table, and with extravagant beatings of the breast began an outlandish but faithful mockery of a Mexican Catholic congregation at vespers." With the ethnographer thus enlisted as votive figure, the parody continued, "to the uncontrolled merriment of the red-skinned listeners," with the mock priest delivering a passionate sermon and, after a brief interlude, a most surprising communion: "A squaw entered, carrying an

59

'olla' of urine, of which the filthy brutes drank heartily." Two or three gallons were thus consumed, we are told, and one of the participants expressed regret that the dance had not been held out of doors, in one of the plazas, for there they always made it a point of honor to eat the excrement of men and dogs. "For my part," write Captain Bourke, "I felt satisfied with the omission, particularly as the room stuffed with one hundred Zuñis had become so foul and filthy as to be almost unbearable" (p. 6). As soon as the dance was over, he ran, he tells us, into the refreshing night air.

One should remark at once that Captain Bourke was not hallucinating; the dance is described elsewhere, and the fraternity in question (the Ne'wekwe, or Galaxy) noted for its particular fondness for mimicking priests and army officers. Moreover, the remark about the plaza was not simply designed to heighten the visitor's no doubt amusing disgust; as another early ethnographer relates, the consumption of excrement is an essential part of the fraternity's vaunted medical powers as well as a kind of contest: "The one who swallows the largest amount of filth with the greatest gusto is most commended by the fraternity and onlookers."[2] And in a sense, Captain Bourke paid the dancers an appropriate compliment: he may indignantly deny the implicit suggestion that communion is the eating of excrement in both kinds, and may write, with evident relief and snobbery, that "Hebrews and Christians will discover a common ground of congratulation in the fact that believers in their system are now absolutely free from any suggestion of this filth taint," but he does so in the preface to a work directly inspired by his disquieting experience, a 500-page study—the result of ten years' obsessive research—the *Scatologic Rites of All Nations.*

Like all resonant stories, Captain Bourke's is the focal point for several distinct lines of cultural and psychic force. In it we encounter a minor, but intense, version of an interesting, even haunting phenomenon: the role of loathing and disgust in the development of the human sciences. Ethnography is, in effect, the study of those who do not live by one's own rules; to study one's immediate surroundings is to change the very essence of the project, whose enabling condition is the otherness of the object of study. (There are, to be sure, attempts at ethnographic studies of one's own culture, but these must begin with a certain deliberate self-estrangement, so that familiar rules seem alien and in need of explication and representation.) Now in the West, since the onset of the early modern period, the archetypal rules, the earliest and most systematic to which the child is exposed and in which he is trained, are those governing the definition and control of wastes. The behavior manuals of the fifteenth through eighteenth centuries return again and again to codes elaborated for the management of the body's products: urine, feces, mucus, saliva, and wind.[3] Proper control of each of these products, along with the acquisition of the prevailing table manners and modes of speech, mark the entrance into civility, an entrance that distinguishes not only the child from the adult, but the members of a privileged group from the vulgar, the upper classes from the lower, the courtly from the rustic, the civilized from the savage.

Force plays a role in the imposition of these codes, but a far greater role is played by the arousal of disgust, embarrassment, "delicacy of feeling," contempt, distaste, modesty—in short, the complex shaping of a sense of social decency and social horror. When the behavioral codes are successfully implanted, the individual will experience physical and psychic discomfort in the presence of violations: blushing, an acute sense of shame, nausea. To hold back wind is dangerous, writes Erasmus in the 1530s, but one should hide the sound with a cough, for "the sound of farting, especially of those who stand on elevated ground, is horrible." "It does not befit a modest, honorable man to prepare to relieve nature in the presence of other people," counsels della Casa's *Galateo* (1558); "similarly, he will not wash his hands on returning to decent society from private places, as the reason for his washing will arouse disagreeable thoughts in people"; at table, a seventeenth-century manual declares, "to blow your nose openly into your handkerchief, without concealing yourself with your serviette, and to wipe away your sweat with it . . . are filthy habits fit to make everyone's gorge rise."[4]

As these few examples should make clear, such regulations have little or nothing to do with hygiene, though health is occasionally involved as a rationale. Their concern, rather, is the fashioning of social and personal identity, identity dependent not only on shared norms, but on differences as well. Since one of the principal agents in this process of fashioning is disgust—or more accurately, a wide range of negative sensations, from "disagreeable thoughts" and queasiness to amused contempt—there is a high likelihood that the observer of an alien culture, even the observer well disposed to the object of his study, will experience bouts of revulsion. For the very conception that a culture is alien rests upon the perceived difference of that culture from one's own behavioral codes, and it is precisely at the points of perceived difference that the individual is conditioned, as a founding principle of personal and group identity, to experience disgust.

Early European accounts of foreign peoples are rich in the expression of revulsion, though one should note that this is by no means the only reaction, for the shifting codes of manners themselves bear witness to the mobility and learned character of "disagreeable thoughts." What is perhaps most striking in the early accounts—in Bernal Díaz del Castillo's description of the Aztec priests or Edmund Scot's account of the Javanese—is the undisguised openness of revulsion, a revulsion that often coexists with understanding and admiration.[5] One should add that the natives' response to the first Europeans, insofar as it is recorded, provides evidence of a comparable reaction: one Amerindian, astonished at the French custom of collecting and carrying about mucus in handkerchiefs, wryly declared: "If thou likest that filth, give my thy handkerchief and I will soon fill it."[6] The rise of "scientific" methodology brought about the systematic suppression of the articulation of disgust in ethnographic writing, but as Malinowski's diaries eloquently attest, the experience itself remained quite strong and underlay pursuit of the objective knowledge of the other. Here too the response could be reciprocal: when Malinowski ventured to suggest to the Trobriand islanders that they should discipline recalcitrant children by beating them, the islanders considered the idea "unnatural and immoral."[7]

All of this returns us to Captain Bourke, who witnessed among the Zuñi Indians extreme and simultaneous violations of the codes governing food and waste, and hence experienced extreme disgust. This reaction is not simply an occupational hazard; after all, it is the ethnographer's nausea that gives him his particular discursive field. The boundaries of his long study are defined precisely by the rising of his gorge; thus *Scatologic Rites* includes the consumption of garlic and hashish as well as earwax and sweat. In the absence of a stable and universal enumeration of those things that must be regarded as filthy, Bourke relies upon the felt distance between himself and aspects of the world to provide him with his subject matter, and that distance is registered in the level of his disgust. His disgust is, moreover, an affirmation of his own cultural identity, a mark of his participation in that civilized world that takes the primitive as one of its characteristic intellectual and moral concerns, the very emblem of that which is alien.[8] It would be absurd to conclude that a similar, if better disguised, revulsion lies at the constitutive moment of *all* ethnography, but one may easily find other and more respectable instances than the work of Captain Bourke, in which aversion serves to transform behavior and material substances into the objects of representation and interpretation.

The ethnographic project that reflects this revulsion also helps to alleviate it, not necessarily because the attempt at understanding breeds tolerant acceptance—*Scatologic Rites* bears eloquent, if eccentric, witness that it need not—but because the act of recording assumes the eventual, perhaps imminent disappearance of the observed behavior. It is recorded in part because, as a survival of an earlier stage of human development, it cannot long endure; indeed, much early anthropology is engaged quite consciously in helping to bring about a more hasty demise. At the same time, the ethnographer's disgust often seems to be the other side of longing: it may be complacently psychoanalytical to say so, but there appears to be at least as much "philia" as phobia in Captain Bourke's ten-year labor, a kind of *nostalgie de la merde.*

It is tempting to reverse this formulation for the Zuñis and to argue that there is as much disgust as relish in their coprophagous ritual. Captain Bourke's explanation is along these lines: citing Isaiah 36:12, he suggests that the abominable dance represents a catastrophic famine that the Zuñis had at some time, perhaps centuries earlier, endured during an enemy siege. But festivals that commemorate a national disaster—the Jewish Tisha b'Av would be an example—are not usually pervaded by the spirit of clowning, uncontrolled merriment, and, above all, malicious parody. The transcription of portions of a recent oral history project, *Self-Portrayals by the Zuñi People,* raises the possibility of a different semiotic relation between the dance and the Zuñis' historical experience, a relation not of commemoration, but of festive travesty. "Our grandparents," it is said, prophesied to their children that "drinkers of dark liquids will come upon the land, speaking nonsense and filth. Then the end shall be nearer."[9] Were the Ne'wekwe dancers, then, in the presence of the representatives of the conquering institutions, comically enacting the roles of their oppressors, displacing and absorbing alien cultural symbols in a ritual of mockery, warding off, as it were, eschatology with scatology?

Captain Bourke speculates that the dancers were recalling their ancient Apache enemies, but it seems far more likely that he himself was the object of their abusive mirth, along with all the other army officers and priests who tirelessly struggled to bring civilization to the heathen. One should perhaps add enthnographers, not only because of Captain Bourke's own dual function, but because an observer in 1918 noticed one of the dancers holding a ceremonial stave composed of cattails, cornstalks, and the measuring stick that Alfred Kroeber had used in a survey three years before.[10]

The Ne'wekwe ceremony cannot, however, be reduced to its element of mockery; after all, if the filth is symbolically directed at the white man, it is swallowed by the Indians. The gesture of insult is at the same time an acknowledgement of defeat, for the satiric humor of the oppressed, no matter how telling it may be, always assumes the condition of oppression, perhaps even reinforces that condition, both by releasing aggression nonviolently through laughter and by confirming in the minds of the conquerors the impotence of the conquered. And yet this duality may not be the most important point, for we may recall that the ritual is conceived as powerful medicine, "the most powerful known to the Zuñi people."[11] I would like to argue not that this medical function explains, or is explained by, the dialectic of aggression and submission, but rather the reverse; the elements are not fully integrated, they defy hierarchical organization, they do not form a unified whole. Somehow the magical healing has survived alongside all of the portentous significance of the encounter with white civilization, and has resisted semantic organization by that encounter. In this indifference to unity, this refusal of conceptual integration, we may grasp one of the sources of the Zuñis' dogged resistance, to this day, to assimilation.

Where does this leave Captain Bourke? Beside the point, I suppose—not, as it seemed, the symbolic center of the ceremony, but utterly marginal. Yet if he found no place in Zuñi culture, he may have encountered something important about his own. I refer now not to his disgust, but rather to his very shrewd speculation that what he had witnessed bore a striking resemblance to the accounts of the Feast of Fools in early modern Europe. For him, this resemblance could only signify the "filth taint" from which is own culture had cleansed itself, but our understanding of the Feast of Fools has been deepened in the last decades, especially by the Russian semiologist Mikhail Bakhtin's brilliant study, *Rabelais and His World.*[12]

Laughter, Bakhtin suggests, which had been eliminated in the Middle Ages from official cult and ideology, survived in the unofficial, but widely tolerated, carnival aspect of virtually every feast. The festivities often included masking, hiding, parades, dancing, noise-making, gambling, and costuming: fools dressed as dignitaries, peasants as lords, men as women, women as men. Festive laughter—popular, universal, ambivalent in its triumph and derision, gaiety and degradation—has at its center what Bakhtin calls the "grotesque body," ever unfinished, ever creating, ever exceeding its limits in copulation, pregnancy, childbirth, dying, eating, drinking, and defecating. The grotesque body—open to the world in all its orifices, unbounded, abusive, devouring, and nurturing—receives its fullest visual representation in the art of Bosch and Breughel, its most masterful literary expression in Rabelais' *Gargantua and Pantagruel.* Rabelias's scatology, Bakhtin suggests, must be understood in the context of rituals like the mock mass, in which excrement was used instead of incense, or processions in which the festive clergy, eating boudins, rode in carts loaded with dung and tossed it at the crowd. And, as we might expect in a writer who was both monk and doctor, the protagonists of these rituals are medical as well as clerical: the Rabelaisian image of the physician, Bakhtin writes, is an ambivalent composite of Hippocrates's noble physician and of the scatophage who devours excrement in antique comedies, mimes, and medieval *facéties*.

The comic force of Rabelais's scatological improvisations on carnivalesque themes is felt from the first pages of his work in the account of Gargantua's birth. The hero's mother, Gargamelle, has been carrying him in her belly for eleven months, when, after the slaughter of three hundred sixty-seven thousand fourteen fat oxen, she indulges her voracious appetite at a feast of tainted tripe. Her husband warns her to eat modestly—"Anyone who eats the bag," he said, "might just as well be chewing dung"—but she consumes a vast amount: "Oh, what fine faecal matter to swell up inside her!"[13] After a frolicking dance and a drinking party, Gargamelle believes that she feels the first birth pangs. The midwives who reach underneath find "some rather ill-smelling excrescences, which they thought were the child; but it was her fundament slipping out because of the softening of her right intestine—which you call the bum-gut—owing to her having eaten too much tripe." In response, "a dirty old hag of the company who had the reputation of being a good she-doctor" applies an astringent "so horrible that all her sphincter muscles were stopped and constricted." "By this misfortune," the narrator continues, "the cotyledons of the matrix were loosened at the top, and the child leapt up through them to enter the hollow vein. Then, climbing through the diaphragm to a point above the shoulders where this vein divides in two, he took the left fork and came out by the left ear." The newborn does not cry like other babies, but instead shouts, "Drink! Drink! Drink!"

This remarkable episode is in part an exuberant parody of classical legends of the birth of heroes: the narrator invokes Bacchus, Minerva, Adonis, and Castor and Pollux. We shall have occasion to return to this learned comedy, which it is all too easy to neglect in the context of the riotous popular festivities Bakhtin invokes. Those festivities often included, we have noted, parodies of the most sacred mysteries in the official religion, and Rabelais daringly pursues the same impulse: "I doubt whether you will truly believe in this strange nativity," the narrator remarks, "but an honest man, a man of good sense, always believes what he is told and what he finds written down." The first edition then continues with a passage that was suppressed in 1542 (and that is omitted from the Urquhart-Motteux translation and from J. M. Cohen's influential modern translation):

Ne dict pas Solomon Proverbiorum 14: "Innocens credit omni verbo etc.," et Saint Paul, prime Corinthio. 13: "Charitas omnia credit." Pourquoy ne le croyriez vous? Pour ce (dictez vous) qu'il n'y a nulle apparence. Je vous dicz que pour ceste seule cause vous le debvez croyre en foy parfaicte. Car les Sorbonistes disent que foy est argument des choses de nulle apparence.[14]

This passage not only mocks the Paris theologians, as More and Erasmus had done a few years earlier, but goes very far toward mocking the miraculous nativity at the heart of Christianity itself. To be sure, such mockery could be accommodated, if somewhat uneasily, to the larger rhythms of faith: thus for centuries periodic outbursts of parodic festivity had been tolerated as a release of pent-up frustrations, a safety valve that would enable the participants to return with renewed obedience to the discipline of true faith. Moreover, in works of art such as the English *Second Shepherd's Play*, the element of parody— the lamb in the manger instead of the holy babe—could be viewed as a moving comic tribute to the Christian mystery.

Rabelais's parody of the sacred, however, cannot be so easily absorbed or domesticated. Gargantua is no lamb, and the overarching symbolic and institutional constraints that enclose the carnival and return its participants to the everyday world are altogether missing from Rabelais's novel. Moreover, the mockery in the suppressed passage strikes at one of the central doctrinal tactics since St. Paul for the suppression of doubt: the definition of faith comically attributed to the Sorbonistes is from Paul's Epistle to the Hebrews. This definition was invoked to defend doctrines like the Virgin Birth and the Real Presence against the skeptical challenge of materialism; Rabelais's deadpan parody—"For I say to you that to God nothing is impossible"—is solemnly invoked as the justification for a grotesque hypermaterialism, the realm (in Bakhtin's phrase) of the "lower bodily stratum."

Rabelais's exuberant laughter turns the world topsy-turvy, challenges the dominant structures of authority, triumphs over fear and constraint, breaks down what had seemed essential boundaries. The birth of Gargantua celebrates a primal, animal energy, difficult to moralize conventionally and impossible to contain; when Gargamelle's sphincter muscles are closed, the infant—in a comic prefiguration of what Freud called "displacement upward"—forces his way through a different orifice. This miraculous birth is not transcendence of the human condition—*inter urinas et faeces nascimur*—but a radical confirmation in which the veins of the head, the birth canal, and the intestines are confounded with one another. Acts of degradation—

including the eating of excrement—are linked inseparably with birth, fertility, renewal; acts of renewal are linked, in turn, with decay and death. The birth of Gargantua, Bakhtin writes, "ties into one grotesque knot the slaughter, the dismemberment and disemboweling, bodily life, abundance, fat, the banquet, merry improprieties, and finally childbirth" (p. 222).

With this blend of laughter, religious parody, and exuberant self-affirmation, and its carnivalesque context compounded of rebellion, celebration, humiliation, and excremental medicine, we are, as Captain Bourke dimly grasped, quite close to the Ne'wekwe dances. What he witnessed in a state of shock, and in the conviction of profound cultural distance, was something his own European and American forebears had relatively recently suppressed. What the Zuñis did to Bourke—brazenly performing filthy rites in his presence, mocking him under the pretense of doing him honor, making him at once comically central and yet in a deeper sense quite peripheral—Rabelais in effect did again and again to the Sorbonists, who responded by trying to destroy him and suppress his book. Indeed, the Indian fighter/ethnographer's response to the savages, a response composed of disgust, self-congratulation, and obscure, nostalgic longing, strikingly resembles the response of the European elite to the unreformed carnivalesque customs of the lower orders. The connection is perfectly explicit as early as the sixteenth century, and had important historical consequences; as Karen Kupperman has recently demonstrated, colonial policy in Virginia was deeply conditioned by the widespread notion that the natives resembled the common people of England, Algonkian culture being a curious anamorphic representation of European popular culture.[15]

But we must caution ourselves at this point against simply equating Renaissance popular culture with Rabelais's novel: *Gargantua and Pantagruel* is not carnival, but the brilliant aesthetic representation of carnival motifs; not the communal laughter of a largely illiterate populace, but the highly crafted, classicizing of a supremely literate individual; not festive mayhem in the streets, but words on a page. The difference—like the difference between the traditional Whitsun-ale an Englishman could still have seen in 1611 in dozens of country villages, and the Whitsun-ale he could have seen represented at the Globe Theater in *The Winter's Tale*—signals as much the break away from the festive mode as its continued vigor. Though they would not vanish until quite late—despite the efforts of the Society for the Suppression of Vice, there are records of wakes and popular fairs in England until well into the nineteenth century—the Feast of the Fools and other carnivalesque recreations had come under increasingly effective attack in the Renaissance from clerical authorities, social reformers, city fathers, popular preachers, and significant elements of the folk itself.[16] Rabelais does not seem to share in any way our ethnographer's revulsion, but his act of recording implies the evanescence, as well as the aesthetic and social power, of the popular rituals from which his art draws its inspiration.

Indeed, some of Rabelais's power derives *from* the evanescence of the festive tradition, or more accurately, from the sense of a literary, social, and religious world hardening in its commitment to order, discipline, and decorum. In the realm of manners, bodily functions that had been largely ignored come under increasing scrutiny and regulation; in the family, patriarchal authority is asserted with a new and intense insistence, while children are subjected to increased disciplinary attention; in religion, a sharp intensification of dogmatic rigidity is fueled by the crisis of the Reformation; in literature, there is a growing self-consciousness about decorum. Rabelais's work must be understood not as the naive self-expression of an unregenerate popular spirit, but as a sophisticated and brilliant response to such developments: hence the grotesque violations of "good manners," the hyperbolic celebration of the unconstrained instinctual energies of childhood, the mockery of the theological rage for order, the comic breaches of literary decorum. Rabelais's festive representations derive at least some of their intensity from this new agonistic situation: not Carnival in its recurrent, cyclical struggle with Lent, but the carnivalesque threatened in its very existence. The excessiveness and the dense particularity of *Gargantua and Patagruel* are in compensatory relation to the long day's dying of all that Rabelais hyperbolically depicts.

So too in just this period, European humanists begin to compile vast collections of folk proverbs, and the attention, even when closer to admiration than amused contempt, reflects less the continued vitality of popular culture than its slow contraction into an object of learned study, literary representation, and pastoral reform.[17] Rabelais shows no interest in reforming the people, but his work has a certain quality of inspired compilation, as if to suggest that from now on the carnivalesque will live more authentically and fully in the pages of *Gargantua and Pantagruel* than in actual folk experience. And this proposition is inadvertently confirmed when Bakhtin draws virtually all of his best evidence for the realm of the "grotesque body" from this novel written by a highly learned humanist/monk/physician writing under the protection of aristocratic, clerical, and royal patrons.

The folk culture forged by Rabelais into a devastating comic weapon is in effect presented to those patrons, as scatological and bawdy tales were traditionally presented, alongside chivalric romances and allegories of love, to the aristocratic audiences of the Merovingian court.[18] The presence of the book's noble protectors is registered not only in the circumstances of its composition and publication, but in some of its most characteristic values as well. Thus, when in the famous description of the Abbey of Thélème, Rabelais imagines a world of freedom and delight, he does so, not as a peasant dream of abundance, but as an elegant aristocratic retreat, comically reconceived as a monastery. The monks and nuns are all "free, well-born, well-bred, and easy in honest company," and their elegant lives are simplified and sweetened by armies of servants in discreet attendance: "These attendants also provided the ladies' rooms each morning with rose-water, orange-water, and myrtle-water, and brought for each lady a precious casket, which breathed of every aromatic scent" (p. 156). The excremental aggression and reckless exuberance have vanished, as if they were only called into being by resistance and constraint. In a world whose sole rule is *"Do what you will,"* excrement is completely transformed, as Artemidorus's ancient dream interpretation had foretold, into showers of superfluous wealth: gold, precious jewels, costly clothes, and those sweet-smelling caskets.[19]

Rabelais's fantasy of perfect aristocratic liberty, like his fantasy of unending popular carnival, is generated in response to a culture increasingly intolerant of disorder in society, in the individual, and in art. Scatology, of course, did not vanish—indeed, its endurance has surpassed that of the aristocracy—but what Norbert Elias calls "the threshold of shame and embarrassment" altered, so what was once acceptable in the central zone of the social system was pushed out to the periphery, and what was once tolerated on the periphery was declared altogether unacceptable. The expurgation of Rabelais's novel began in his own lifetime, and the process of cleansing extended, of course, well beyond this single scandalous French text. Shakespeare's distinguished eighteenth-century editor Warburton, to cite one of the more subtle examples, proposed a decorous textual emendation: where, in the folio text of the tragedy, Cleopatra, contemplating suicide, declares that it is great "to do that thing that ends all other deeds ... Which sleeps, and never palates more the dung" (V. ii. 5–7), he suggests that Shakespeare had intended to write, "and never palates more the dug"—that is, the nipple. Excrement is transformed into milk.[20]

But conscious or unconscious attempts at bowdlerizing are probably less significant than disciplinary pressures brought to bear upon scatology itself and consequent changes in the symbolic significance of the "lower bodily stratum." In Rabelais, as in the Ne'wekwe dances, excrement was the material sign of abundance as well as humiliation, magical medicine as well as corruption, renewal as well as death. From the early Renaissance onward, such paradoxical doubleness is more and more widely repudiated, and then repressed, so that by the nineteenth century, it is recoverable only in ethnographic descriptions of savage rituals. In England, this transformation may be traced at the symbolic center of society in the history of the royal Privy Chamber. During the regime of Rabelais's contemporary, Henry VIII, the working head of the Privy Chamber was a high-ranking and influential gentleman, called the Groom of the Stool, whose status originated in his duty to attend on the king when he made use of the royal close-stool. This attendance signaled the groom's publicly acknowledged intimacy with the king, an intimacy that conferred power not only by virtue of the king's evident confidence, but by virtue as well of a charisma that extended even to the barest functions of the king's body. By the later seventeenth century, that charisma had drastically waned, and royal body service had begun to seem an embarrassment. As early as 1669, a writer on court offices solemnly explained that the correct title of the First Gentleman of the Bedchamber was Groom of the Stole, "he having the office and honour to present and put on his Majesty's first garment or shirt every morning."[21] By the eighteenth century, the office had become a sinecure having little or nothing to do with the king's body, and at the accession of Victoria, the groomship was abolished altogether in an attempt to reduce costs.

This brief history reflects not only the waning of royal charisma, but a separation of body and spirit whose implications extend well beyond the fate of the monarchy. In this separation, the "lower bodily stratum" steadily loses any connection with renewal and potency, except in the increasingly disreputable dreams of alchemists and cranks. Eventually, all of the body's products, except tears, become simply unmentionable in decent society, but long before this repression, scatology is reconceived symbolically, so that it can have none of the festive ambivalence it possesses in Rabelais's novel or in the Zuñi ceremony. We may glimpse this refiguration in Thomas More's *Utopia*, written at a time, we may recall, when Henry VIII's Groom of the Stool derived prestige from his important function and would be rewarded, at the king's death, with the precious collection of royal close-stools.[22] While the Utopians, More writes,

> eat and drink from earthenware and glassware of fine workmanship but of little value, from gold and silver they make chamber pots and all the humblest vessels for use everywhere. . . . Moreover, they employ the same metals to make the chains and solid fetters which

they put on their slaves. Finally, as for those who bear the stigma of disgrace on account of some crime, they have gold ornaments hanging from their ears, gold rings encircling their fingers, gold chains thrown around their necks, and, as a last touch, a gold crown binding their temples. Thus by every means in their power they make gold and silver a mark of ill fame.[23]

In More's dream of a communal society, a society with neither charismatic absolutism nor private property, men can be freed from excessive, anxious attachment to wealth by means of the social power of shaming. Defecation is used, along with slavery and disgrace, to stigmatize gold and silver, and these metals, bearing the weight of the communal judgment, may subsequently be used elsewhere to symbolize dishonor.

The "lower bodily stratum" plays an important role, then, in the technology of social control that makes possible Utopian communism, but we should not conclude that the values of More's imaginary society revolve around a loathing of the flesh such as we find in certain strains of medieval monasticism. Utopia is not an ascetic community but one officially dedicated to the pursuit of pleasure, including the humblest pleasures of the body. All pleasures are, however, carefully ranked in an order that represents the objective standard of the community and permits no individual deviation. At the top of the hierarchy are the pleasures of the soul; below are the bodily pleasures, which the Utopians divide into two general categories. The first is "a calm and harmonious state of the body," that is, the pleasure of overall good health; the second is the pleasure of the senses. This latter is in turn divided into two kinds: the intangible, but sweet, pleasure of music; and the pleasure of the body's organs. And this last and lowest form of pleasure is also divided into two parts: pleasure that arises from renewal, that is, from eating and drinking; and the pleasure that arises from elimination. The latter sensation "occurs when we discharge feces from our bowels or perform the activity generative of children or relieve the itching of some part by rubbing or scratching."[24] The Utopians, then, embrace bodily pleasures, but they do so in a scheme that seems designed to curb sexuality by equating it with defecation and scratching. As so often happens in More's Utopia, what is at first heralded as a central value turns out, on closer inspection, to be hedged about with restrictions:

If a person thinks that his felicity consists in this kind of pleasure, he must admit that he will be in the greatest happiness if his lot happens to be a life which is spent in perpetual hunger, thirst, itching, eating,

drinking, scratching, and rubbing. Who does not see that such a life
is not only disgusting but wretched? (p. 101)

In More's representation of the pleasures of the body, there is none
of the festive excess, the mingled degradation and exuberance, that
characterize Rabelais's scatological representation. For More, the instinctual demands of the flesh take their appointed place in a great,
integrated social body, into which every individual must merge himself. Utopia is in this respect the secular equivalent of the Catholic
*corpus Christianorum*, for which More gave his own life. In More's
Christianity, the body is not utterly despised, but it is subordinated
to higher values, the values embodied in the universal, visible Catholic
Church. In the service of this ultimate authority, even the grossest
bodily functions must play their part, that of the agents of shame and
disgrace. During the years of violent religious controversy in England,
More calls upon those functions to bear the full charge of aggression
against any individual who dares to challenge the Catholic consensus.
Writing on behalf of Henry VIII, More tells Luther that

> as long as your reverend paternity will be determined to tell these
> shameless lies, others will be permitted, on behalf of his English
> majesty, to throw back into your paternity's shitty mouth, truly the
> shit-pool of all shit, all the muck and shit which your damnable
> rottenness has vomited up, and to empty out all the sewers and
> privies onto your crown.[25]

More is not inaccurate when he claims to be throwing back at Luther
something Luther himself threw with reckless abandon. Significantly,
More speaks for his ruler and in his opponent's idiom; Luther speaks
for himself, and his scatological imagery far exceeds in quantity,
intensity, and inventiveness anything that More could muster. If for
More scatology normally expresses a communal disapproval, for Luther, it expresses a deep personal rage. This rage has many external
objects, from the pope and his bishops ("They are no part of the body,
or clean and healthy members but merely the filth of squiredom, merd
spattered on the sleeve and veritable ordure"[26]) to the Jews ("You
should read only the bible that is found under the sow's tail, and eat
and drink the letters that drop from there"[27]). But all of these hated
enemies—priest, temporizing princes, rebellious peasants, usurers,
Jews—resolve themselves into a single, supreme enemy, the Devil.[28]
For Luther, the Devil dwells in excrement, and his dominion over the
world is made possible by the world's excremental character: its
obsession with gold and silver, its lies and trickery, its filthy desires.
If the Devil assaults with excrement—"A Christian should and could

be gay, but then the devil shits on him"—so too the Christian must counterattack with excrement: "For note this down," Luther tells Satan, "I have shit in the pants, and you can hang them around your neck and wipe your mouth with it."[29]

Powerful psychohistorical explorations by Norman O. Brown and by Erik H. Erickson of Luther's "excremental vision" have enabled us to understand this extraordinary scatological language, not as the incidental reflection of the reformer's peasant origins, but as a central element in Luther's conception of the world and of himself. In the present context, we can begin to understand that Luther's symbolic use of the "lower bodily stratum" is set against both the festive celebrations of the grotesque body expressed by Rabelais and the communal judgments expressed by More. If in these expressions Rabelais and More reflect conflicting aspects of Catholic culture in the late Middle Ages and early Renaissance, so Luther's scatology is powerfully linked to early Protestantism: there is, in short, a telling difference between the Catholic and Protestant semiotics of excrement. Where the excremental in Rabelais is bound up with renewal as well as decay, in Luther it is a sign of the Church's corrupt compromise with pagan idolatry and evil. Where Rabelais cheerfully acknowledges an ineradicable connection between human ideals and man's grossest functions, Luther regards that connection as proof of man's depravity, and proclaims that salvation lies only in God's utter eradication of the filth taint. Where defecation in More is a necessity that God has rendered mildly, if embarrassingly, pleasurable, it is for Luther a mark of sinfulness and spiritual violence, though the violence can be turned back against the enemy. Most significantly perhaps, where scatology in More is part of an institutional rhetoric—an agent of the shared wrath of the visible *consensus fidelium* against heresy, or a device in the Utopians' collective dishonoring of gold and silver—scatology in Luther is part of a personal vision, a weapon in the struggle of an isolated believer against Satan, or an expression of the inward state of the individual fleshly man. For More, the emotion principally associated with excrement is shame; for Luther, it is not shame, the social sense of disgrace in the eyes of the community, but guilt. When Luther looks into himself, that is, into his natural inwardness unaided by divine grace, what he perceives is filth: "I am like ripe shit, and the world is a gigantic ass-hole. We probably will let go of each other soon."[30] There is intense self-loathing in this excremental vision—a nauseated perception of utter worthlessness and damnation—but there is also a paradoxical self-importance, a sense of the immensity of individual depravity that makes possible a corresponding sense of the immensity of God's mercy in cleansing man of his guilt.

With shame and guilt, communal regulation and individual anxiety, we have the two forces that between them will stamp out over the ensuing centuries almost all popular manifestations of the "grotesque body." Yet it will not do to conclude simply that a repressive disciplinary scatology destroyed the radical, liberated excrementalism represented in *Gargantua and Pantagruel*. Out of the midst of his unbridled, carnivalesque exuberance, the energies of the "lower bodily stratum," Rabelais produced the aristocratic fantasy of the Abbey of Thélème; out of the midst of their conservatism and repressiveness, More and Luther generated and inspired some of the most radical social thought of the early modern period. We may glimpse, before we close, a daring attempt by one seventeenth-century visionary to forge a liberating social and religious practice out of ideological materials, including scatology, drawn from More and Luther.

On April 1, 1649, a half-dozen poor men began to dig on the common land at St. George's Hill, Surrey, to prepare the ground for planting. They were followers of Gerrard Winstanley, to whom, in a trance, a voice had come, saying, "Worke together, Eat bread together."[31] The actions of these men and women—and the group, known as the Diggers, quickly grew—were modest and scrupulously nonviolent, but their project, like others undertaken by religious radicals in the wake of the execution of Charles I, was millennial: "That we may work in righteousness and lay the Foundation of making the Earth a Common Treasure for All, both Rich and Poor" (p. 257). To this end, the Digger community outlawed private property and wage labor, struggled to overturn the patriarchal oppression of women and children, shared their goods in common, and attempted to live exemplary, decent lives, free from fear, subservience, and hunger:

> Therefore we are resolved to be cheated no longer, nor be held under the slavish fear of you no longer, seeing the Earth was made for us, as well as for you. . . . If we lie still, and let you steale away our birthrights, we perish; and if we Petition we perish also. . . . Therefore we require, and we resolve to take both Common Land, and Common woods to be a livelihood for us, and look upon you as equal with us, not above us. (p. 273)

The project drew from local freeholders and magistrates immediate and predictable hostility, to which Winstanley responded in a remarkable series of pamphlets explaining and defending his "experimental" religion (p. 93) and social reform. In the beginning of time, he writes, "there was an evenness between man and all creatures, and an evenness between man and his Maker" (p. 156). But when man fell, he began to imagine that all of his happiness lay in possessing external

objects for himself, tyrannizing over others, enclosing the earth, en-
riching himself with the labor of his fellows, and upholding by force
the principle, *"This is mine"* (p. 158). The fall is at once an inward
condition and a specific set of external injustices, a spiritual darkness
and a social evil. Hence, there can be no personal righteousness without a transformation of the oppressive circumstances in which the
common people live, and no lasting social reform without inward
salvation.

Man can be ruled, Winstanley writes, by "a particular, confining,
selfish power, which is the Devil," or by "a universall spreading power,
that delights in the liberty of the whole Creation, which is Christ" (p.
172). The Devil does not dwell in an external hell, but in the "bottom-
less pit, your very fleshly self," and all torments and miseries are "but
the breakings forth of that stinking dunghill, that is seated within
you" (p. 216). The whole of mankind can be conceived as a great
creature, whose "face is called the universal power of Love," but whose
"back parts is called the selfish power" (p. 376). All men and women
have an equal birthright in the earth, but under the dominion of the
"back parts," men have enslaved each other, while through buying
and selling, "the earth stinks, because this hath been established by a
compulsive binding power" (p. 188). The earth must be made clean
again by returning it to those things that belong by "the Law of
Creation" to all mankind: "Be not like the Rats and Mice, that drawes
the treasures of the Earth into your holes to looke upon, whil'st your
fellow-members . . . doe starve for want" (p. 448). All that is locked up
covetously becomes inner filth, and at the appointed time, those who
are ruled by the dark power of possessiveness "must and shall be torne
in pieces, and scattered, and shamed; . . . and be cast out, as stinking,
imaginary dung" (p. 447). To avoid this fate, men and women, governed by "the Spirit of Community," must come together "to plant
and manure the Common land" (p. 274), so that the poor may once
again "suck the Brests of their mother Earth" (p. 265). "The voyce is
gone out." Winstanley writes, "freedome, freedome, freedome: he that
hath eares to heare, let him heare, he that is filthie, let him be filthie
still, till he be cast out as dung" (p. 448).

If we consider the excremental imagery scattered throughout Winstanley's writings not as a psychic aberration but as part of a continuing social dialogue about body, spirit, property, and power, we can
understand that he is trying to fuse, in a revolutionary synthesis,
elements of the bitterly opposed visions expressed by More and Luther. He shares with Luther the perception that covetous men are
dominated by the "back part"—the "dunghill" within—and that this
"back part" is in fact the Devil. But for Winstanley, this perception is

not an acknowledgement of universal depravity, the worthlessness of human "works," and his own personal guilt. Instead, he shares with More a conviction that communal actions can arouse men's sense of shame, liberate them from their attachment to property, and return them to righteousness and peace. But for Winstanley, this conviction is not an adherence to any visible church or formal ritual or hierarchical institution, and he utterly rejects both the enslavement of criminals that More contemplated in *Utopia* and the persecution of heretics that More supported in his own life. Winstanley feels angry at his oppressors, but he struggles to transform scatological aggression into its opposite: not an inward feeling of love, but an active social practice—manuring the earth.

On June 11, 1649, four unarmed Diggers on St. George's Hill were set upon and severely beaten by two freeholders on horseback and a club-wielding gang of men in women's apparel. The cross-dressing was perhaps a disguise—though the magistrates were far more interested in prosecuting than in protecting the Diggers—but it was also a familiar and traditional emblem of the carnivalesque. The festive gesture seems calculated to deride the Diggers, to avoid the impression of an official military or judicial repression, to deprive them of the possibility of dignity in defeat, and to pit one conception of the common people against another. In the weeks of harassment and violence that followed, Winstanley acknowledged the symbolism: the fury of their enemies is so great, he writes,

> that they would not only drive away all the Cowes upon the ground, but spoyl the corn too, and when they had done this mischief, the Bayliffs, & the other . . . snapsack boyes went hollowing and shouting, as if they were dancing at a whitson Ale; so glad they are to do mischief to the Diggers, that they might hinder the work of freedome."
> (p. 335)

By the spring of 1650, the Diggers were destroyed. The old exuberant spirit of carnival, safely in the pay of the landlords, had played its part in the destruction.

### Notes

1. John G. Bourke, *Scatologic Rites of All Nations* (Washington, D.C.: Lowdermilk and Company, 1891), p. 4. The introductory pages of the present essay appeared in *University Publishing* 8 (1979): 5–6.

2. Matilda Coxe Stevenson, "The Zuñi Indians," *U.S. Bureau of American Ethnology.* Annual Report, 1901–2, p. 437.

3. Semen and menses are also, of course, the object of complex regulations, but rarely in behavior manuals. For a brilliant study of these manuals, see Norbert Elias, *The Civilizing Process*, translated by Edmond Jephcott (New York: Urizen Books, 1978; original German edition, 1939). On the cultural definition of filth, see Mary Douglas, *Purity and Danger: An Analysis of Concepts of Pollution and Taboo* (New York: Praeger, 1966).

4. Erasmus, *De civilitate morum puerilium;* Giovanni della Casa, *Galateo;* Antoine de Courtin, *Nouveau traité de civilité,* quoted in Elias, *The Civilizing Process,* pp. 130, 131, 146.

5. In a provocative essay, "Paradox and Limits in the History of Ethnology" *(Daedalus* 109 [1980]; 73–91), James A. Boon challenges the conventional distinction between pre-Enlightenment prejudice and Enlightenment objectivity. He cites Darwin on the Fuegians: they were "quite naked . . . stunted in their growth, their hideous faces bedaubed with white paint, their skins filthy and greasy, their hair entangled, their voices discordant, and their gestures violent. Viewing such men, one can hardly make one's self believe that they are fellow-creatures" (p. 86).

6. *The Jesuit Relations and Allied Documents,* edited by R. G. Thwaites (Cleveland: Burrows Company, 1896–1901), 47:297. The same correspondent reports that "some time ago a Savage, looking into a Frenchman's face with most extraordinary attention and in profound silence, suddenly exclaimed, after considering him a long time, 'Oh, the bearded man! Oh, how ugly he is!' " (47:287). See also Cornelius J. Jaenen. "Amerindian Views of French Culture in the Seventeenth Century," *Canadian Historical Review* 55 (1974): 261–91.

7. Bronislaw Malinowski, *The Sexual Life of Savages in North-Western Melanesia* (New York: Harcourt, Brace & World, 1929), pp. 52–53. Malinowski remarks of the Trobriand pastime, during the *kwakwadu,* or amorous excursion, of eating the lice found in one's lover's hair, that it is "a practice disgusting to us and ill associated with love-making," but he quickly adds that to the Trobriands, "the idea of European boys and girls going out for a picnic with a knapsack full of eatables is as disgusting and indecent as their *kwakwadu* would be to a Puritan" (p. 327). See also Bronislaw Malinowski, *A Diary in the Strict Sense of the Term,* translated by Norbert Guterman (New York: Harcourt, Brace, 1967).

8. We may look beyond ethnology in this regard to the work of Bourke's great contemporary, Sigmund Freud, who speculates that the experience of revulsion at the intertwining of "excremental things" and "sexual things" leads to the splitting off of the conscious from the unconscious and hence to the human condition itself. ("The Most Prevalent Form of Degradation in Erotic Life" [1912], in *Collected Papers,* edited by J. Riviere and J. Strachey, 5 vols. [New York: International Psycho-Analytical Press, 1924–50], 4:215). Freud knew Bourke's *Scatologic Rites.*

9. *The Zuñis: Self-Portrayals,* translated by Alvina Quam (Albuquerque: University of New Mexico Press, 1972), p. 3.

10. Elsie Clews Parson, "Winter and Summer Dance Series in Zuñi in 1918," *University of California Publications in American Archaeology and Ethnology* 17 (1922): 189.

11. In Freudian theory, the source of this powerful medicine is the infantile narcissistic project of becoming father of oneself; in Norman O. Brown's words, "The project of becoming father of oneself and thus triumphing over death, can be worked out with things, and at the same time retain bodily meaning, only if the things produced by the body at the same time nourish it" *(Life Against Death* [New York: Vintage Books, 1959], p. 293).

12. Mikhail Bakhtin, *Rabelais and His World*, translated by Helene Iswolsky (Cambridge, Mass.: MIT Press, 1968).

13. François Rabelais, *The Histories of Gargantua and Pantagruel*, translated by J. M. Cohen (Baltimore: Penguin, 1955), book 1, chapters 4–6, pp. 47–53.

14. Rabelais, *Oeuvres*, edited by Abel Lefranc, 6 vols. (Paris: Champion, 1913), I:72. "Does not Solomon say, in Proverbs 14, 'The simple believeth every word etc.,' and St. Paul in 1 Corinthians 13, 'Charity believeth all things.' Why should you not believe what I tell you? Because, you say, there is no evidence. I tell you that for this reason alone you ought to believe with perfect faith. For the gentlemen of the Sorbonne say that faith is the evidence of things not seen."

15. Karen Kupperman, *Settling with the Indians: The Meeting of English and Indian Cultures in America. 1580–1649* (Totowa, N.J.: Rowman and Littlefield, 1980).

16. See Robert W. Malcolmson, *Popular Recreations in English Society, 1700–1850* (Cambridge: Cambridge University Press, 1973).

17. See Natalie Zemon Davis, "Proverbial Wisdom and Popular Errors," in *Society and Culture in Early Modern France* (Stanford: Stanford University Press, 1975), pp. 227–67.

18. See Per Nykrog, *Les Fabliaux: Etude d'histoire littéraire et de stylistique médiévale* (Copenhague: E. Munksgaard, 1957); *Bawdy Tales from the Courts of Medieval France*, translated and edited by Paul Brians (New York: Harper & Row, 1972), pp. vii–x.

19. In dreams, according to Artemidorus of Daldis, human excrement is both a sign of dishonor and a sign of the release of retained surpluses of wealth *(The Interpretation of Dreams*, translated by Robert J. White, Noyes Classical Studies [New Jersey: Noves Press, 1975], pp. 106, 171). I owe this reference to Peter Brown. Rabelais refers to Artemidorus's volume in *Gargantua and Pantagruel*, book 3, chapter 13.

20. The modern editor of the Pelican edition leaves "dung," but suggests as a gloss, "i.e., the fruits of the earth."

21. David Starkey, "Representation Through Intimacy: A study in the symbolism of monarchy and court office in early-modern England," in *Sym-*

*bols and Sentiments: Cross-Cultural Studies in Symbolism*, edited by Joan Lewis (London: Academic Press, 1977), p. 218.

22. Ibid., p. 205. For a zany and learned meditation of Elizabethan close-stools, see Sir John Harrington, *The Metamorphosis of Ajax* (1956), edited by Elizabeth Story Donno (New York: Columbia University Press, 1962).

23. St. Thomas More, *Utopia*, edited by Edward Surtz, S.J. (New Haven: Yale University Press, 1964), p. 86.

24. *Utopia*, p. 173. The linking of excretion with other types of "evacuation" was evidently medical, as well as moral, wisdom. Robert Burton connects feces with sex, sweat, menstruation, and nosebleed, and remarks that it is dangerous to attempt to stop any of these too suddenly. "The extremes being both bad, the medium is to be kept, which cannot easily be determined." *(The Anatomy of Melancholy*, edited by Holbrook Jackson, 3 vols. [London: Dent, 1932], 2:34.)

25. *Responsio ad Lutherum*, in *The Complete Works of St. Thomas More*, edited by John M. Headley, translated by Sister Scholastica Mandeville (New Haven: Yale University Press, 1969), 5:1, p. 311.

26. Quoted in Brown, *Life Against Death*, p. 225.

27. "On the Jews and Their Lies" (1543), in *Luther's Works*, edited by Helmut T. Lehmann, 55 vols. (Philadelphia: Fortress Press, 1971), 47:212.

28. Thus, for example, "Wherever you see a genuine Jew, you may with good conscience cross yourself and bluntly say: 'There goes a devil incarnate,' " *Luther's Works* 47:214.

29. These and similar outbursts are from *Table Talk* (#522, #1557). As the English translation in *Luther's Works*, vol. 54, is deliberately colorless, I have followed the translation in Erik H. Erikson, *Young Man Luther* (New York: Norton, 1958), pp. 244, 245. In Erikson's sensitive account, "Martin's tortured attempt to establish silence, self-restraint, and submission to the Church's authority and dogma had led to rebellious self-expression" (p. 245). I would only add that passages like those from the essay on the Jews are useful reminders of some of the external consequences of this internal drama.

30. *Table Talk*, #5537, cited in Erikson, *Young Man Luther*, p. 206.

31. *The Works of Gerard Winstanley*, edited by George H. Sabine (Ithaca: Cornell University Press, 1941; reissue by Russell & Russell, 1965), pp. 190. I am indebted throughout my discussion of Winstanley to George Shulman, "The Lamb and the Dragon: Gerrard Winstanley and Thomas Hobbes in the English Revolution" (Ph.D. dissertation, University of California, Berkeley, Department of Political Science, 1982).

# 5

# The Cultivation of Anxiety:
# King Lear and His Heirs

I want to begin this essay far from the Renaissance, with a narrative of social practice first published in the *American Baptist Magazine* of 1831. Its author is the Reverend Francis Wayland, an early president of Brown University and a Baptist minister. The passage concerns his infant son, Heman Lincoln Wayland, who was himself to become a college president and Baptist minister:

> My youngest child is an infant about 15 months old, with about the intelligence common to children of that age. It has for some months been evident, that he was more than usually self willed, but the several attempts to subdue him, had been thus far relinquished, from the fear that he did not fully understand what was said to him. It so happened, however, that I had never been brought into collision with him myself, until the incident occurred which I am about to relate. Still I had seen enough to convince me of the necessity of subduing his temper, and resolved to seize upon the first favorable opportunity which presented, for settling the question of authority between us.
>
> On Friday last before breakfast, on my taking him from his nurse, he began to cry violently. I determined to hold him in my arms until he ceased. As he had a piece of bread in his hand, I took it away, intending to give it to him again after he became quiet. In a few minutes he ceased, but when I offered him the bread he threw it away, although he was very hungry. He had, in fact, taken no nourishment except a cup of milk since 5 o'clock on the preceding afternoon. I considered this a fit opportunity for attempting to subdue his temper, and resolved to embrace it. I thought it necessary to change his disposition, so that he would receive the bread *from me*, and also be so reconciled to me that he would *voluntarily* come to me. The task I found more difficult than I had expected.
>
> I put him into a room by himself, and desired that no one should speak to him, or give him any food or drink whatever. This was about 8 o'clock in the morning. I visited him every hour or two during the

day, and spoke to him in the kindest tones, offering him the bread and putting out my arms to take him. But throughout the whole day he remained inflexibly obstinate. He did not yield a hair's breadth. I put a cup of water to his mouth, and he drank it greedily, but would not touch it with his hand. If a crumb was dropped on the floor he would eat it, but if *I* offered him the piece of bread, he would push it away from him. When I told him to come to me, he would turn away and cry bitterly. He went to bed supperless. It was now twenty-four hours since he had eaten anything.

He woke the next morning in the same state. He would take nothing that I offered him, and shunned all my offers of kindness. He was now truly an object of pity. He had fasted thirty-six hours. His eyes were wan and sunken. His breath hot and feverish, and his voice feeble and wailing. Yet he remained obstinate. He continued thus, till 10 o'clock, A.M when hunger overcame him, and he took from me a piece of bread, to which I added a cup of milk, and hoped that the labor was at last accomplished.

In this however I had not rightly judged. He ate his bread greedily, but when I offered to take him, he still refused as pertinaciously as ever. I therefore ceased feeding him, and recommenced my course of discipline.

He was again left alone in his crib, and I visited him as before, at intervals. About one o'clock, Saturday, I found that he began to view his condition in its true light. The tones of his voice in weeping were graver and less passionate, and had more the appearance of one bemoaning himself. Yet when I went to him he still remained obstinate. You could clearly see in him the abortive efforts of the will. Frequently he would raise his hands an inch or two, and then suddenly put them down again. He would look at me, and then hiding his face in the bedclothes weep most sorrowfully. During all this time I was addressing him, whenever I came into the room, with invariable kindness. But my kindness met with no suitable return. All I required of him was, that he should come to me. This he would not do, and he began now to see that it had become a serious business. Hence his distress increased. He would not submit, and he found that there was no help without it. It was truly surprising to behold how much agony so young a being could inflict upon himself.

About three o'clock I visited him again. He continued in the state I have described. I was going away, and had opened the door, when I thought that he looked somewhat softened, and returning, put out my hands, again requesting him to come to me. To my joy, and I hope gratitude, he rose up and put forth his hands immediately. The agony was over. He was completely subdued. He repeatedly kissed me, and would do so whenever I commanded. He would kiss any one when I directed him, so full of love was he to all the family. Indeed, so entirely and instantaneously were his feelings towards me changed, that he preferred me now to any of the family. As he had never done before, he moaned after me when he saw that I was going away.

Since this event several slight revivals of his former temper have occurred, but they have all been easily subdued. His disposition is, as it never has been before, mild and obedient. He is kind and affectionate, and evidently much happier than he was, when he was determined to have his own way. I hope and pray that it may prove that an effect has been produced upon him for life.[1]

The indignation and disgust that this account immediately excited in the popular press of Jacksonian America, as it does in ourselves, seem to me appropriate but incomplete responses, for if we say that tyranny here masquerades as paternal kindness, we must also remember that, as Kafka once remarked of his father, "love often wears the face of violence." Wayland's behavior reflects the relentless effort of generations of evangelical fathers to break the child's will, but it would be a mistake to conceive of this effort as a rejection of affective familial bonds or as a primitive disciplinary pathology from which our own unfailing decency toward the young has freed itself. On the contrary, Wayland's struggle is a strategy of intense familial love, and it is the sophisticated product of a long historical process whose roots lie at least partly in early modern England, the England of Shakespeare's *King Lear*.

Wayland's twin demands—that his son take food directly from him and come to him voluntarily, as an act of love and not forced compliance—may in fact be seen, from the perspective of what French historians call the *longue durée*, as a domesticated, "realistic," and, as it were, bourgeoisified version of the love test with which Shakespeare's play opens. Lear too wishes to be the object—the preferred and even the sole recipient—of his child's love. He can endure a portion of that love being turned elsewhere, but only when he directs that it be so divided, just as Reverend Wayland was in the end pleased that the child "would kiss any one when I directed him." Such a kiss is not a turning elsewhere but an indirect expression of love for the father.

Goneril, to be sure, understands that the test she so successfully passes is focused on compliance: "you have obedience scanted," she tells Cordelia, "And well are worth the want that you have wanted" (I,i). But Lear's response to his youngest daughter's declaration that she does not love him all suggests that more than outward deference is at stake: "But goes thy heart with this?" From Cordelia at least he wants something more than formal obedience, something akin to the odd blend of submission to authority and almost erotic longing depicted at the close of Wayland's account: "He repeatedly kissed me, and would do so whenever I commanded. . . . As he had never done before, he moaned after me when he saw that I was going away."

To obtain such love, Wayland withholds his child's food, and it is tempting to say that Lear, in disinheriting Cordelia, does the same. But what is a technique for Wayland is for Lear a dire and irreversible punishment: the disinheriting and banishment of Cordelia is not a lesson, even for the elder sisters, let alone for Cordelia herself, but a permanent estrangement, sealed with the most solemn oaths. Wayland's familial strategy uses parental discipline to bring about a desired relationship rather than to punish when the relationship has failed. In his account, the taking away of the child's food *initiates* the love test, whereas in *King Lear* the father's angry cancellation of his daughter's dowry signals the abandonment of the love test and the formal disclaimer of all paternal care. In the contrast between this bitter finality and a more calculating discipline that punishes in order to fashion its object into a desired shape, we glimpse the first of the differences that help to account for the resounding success of Wayland's test and the grotesque and terrifying failure of Lear's.

A second crucial difference is that by the early nineteenth century the age of the child who is tested has been pushed back drastically; Wayland had noticed signs of self-will in his infant son for some months, but had not sought to subdue it until he was certain that the child could "fully understand what was said to him." That he expected to find such understanding in a fifteen-month-old reflects a transformation in cultural attitudes toward children, a transformation whose early signs may be glimpsed in Puritan child-rearing manuals and early seventeenth-century religious lyrics and that culminates in the educational philosophy of Rousseau and the poetry of Wordsworth.

*King Lear*, by contrast, locates the moment of testing, for Cordelia at least, precisely in what was for Shakespeare's England the age that demanded the greatest attention, instruction, and discipline, the years between sexual maturity at about fifteen and social maturity at about twenty-six. This was, in the words of a seventeenth-century clergyman quoted by Keith Thomas, "a slippery age, full of passion, rashness, wilfulness," upon which adults must impose restraints and exercise shaping power. The Elizabethan and Jacobean theater returned almost obsessively to the representation of this age group, which, not coincidentally, constituted a significant portion of the play-going population. Civic officials, lawyers, preachers, and moralists joined dramatists in worrying chiefly about what Lawrence Stone in *The Family, Sex and Marriage in England 1500–1800* calls "potentially the most unruly element in any society, the floating mass of young unmarried males," and it was to curb their spirits, fashion their wills, and delay their full entry into the adult world that the educational system and the laws governing apprenticeship addressed themselves. But girls were also the objects of a sustained cultural scrutiny that focused on the critical passage from the authority of the father or guardian to the authority of the husband. This transition was of the highest structural significance, entailing complex transactions of love, power, and material substance, all of which, we may note, are simultaneously at issue when Lear demands of his youngest daughter a declaration she is unwilling or unable to give.

Love, power, and material substance are likewise at issue in the struggle between Reverend Wayland and his toddler, but all reduced to the proportions of the nursery: a kiss, an infantile gesture of refusal, a piece of bread. In the nineteenth-century confrontation, punishment is justified as exemplary technique, and the temporal frame has shifted from adolescence to infancy. Equally significant, the spatial frame has shifted as well, from the public to the private. Lear is of course a king, for whom there would, in any case, be no privacy, but generally Renaissance writers do not assume that the family is set off from public life. On the contrary, public life is itself most frequently conceived in familial terms, as an interlocking, hierarchical system of patriarchal authorities, while conversely the family is conceived as a little commonwealth. Indeed the family is widely understood in the sixteenth and early seventeenth centuries as both the historical source and the ideological justification of society: "for I admit," writes Bacon, "the law to be that if the son kill his father or mother it is petty treason, and that there remainith in our laws so much of the ancient footsteps of *potestas patria* and natural obedience, which by the law of God is the very instance itself, and all other government and obedience is taken but by equity." In other words, the Fifth Commandment— "Honor thy father and mother"—is the original letter of the law which equity "enlarges," as the Elizabethan jurist Edmund Plowden puts it, to include all political authority.

This general understanding of the enlargement by which the state is derived from the family is given virtually emblematic form in representations of the ruling family; hence the supremely public nature of Lear's interrogations of his daughters' feelings toward him does not mark him off, as other elements in the play do, from the world of Shakespeare's audience, but rather registers a central ideological principle of middle- and upper-class families in the early modern period. Affairs of family shade into affairs of state, as Gloucester's anxious broodings on the late eclipses of the sun and moon make clear: "Love cools, friendship falls off, brothers divide: in cities mutinies; in countries, discord; in palaces, treason; and the bond crack'd twixt son and father" (I, ii). The very order of the phrases here, in their failure to move decisively from private to public, their reversion at the close to the familial bond, signals the interinvolvement of household and society. By the time of Jacksonian America, the family has moved indoors, separated from civil society, which in turn has been separated from the state. Reverend Wayland's account of his domestic crisis is also, of course, intended for public consumption, but it was published anonymously, as if to respect the protective boundaries of the family, and more important still, it makes public a private event in order to assist the private lives of others, that is, to strengthen the resolve of loving parents to subdue the temper of their own infants.

We will return later to the temporal and spatial problems touched upon here—the cultural evaluation of differing age groups and the status of privacy—but we should first note several of the significant continuities between Renaissance child-rearing techniques and those of nineteenth-century American evangelicals. The first, and ground of all the others, is the not-so-simple fact of observation: these parents pay attention to their children, testing the young to gauge the precise cast of their emotion and will. This is more obviously the case with Reverend Wayland, who when his child was scarcely a year old was already scrutinizing him for signs of self-will. The fathers in Shakespeare's play seem purblind by comparison: Lear apparently cannot perceive the difference between his eldest daughters' blatant hypocrisy and his youngest daughter's truth, while Gloucester evidently does not know what his eldest (and sole legitimate) son's handwriting—his "character"—looks like and is easily persuaded that this son (with whom he had talked for two hours the night before) wishes to kill him. This seeming obliviousness, however, signifies not indifference but error: Lear and Gloucester are hopelessly inept at reading their children's "characters," but the effort to do so is of the utmost importance in the play, which, after all, represents the fatal consequences of an incorrect "reading." We may say, with the Fool, that Lear was "a pretty fellow" when he had "no need to care" for his daughter's frowns (I, iv), but this indifference only exists outside the play itself, or perhaps in its initial moments; thereafter (and irreversibly) parents must scrutinize their children with what Lear, in a moment of uncharacteristic self-criticism, calls a "jealous curiosity" (I, iv). In initiating the plot against Edgar, Edmund gauges perfectly his father's blend of credulity and inquisitorial curiosity: "Edmund, how now! what news? . . . Why so earnestly seek you to put up that letter? . . . What paper were you reading? . . . What needed then that terrible dispatch of it into your pocket? . . . Let's see: come; if it be nothing, I shall not need spectacles" (I, ii). Children in the play, we might add, similarly scrutinize their fathers: "You see how full of changes his age is," Goneril remarks to Regan in their first moment alone together; "the observation we have made of it hath not been little" (I, i). The whole family comes to exist *sub specie semioticae;* everyone is intent on reading the signs in everyone else.

This mode of observation is common to Shakespeare's play and Wayland's account, but not because it is intrinsic to all family life: intense paternal observation of the young is by no means a universal practice. It is, rather, learned by certain social groups in particular cultures and ages. Thus there is virtually no evidence of the practice in late medieval England, while for the seventeenth century there is (given the general paucity of materials for intimate family history) quite impressive evidence, especially for the substantial segment of the population touched by Puritanism. For example, the Essex vicar Ralph Josselin (1617–83) has left in his diary a remarkably full record of his troubled relationship with his son, particularly during the latter's adolescence. "My soule yearned over John," notes one characteristic entry, "oh lord overcome his heart." The conflict between them reached a crisis in 1674, when, in a family discussion held in the presence of his wife and four daughters, Josselin put the following proposition before his twenty-three-year-old heir:

> John set your selfe to fear God, & bee industrious in my business, refrain your evill courses, and I will passe by all past offences, setle all my estate on you after your mothers death, and leave you with some stocke on the ground and within doores to the value of an £100 and desire of you, out of your marriage portion but £400 to provide for my daughters or otherwise to charge my land with so much for their porcions; but if you continue your ill courses I shall dispose of my land otherwise, and make only a provision for your life to put bread in your hand.

The father's strategy was at least temporarily successful, as John prudently accepted the offer and "ownd his debauchery."

Josselin's insistence upon the economic consequences of disobedience provides an immediate link to *King Lear,* where the father's power to alter portions and to disinherit is of crucial importance. We should note that primogeniture was never so inflexibly established in England, even among the aristocracy, as to preclude the exercise of paternal discretion, the power to bribe, threaten, reward, and punish. Lear's division of the kingdom, his attempt both to set his daughters in competition with each other and to dispose of his property equitably among them, seems less a wanton violation of the normative practice than a daring attempt to use the paternal power always inherent in it. This power is exhibited in more conventional form in the subplot: "And of my land, / Loyal and natural boy," the deceived Gloucester tells his conniving bastard son, "I'll work the means / To make thee capable" (II, i). This economic pressure is not, of course, immediately apparent in Reverent Wayland's dealings with his infant, but Josselin's threat to "make only a provision . . . to put bread in your hand" curiously anticipates the symbolic object of contention in the Wayland nursery and suggests that there too the paternal power to withhold or manipulate the means of sustenance is at issue.

This power should not be regarded as exclusively disciplinary. It is instead an aspect of a general familial concern with planning for the future, a concern that extends from attempts to shape the careers of individual children to an overarching interest in the prosperity of the "house." Francis Wayland's struggle with his son is not a flaring-up of paternal anger but a calculated effort to fashion his child's future: "I hope and pray that it may prove that an effect has been produced upon him for life." Similarly, Lear's disastrous division of the kingdom is undertaken, he claims, so that "future strife / May be prevented now" (I, i), and the love test marked the formal entry into his planned retirement.

These efforts to shape the future of the family seem to reflect a conviction that there are certain critical moments upon which a whole train of subsequent events depends, moments whose enabling conditions may be irrecoverable and whose consequences may be irreversible. Such a conviction is formally expressed most often in relation to great public events, but its influence is more widespread, extending, for example, to rhetorical training, religious belief, and, I would suggest, child rearing. Parents must be careful to watch for what we may call, to adapt the rhetorical term, kairotic moments and to grasp the occasion for action. Hence Francis Wayland, wishing to alter his son's nature for life, "resolved to seize upon the first favorable opportunity which presented, for settling the question of authority between us." Had the father not done so, he would not only have diminished his own position but risked the destruction of his child's spiritual and physical being. Moreover, Wayland adds, had he received his stubborn child on any other terms than "the unconditional surrender of his will," he would have permitted the formation of a topsy-turvy world in which his entire family would have submitted to the caprices of an infant: "He must have been made the center of a whole system. A whole family under the control of a child 15 months old!" This carnivalesque reversal of roles would then have invited further insurrections, for "my other children and every member of my family would have been entitled to the same privilege." "Hence," Wayland concludes, "there would have been as many supreme authorities as there were individuals, and contention to the uttermost must have ensued."

*King Lear* depicts something very much like such a world turned upside down: Lear, as the Fools says, has made his daughters his mothers, and they employ on him, as in a nightmare, those disciplinary techniques deemed appropriate for "a slippery age, full of passion, rashness, wilfulness." "Old fools are babes again," says Goneril, "and must be us'd / With checks as flatteries, when they are seen abus'd" (I, iii). In the carnival tradition, tolerated—if uneasily—by the medieval church and state, such reversals of role, provided they were temporary, could be seen as restorative, renewing the proper order of society by releasing pent-up frustrations and potentially disruptive energies. As we know from a family account, even Francis Wayland could allow his children occasional bursts of festive inversion, always returning in the end to the supreme paternal authority that his early discipline had secured. But in Lear the role reversal is permanent, and its effect is the disintegration of the entire kingdom. Wayland similarly links permanent disorder in the family to chaos in the political, moral, and theological realms; indeed his loving struggle with his son offers, he suggests, a precise and resonant analogy to God's struggle with the sinner: it is infinitely kind in God to resist the sinner's will, "for if he were not resisted, he would destroy the happiness of the universe and himself together."

Here again, in Wayland's conviction that the fate of the universe may be linked to the power struggle in his nursery, we may hear an echo of Lear:

> O Heavens,
> If you do love old men, if your sweet sway
> Allow obedience, if you yourselves are old,
> Make it your cause; send down and take my part.
> (II, iv)

Of course, as these very lines suggest, what is assumed in Wayland is deeply problematical in Lear: the fictive nature of the play, reinforced by its specifically pagan setting, seems to have licensed Shakespeare to anatomize the status and the underlying motives of virtually all of the elements that we have noted as common to the two texts. This difference is crucial, and it comes as no surprise that King Lear is more profound than Francis Wayland's account of his paternal authority: celebration of Shakespeare's profundity is an institutionalized rite of civility in our culture. We tend to assume, however, that Shakespearean self-consciousness and irony lead to a radical transcendence of the network of social conditions, paradigms, and practices in the plays. I would argue, by contrast, that Renaissance theatrical representation itself is fully implicated in this network and that Shakespeare's self-consciousness is in significant ways bound up with the institutions and the symbology of power it anatomizes.

But if its local ideological situation, its historical embeddedness, is so crucial to Shakespeare's play, what accounts for the similarities I have sketched between *King Lear* and Wayland's family narrative? The explanation lies first in the fact that nineteenth-century evangelical child-rearing techniques are the heirs of more widely diffused child-rearing techniques in the late sixteenth and early seventeenth centuries—Wayland's practices may be seen almost fully articulated in a work like John Robinson's *Of Children and Their Education*, published in 1628 though written some years earlier—and second in the fact that the Renaissance English drama was one of the cultural institutions that expressed and fashioned just those qualities that we have identified as enabling the familial love test in the first place. That is, the mode of the drama, quite apart from any specific content, depended upon and fostered in its audience *observation*, the close reading of gesture and speech as manifestations of character and intention; *planning*, a sensitivity to the consequences of action (i.e., plot) and to kairotic moments (i.e., rhetoric); and a sense of *resonance*, the conviction, rooted in the drama's medieval inheritance, that cosmic meanings were bound up with local and particular circumstances.

I am not, of course, suggesting that the nineteenth-century American minister was fashioned by the Renaissance theater (a theater his seventeenth-century religious forebears detested and sought to close) nor that without the theater Renaissance child-rearing techniques would have been far different. But the theater was not merely the passive reflector of social forces that lay entirely outside of it; rather, like all forms of art, indeed like all utterances, the theater was itself a *social event*. Artistic expression is never perfectly self-contained and abstract, nor can it be derived satisfactorily from the subjective consciousness of an isolated creator. Collective actions, ritual gestures, paradigms of relationship, and shared images of authority penetrate the work of art and shape it from within, while conversely the socially overdetermined work of art, along with a multitude of other institutions and utterances, contributes to the formation, realignment, and transmission of social practices.

Works of art are, to be sure, marked off in our culture from ordinary utterances, but this demarcation is itself a communal event and signals not the effacement of the social but rather its successful absorption into the work by implication or articulation. This absorption— the presence within the work of its social being—makes it possible, as Bakhtin has argued, for art to survive the disappearance of its enabling social conditions, where ordinary utterance, more dependent upon the extraverbal pragmatic situation, drifts rapidly toward insignificance or incomprehensibility. Hence art's genius for survival, its delighted reception by audiences for whom it was never intended, does not signal its freedom from all other domains of life, nor does its inward articulation of the social confer upon it a formal coherence independent of the world outside its boundaries. On the contrary, artistic form itself both expresses and fashions social evaluations and practices.

Thus the Renaissance theater does not by virtue of the content of a particular play reach across a void to touch the Renaissance family; rather the theater is itself already saturated with social significance and hence with the family as the period's central social institution. Conversely, the theater contributes, in a small but by no means entirely negligible way, to the formal condensation and expression of patterns of observation, planning, and a sense of resonance. Hence it is fitting that when Cordelia resists Lear's paternal demand, she does so in an antitheatrical gesture, a refusal to perform: the theater and the family are simultaneously at stake.

To these shared patterns that link the quasi-mythical family of King Lear to the prosaic and amply documented family of Francis Wayland, we may now add four further interlocking features of Wayland's account that are more closely tied not to the mode of the theater as a whole but to the specific form and content of Shakespeare's tragedy: these are the absence or displacement of the mother, an affirmation of absolute paternal authority, an overriding interest in the will and hence in differentiating voluntary from merely forced compliance, and a belief in salutary anxiety.

Francis Wayland's wife was alive in 1831, but she is entirely, even eerily, missing from his account. Where was she during the long ordeal? In part her absence must depend upon her husband's understanding of the theological significance of the incident: in Francis Wayland's Christianity, there is no female intercessor, no Mother of Mankind to appeal to the stern Father for mercy upon a wayward child. Even if Mrs. Wayland did in fact try to temper (or reinforce) her husband's actions, he might well have regarded such intervention as irrelevant. Moreover, we may speculate that the timing of the incident—what we have called the perception of the kairotic moment—is designed precisely to avoid such irrelevant interventions. We do not know when any of the Wayland children were weaned, but fifteen months would seem about the earliest age at which the disciplinary withdrawal of food—the piece of bread and the cup of milk—could be undertaken without involving the mother or the nurse.

Thus the father is able entirely to displace the nurturing female body and with this displacement make manifest his "supreme authority" in the family, a micropolitics that, as we have seen, has its analogue both in the human world outside the home and in the divine realm. Between the law of the father and the law of God there is a perfect fit; between the father's authority and worldly authorities there is a more complicated relation, since Wayland, though an absolutist within his family, could not invoke in Jacksonian America a specific model of absolute power. The most he can do is to invoke, in effect, a generalized image of the social world and of the child as misfit: had his son been left unchecked, he "would soon have entered a *world where other and more powerful beings than he* would have opposed his will, and his disposition which I had cherished must have made him miserable as long as he lived."

This social vision does not mean that Wayland's primary interest is in outward compliance; on the contrary, a "forced yielding," as he terms it, is worthless. "Our voluntary service he requires," says Milton's Raphael of the Divine Father in *Paradise Lost*,

> Not our necessitated, such with him
> Finds no acceptance, nor *can* find, for how
> Can hearts, not free, be tri'd whether they serve
> Willing or no . . .
> . . . freely we serve.
> Because we freely love.

The proper goal is conversion, and to achieve this the father cannot rely on physical compulsion. He employs instead a technique of disciplinary kindness designed to show the child that his misery is entirely self-inflicted and can only be relieved by a similarly voluntary and inward surrender. In short, Wayland attempts to generate in his son a salutary anxiety that will lead to a transformation of the will.

With salutary anxiety we return powerfully to the mode and the content of *King Lear*. The very practice of tragedy depends upon a communal conviction that anxiety may be profitably and even pleasurably cultivated. That is, tragedy goes beyond the usual philosophical and religious *consolations* for affliction, and both exemplifies and perfects techniques for the creation or intensification of affliction. To justify such techniques, Renaissance artists could appeal to the theoretical account of tragedy that originated with Aristotle and was substantially elaborated in the sixteenth century, especially in Italy. But like most such theories, this one was inert until it intersected with a set of powerful social practices in the period.

From the perspective of Wayland's account, we may say that the most enduring of these practices is the Protestant cultivation of a sense of sin, the deliberate heightening of an anxiety that can only be relieved by a divine grace whose effect can only be felt by one who has experienced the anxiety. (I should emphasize that I am speaking here not simply of a set of theological propositions but of a program, prescribed in great detail and carried out by English Protestants from Tyndale onward.) To this religious practice, we may add the child-rearing techniques that also appear in Wayland's account, techniques that once again made a self-conscious and programmatic attempt to arouse anxiety for the child's ultimate good. But what is lost by early nineteenth-century America is the practice of salutary anxiety at the symbolic center of society, that is, in the characteristic operations of royal power. That power, concentrated and personalized, aroused anxiety not only as the negative limit but as the positive condition of its functioning. The monarchy, let us remind ourselves, did not conceive its purpose as the furthering of the subject's pursuit of happiness, nor was the political center of society a point at which all tensions and contradictions disappeared. On the contrary, Elizabethan and Jacobean charismatic absolutism battened on as well as suffered from the anxiety that arose from the instability of favor, the unresolved tensions in the religious settlement, the constantly proclaimed threats of subversion, invasion, and civil war, the spectacular public maimings and executions, and even the conspicuous gap between the monarch's ideological claim to perfect wisdom, beauty, and power and the all-too-visible limitations of the actual Elizabeth and James. The obedience required of the subject consisted not so much in preserving a genuine ignorance of this gap but in behaving as if the gap, though fully recognized, did not exist. The pressure of such a performance, demanded by the monarch's paradoxical yoking of the language of love and the language of coercion and registered in the subject's endless effusions of strained but not entirely hypocritical admiration, was itself an enhancement of royal power.

Throughout his career Shakespeare displays the deepest sensitivity to this production of salutary anxiety, a production he simultaneously questions and assimilates to his own authorial power. The fullest metatheatrical explorations of the phenomenon are in *Measure for Measure* and *The Tempest*, where both Dukes systematically awaken anxiety in others and become, for this reason, images of the dramatist himself. But Shakespeare's fullest embodiment of the practice is *King Lear*, and the vast critical literature that has grown up around the play, since the restoration of the text in the early nineteenth century, bears eloquent witness to the power of this anxiety to generate tireless expressions of love. *King Lear* characteristically incorporates several powerful and complex representations of salutary anxiety, the most notable of which, for our purposes, is the love test itself, a ritual whose intended function seems to have been to allay the retiring monarch's anxiety by arousing it in others. As the opening words of the play make clear, the division of the kingdom has in effect already taken place, with the shares carefully weighed. Lear's pretence that this prearranged legal agreement is a contest—"which of you shall we say doth love us most?"—infuses symbolic uncertainty into a situation where apparently no real uncertainty exists. This is confirmed by his persistence in the test even when its declared occasion has been rendered wholly absurd by the disposition of the first two-thirds of the kingdom, complete with declarations that possession is "perpetual," "hereditary ever." Lear wants his children to experience the anxiety of a competition for his bounty without having to endure any of the actual consequences of such a competition; he wants, that is, to produce in them something like the effect of a work of art, where emotions run high and practical effects seem negligible.

Why should Lear want his children, even his "joy" Cordelia, to experience such anxiety? Shakespeare's sources, going back to the distant folk tale with its salt motif, suggest that Lear wishes his full value to be recognized and that he stages the love test to enforce this recognition, which is crucially important to him because he is about to abdicate and hence lose the power to compel the deference of his children. Marks of deference such as kneeling for blessings, removing the hat, and sitting only when granted leave to do so, were of great significance in medieval and early modern families, though John Aubrey testifies that by the mid-seventeenth century they seemed strained and arbitrary. They figured as part of a complex, interlocking system of public signs of respect for wealth, caste, and, at virtually every level of society, age. The period had a deep gerontological bias. It told itself constantly that by the will of God and the natural order of things authority belonged to the old, and it contrived, through such practices as deferral of marriage, prolonged apprenticeships, and systematic exclusion of the young from office, to ensure that this proper arrangement of society be observed. At stake, it was thought, was not only a societal arrangement—the protection, in an economy of scarcity, of the material interests of gerontological hierarchy against the counterclaims of the young—but the structure and meaning of a world where the old in each generation formed a link with the old of the preceding generation and so, by contiguity, reached back to the ideal, sanctified order at the origin of time.

But paradoxically the late Middle Ages and the early modern period also kept telling itself that without the control of property and the means of production, age's claim to authority was pathetically vulnerable to the ruthless ambitions of the young. Sermons and, more generally, the writings of moralists over several centuries provide numerously monitory tales of parents who turn their wealth over to their children and are, in consequence, treated brutally. "Your father were a fool," Gremio, echoing the moral of these tales, tells Tranio in *The Taming of the Shrew*, "To give thee all, and in his waning age / Set foot under thy table" (II, i).

The story of King Lear in its numerous retellings from at least the twelfth century on seems to have served precisely as one of these admonitions, and Shakespeare's Edmund, in the forged letter he passes off as Edgar's, gives full voice to the fears of the old, that is, to their fantasy of what the young, beneath the superficial marks of deference, are really thinking:

> This policy and reverence of age makes the world bitter to the best of our times; keeps our fortunes from us till our oldness cannot relish them. I begin to find an idle and fond bondage in the oppression of aged tyranny, who sways, not as it hath power, but as it is suffr'd. (I, ii).

This recurrent nightmare of the old seems to challenge not only the material well-being of fathers but the conception of the natural order of things to which the old appeal in justification of their prerogatives. "Fathers fear," writes Pascal, "that the natural love of their children can be erased. What kind of nature is this, that can thus be erased? Custom is a second nature that destroys the first. But what is nature? Why isn't custom natural? I am very much afraid that this nature is only a first custom, as custom is a second nature." Shakespeare's *King Lear* is haunted by this fear, voiced not in the relative privacy of the *Pensées* but in the public agony of family and state relations: ". . . let them anatomize Regan, see what breeds about her heart. Is there any cause in nature that makes these hard hearts?" (III, vi).

But it would be misleading simply to associate Shakespeare's play with this uneasiness without specifying the practical measures that medieval and early modern fathers undertook to protect themselves when retirement, always frowned upon, could not be avoided. Such situations arose most frequently in Shakespeare's own class of origin, that is, among artisans and small landowners whose income depended upon continual personal productivity. Faced with a precipitous decline in such productivity, the old frequently did have to transfer a farm or workshop to the young, but for all the talk of the natural privileges and supernatural protection of the aged, there was, as we have seen, remarkably little confidence in either the inherent or customary rights of parents. On the contrary, as Alan Macfarlane has noted in *The Origins of English Individualism,* "contemporaries seem to have been well aware that without legal guarantees, parents had no rights whatsoever." There could even be a ritual acknowledgement of this fact, as testimony in a thirteenth-century lawsuit suggests: having agreed to give his daughter in marriage to Hugh, with half of his land, the widower Anseline and the married couple were to live together in one house. "And the same Anseline went out of the house and handed over to them the door by the hasp, and at once begged lodging out of charity."

Once a father had given up his land, he became, even in the house that had once been his own, what was called a "sojourner." The connotations of the word are suggested by its use in the Authorized Version of the Old Testament: "We are strangers before Thee, and sojourners, as were all our fathers. Our days on the earth are as a shadow, and there is none abiding" (1 *Chron.* 29).

Threatened with such a drastic loss of their status and authority, parents facing retirement turned, not surprisingly, to the law, obtaining contracts or maintenance agreements by which, in return for the transfer of family property, children undertook to provide food, clothing, and shelter. The extent of parental anxiety may be gauged by the great specificity of many of these requirements—so many yards of woolen cloth, pounds of coal, or bushels of grain—and by the pervasive fear of being turned out of the house in the wake of a quarrel. The father, who has been, in Sir Edward Coke's phrase, "the guardian by nature" of his children, now has these children for his legal guardians. The maintenance agreement is essentially a medieval device, linked to feudal contractualism, to temper the power of this new guardianship by stipulating that the children are only "depositaries" of the paternal property, so that, in the words of William West's early seventeenth-century legal manual *Simboleography,* the self same thing [may] be restored whensoeuer it shall please him that so leaueth it." Thus the maintenance agreement can "reserve" to the father some right or interest in the property that he has conveyed to his children.

We are, of course, very far from the social world of *King Lear,* which does not represent the milieu of yeomen and artisans, but I would argue that Shakespeare's play is powerfully situated in the midst of precisely the concerns of the makers of these maintenance agreements: the terror of being turned out of doors or of becoming a stranger even in one's own house; the fear of losing the food, clothing, and shelter necessary for survival, let alone dignity; the humiliating loss of parental authority; the dread, particularly powerful in a society that adhered to the principle of gerontological hierarchy, of being supplanted by the young. Lear's royal status does not cancel but rather intensifies these concerns:

experience in the first scene makes clear, royal absolutism is at the same time at war with this feudal legacy. Shakespeare's play emphasizes Lear's claim to unbounded power, even at the moment of his abdication, since his "darker purpose" sets itself above all constraints upon the royal will and pleasure. What enables him to lay aside his claim to rule, the scene suggests, is the transformation of power into a demand for unbounded love, a love that then takes the place of the older contractual bond between parents and children. Goneril and Regan understand Lear's demand as an aspect of absolutist theater; hence in their flattering speeches they discursively *perform* the impossibility of ever adequately expressing their love: "Sir, I love you more than word can wield the matter / . . . A love that makes breath poor and speech unable; / Beyond all manner of so much I love you" (I, i). This cunning representation of the impossibility of representation contaminates Cordelia's inability to speak by speaking it; that is, Goneril's words occupy the discursive space that Cordelia would have to claim for herself if she were truly to satisfy her father's demand. Consequently, any attempt to represent her silent love is already tainted: representation is theatricalization is hypocrisy and hence is misrepresentation. Even Cordelia's initial aside seems to long for the avoidance of language altogether and thus for an escape from the theater. Her words have an odd internal distance, as if they were spoken by another, and more precisely as if the author outside the play were asking himself what he should have his character say and deciding that she should say nothing: "What shall Cordelia speak? Love, and be silent" (I, i). But this attempt to remain silent—to surpass her sisters and satisfy her father by refusing to represent her love—is rejected, as is her subsequent attempt to say nothing, that is, literally to speak the word "nothing." Driven into discourse by her father's anger, Cordelia then appeals not like her sisters to an utter dependence upon paternal love but to a "bond" that is both reciprocal and limited. Against paternal and monarchical absolutism, Cordelia opposes in effect the ethos of the maintenance agreement, and this opposition has for Lear the quality of treason.

Lear, who has, as he thinks, given all to this children, demands all from them. In place of a contract, he has substituted the love test. He wants, that is, not only the formal marks of deference that publicly acknowledge his value, but also the inward and absolute tribute of the heart. It is in the spirit of this demand that he absorbs into himself the figure of the mother; there can be no division for Lear between authority and love. But as the play's tragic logic reveals, Lear cannot have both the public deference and the inward love of his children. The public deference is only as good as the legal constraints that Lear's absolute power paradoxically deprives him of, and the inward love cannot be adequately represented in social discourse, licensed by authority and performed in the public sphere, enacted as in a court or theater. Lear had thought to set his rest—the phrase means both to stake everything and to find response—on Cordelia's "kind nursery," but only in his fantasy of perpetual imprisonment with his daughter does he glimpse, desperately and pathetically, what he sought. That is, only when he has been decisively separated from his public authority and locked away from the world, only when the direct link between family and state power has been broken, can Lear hope, in the dream of the prison as nursery, for his daughter's sustaining and boundless love.

With this image of the prison as nursery we return for the last time to Francis Wayland, who, to gain the love of his child, used the nursery as a prison. We return, then, to the crucial differences, as we sketched them, between the early seventeenth- and early nineteenth-century versions of salutary anxiety, differences between a culture in which the theater was a centrally significant and emblematic artistic practice, profoundly linked with family and power, and a culture in which the theater had shrivelled to marginal entertainment. The love test for Wayland takes place in the privacy of the nursery where he shuts up his fifteen-month-old infant. In consequence, what is sought by the father is not the representation of love in public discourse, but things prior to and separate from language: the embrace, the kiss, the taking of food, the inarticulate moaning after the father when he leaves the room. It is only here, *before* verbal representation, that the love test could be wholly successful, here that the conditional, reciprocal, social world of the maintenance agreement could be decisively replaced by the child's absolute and lifelong love. And, we might add, the father did not in this case have to renounce the public tribute entirely; he had only to wait until he ceased to exist. For upon the death of Francis Wayland, Heman Lincoln Wayland collaborated in writing a reverential two-volume biography of his father, a son's final monument to familial love. Lear, by contrast, dies still looking on his daughter's lips for the words that she never speaks.

### Notes

1. Wayland's letter is reprinted in full in William G. McLoughlin, "Evangelical Childrearing in the Age of Jackson: Francis Wayland's Views on When and How to Subdue the Willfulness of Children," *Journal of Social History* 9 (1975), pp. 20–43; it was first brought to my attention by Philip Greven, *The Protestant Temperament: Patterns of Child-Rearing, Religious Experience, and the Self in Early America* (New York, 1977).

# 6

# Murdering Peasants:
# Status, Genre, and the
# Representation of Rebellion

In 1525, determined to set his country's art on a rational footing by instructing its youth in the skills of applied geometry and perspective, Albrecht Dürer published his *Painter's Manual*, "A Manual of Measurement of Lines, Areas, and Solids by Means of Compass and Ruler." Among the detailed instructions—for the determination of the center of a circle, the construction of spirals and egg-shaped lines, the design of tile patterns, the building of a sundial, and so forth—I would like the dwell upon Dürer's plans for several civil monuments, for, as I hope to show, these plans provide a suggestive introduction to the problematic relation in the Renaissance between genre and historical experience.

Dürer's first proposal is the most straightforward and familiar: a monument to commemorate a victory. "It happens frequently," he writes, "that after a victorious battle a memorial or a column is erected at the place where the enemy was vanquished in order to commemorate the event and to inform posterity about what the enemy was like."[1] If the enemy was rich and powerful, Dürer notes, "some of the booty might be used for the construction of the column," as the Romans had done many centuries before. Insofar as this conception seems classical, it partakes of a cultural dream—the dream of a return to ancient dignity and glory—that extends beyond commemorative architecture. Monuments of this type not only record the achievements of the victors and remind the vanquished of their defeat but provide a proper setting for the noble actions of those who live in their shadows. As such these columns have a special appropriateness to literary tragedy, the genre that concerns itself with the actions and the destiny of rulers. Hence when imagining a stage fit for the performance of classical tragedies, Sebastiano Serlio draws a cityscape dominated by high triumphal columns.[2]

But Dürer's proposed column is anything but classical in design: it

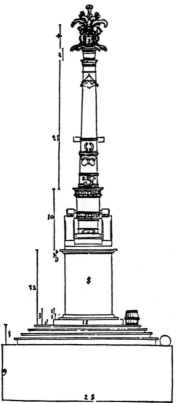

*Figure 1.* Albrecht Dürer. "Monument to Commemorate a Victory"
(in *The Painter's Manual,* 1525).

consists of a massive stone block which supports a ten-foot cannon of
the type known as a mortar, which in turn supports a twenty-one-foot
cannon surmounted by four coats of armor with high plumes (fig. 1). Is
the design seriously intended or a *capriccio?* Difficult to say. Stranger
memorials to military triumphs were actually erected, but Dürer's
plan, which includes powder kegs and cannon balls, is slightly unsettling, as if the artist were wryly—or is it only inadvertently?—recording the triumph of military ordnance over human heroism itself.
Where we might have expected coats of arms, we find only coats of
armor. Dürer had said that the monument should inform posterity
about what the enemy was like; perhaps the enemy, as Ariosto
thought, was the cannon itself.[3] The design, in other words, seems to
generate at least the possibility of an internal distance, a gap, between
the form of the monument and its ethos. From the midst of the genre

of heroic commemoration, there arise doubts about the possibility of sustaining the genre in its traditional form. A victory column, like any other artistic genre, is a received collective practice, but the social conditions of this practice—both the circumstances that make the genre possible and the objects that the genre represents—may change in such a way as to undermine the form. Here the technology of modern warfare literally takes over the column and even in the act of expressing the genre makes it seem rather obsolete.

That Dürer was quite conscious of the complex generic implications of his monument is suggested by the two subsequent designs, a "Monument to Commemorate a Victory over the Rebellious Peasants" and a "Memorial to a Drunkard." If the military monument we have just considered is the proper backdrop to a tragedy, the drunkard's monument—which includes a beer barrel, covered by a board game, surmounted by a basket filled with bread, butter, and cheese—is obviously fit for a comedy, one where mockery and celebration (as with Falstaff) are held in delightful balance (fig. 2). The wit of this design lies not only in its mock heroic mode but in the extreme improbability of its ever being built: neither a notorious drunkard, nor his family and friends could be expected to foot the bill for such a commemoration. Once again, though now in a more pronounced and unambiguous way, the design of the commemorative column undermines the genre itself. This is quite literally a utopian project, a monument that could be built nowhere, as Dürer himself suggests when he explains that he has conceived the design *von abenteur*, for the sake of adventure or oddity. [Latin translation of 1532 translates *"Haec delectationis causa,"* i.e., for amusement's sake.[4]]

Most interesting of all, between the heroic and mock-heroic memorials, and hence between the tragic and the comic, Dürer places the following remarkable design whose description I will quote in full:

> If someone wishes to erect a victory monument after vanquishing rebellious peasants, he might use paraphernalia according to the following instructions: Place a quadrangular stone block measuring ten feet in width and four feet in height on a quadrangular stone slab which measures twenty feet in length and one foot in height. On the four corners of the ledge place tied-up cows, sheep, pigs, etc. But on the four corners of the stone block place four baskets, filled with butter, eggs, onions, and herbs, or whatever you like. In the center of this stone block place a second one, measuring seven feet in length and one foot in height. On top of this second block place a strong chest four feet high, measuring six and a half feet wide at the bottom and four feet wide at the top. Then place a kettle upside down on top of the chest. The kettle's diameter should be four and a half feet at

*Figure 2.*   Albrecht Dürer. "Memorial to a Drunkard" (in *The Painter's Manual*, 1525).

the rim and three feet at its bottom. Surmount the kettle with a cheese bowl which is half a foot high and two and a half feet in diameter at the bottom. Cover this bowl with a thick plate that protrudes beyond its rim. On the plate, place a keg of butter which is three feet high and has a diameter of a foot and a half at the bottom, and of only a foot at the top. Its spout should protrude beyond this. On the top of the butter keg, place a well-formed milk jug, two and a half feet high, and with a diameter which is one foot at its bulge, half a foot at its top, and is wider at its bottom. Into this jug put four rods branching into forks on top and extending five and a half feet in height, so that the rods will protrude by half a foot, and then hang peasants' tools on it—like hoes, pitchforks, flails, etc. The rods are to be surmounted by a chicken basket, topped by a lard tub upon which sits a melancholy peasant with a sword stuck into his back. (fig. 3)

How are we to take this? To our eyes, the monument seems to be the overpowering commemoration not of a victory but of a vicious

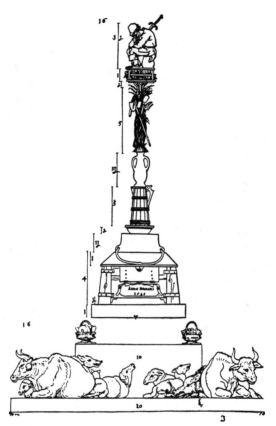

*Figure 3.* Albrecht Dürer. "Monument to Commemorate a Victory over the Rebellious Peasants" (in *The Painter's Manual*, 1525; in Karl-Adolf Kanppe, *Dürer: The Complete Engravings, Etchings, and Woodcuts*, London, Thames and Hudson, 1965, p. 369).

betrayal. The life-sustaining fruits of the peasant's labor are depicted in scrupulous detail—livestock, cheese, milk, butter, eggs, lard, vegetables—as are his tools, carefully bound up, in Dürer's accompanying drawing, with a sheaf of ripe grain. There, on top of it all, the peasant sits, alone, hunched over, unarmed, stabbed in the back. In his solitude, misery, and helplessness, he is the very opposite of the great ruling class nightmare in the Renaissance: the marauding horde, the many-headed multitude, the insatiate, giddy, and murderous crowd. And as there is no image of threat, so there seems to be no image of triumph: no cross rises above the defeated figure, nor does the column bear any symbol of secular order restored. Instead the column itself is composed of all that the peasant provides, while the provider is run through with a sword whose angle of entry suggests that the killer was standing above as well as behind him, in other words, that the

*Figures 4 and 5.*   Left: Albrecht Dürer. "The Man of Sorrows Seated" (title page; proof, 1st state) from *The Little Passion*, 1511; in Karl-Adolf Knappe, *Dürer: The Complete Engravings, Etchings, and Woodcuts*, London, Thames and Hudson, 1965, p. 254. Right: Hans Leinberger, "Christ in Distress," ca. 1525 (in Michael Baxandall, *The Limewood Sculptors of Renaissance Germany, 1475–1525*, New Haven, Yale University Press, 1980, plate 99).

victim was struck treacherously while sitting—resting, perhaps, after his labor.

In sixteenth-century German art there is, of course, one supreme figure of tragic betrayal, and it is precisely this figure that Dürer's drawing evokes: the seated peasant, with his left arm wearily resting on his left thigh and his right arm supporting his drooping head, is closely modelled on the iconographic type known as "Christ in Distress." Dürer himself used this figure on the title page of the *Little Passion* (1511; fig. 4), and there is a moving example in limewood by Hans Leinberger (fig. 5), possibly dating from the year of the *Painter's Manual*. If one dressed Leinberger's bleeding Christ in tattered clothes and substituted a soft cap for the crown of thorns, one would have almost exactly Dürer's image of the murdered peasant.[5]

This is the historical monument that cries out to be built that never gets built because only the victors pay for monuments: it must remain a sketch, a design in a painter's manual, a dark fantasy. The sketch can speak bitterly about more than one period in the history of the European peasantry, but in 1525, in Germany, it refers overwhelmingly to a single, cataclysmic event, then near its bloody close: the Peasants' War. In 1524 and 1525 thousands of peasants and artisans rebelled throughout Swabia, Franconia, and Thuringia. Aroused in part by the struggle of both spiritual and temporal rulers in Germany to free themselves from servitude to Rome, the peasants determined to free themselves from their own servitude. They attacked crucial elements of the existing social, religious, and political system and set about to transform the whole agrarian order. The famous Twelve Articles of the Upper Swabian peasants demanded that the entire community have the power to choose a pastor, that their tithes be distributed to the poor and needy in the same villages in which these tithes were collected, that they be allowed to hunt, fish, and gather wood, that rents be regulated and the death tax abolished, that enclosures of common fields be stopped. Above all, as Luther had proclaimed that Christ had purchased with his own blood the freedom of all Christians, so the peasants proclaimed that they would no longer be owned as property and demanded the abolition of serfdom and the feudal *corvée*.[6]

Though he seemed at moments to sympathize with many of these demands, Luther quickly spoke out against the rebels. "You assert that no one is to be the serf of anyone else," he writes to his "dear friends," the peasants, "because Christ has made us all free. That is making Christian freedom a completely physical matter. Did not Abraham and other patriarchs and prophets have slaves? Read what St. Paul teaches about servants, who, at that time, were all slaves."[7] When the peasants persisted in confusing spiritual and worldly freedom, collapsing the crucial distinction between the Two Kingdoms, Luther wrote in 1525 his notorious pamphlet "Against the Robbing and Murdering Hordes of Peasants." The rebels, he declares, are the agents of the devil, and their revolt is a prelude to the destruction of the world: "Therefore let everyone who can, smite, slay, and stab, secretly or openly, remembering that nothing can be more poisonous, hurtful, or devilish than a rebel."[8]

We may assume that the German princes—who saw to it that over 100,000 peasants were slaughtered in the crushing of the rebellion and its aftermath—did not greatly need Luther's encouragement, but they enthusiastically cited his treatise and may, for all we know, have found genuine spiritual consolation in it. "These are strange times," Luther declares, "when a prince can win heaven with bloodshed better

*Figure 6.* Albrecht Dürer. "Vision of an Inundation," 1525. Water-color and manuscript. Vienna, Kunsthistorisches Museum.

than other men with prayer!"[9] As for the rebel peasants and their sympathizers, those who survived bitterly accused Luther of betraying them. And it is a sense of betrayal, we have said, that suffuses Dürer's monument.

But it is precisely here, at the moment we begin to flesh out the historical situation, that our understanding of Dürer's sketch begins to encounter obstacles. For while it is possible that certain of his associates were sympathetic with the peasants' cause,[10] there are no comparable indications of solidarity, overt or covert, elsewhere in Dürer's art or writings. "Dürer never wavered for a moment in his loyalty to Luther," Panofsky claims,[11] and there is evidence, in a remarkable pen and watercolor sketch done in the year of the *Painter's Manual,* that at the time of the Peasants' War Dürer shared Luther's fear of an impending apocalypse (fig. 6). Dürer writes under the drawing:

> In the year 1525, on the night between the Wednesday and Thursday after Whitsun, I dreamed that I saw four great columns of water descending from heaven. The first fell most furiously, with a dreadful

noise, about four miles away from me, and flooded all the country-
side. I was so terrified by it that I woke. Then the others fell. They
were very great. Sometimes they fell far off, sometimes near. And
they descended from such a height that they seemed to fall slowly.
The falls were accompanied by so much wind and flying spray that
when I awakened my whole body still shook with fear. It was long
before I regained my equanimity. On rising in the morning I painted
what I had seen. May God mend all.[12]

At the height of the Peasants' War and haunted by such hallucina-
tory fears of apocalyptic inundation, Dürer could have taken pleasure,
unmixed by sympathy or ambivalence, in imagining a monument to
commemorate victory over rebellious peasants. What we took for
almost self-evident marks of betrayal would, in such a mood, be the
details of a wish-fulfillment fantasy: the terrifying mobs have been
shattered into defenseless individuals like the unarmed peasant; the
rebel no longer demands anything but sits in melancholy resignation
to his fate; and that fate is justly represented by the sword. "Now
look!" exclaims Luther, "A rebel is a man who runs at his head and
lord with a naked sword. No one should wait, then, until his lord
commands him to defend him, but the first person who can, ought to
take the initiative and run in and stab the rascal, and not worry about
committing murder." And as if he too were thinking about designing
a monument to commemorate such an act, Luther remarks that in
the kingdom of the world—that is, in the kingdom of God's judgments
upon the wicked—the appropriate "tool is not a wreath of roses or a
flower of love, but a naked sword; and a sword is a symbol of wrath,
severity, and punishment."[13]

If Dürer's design was conceived in the spirit of Luther's remarks—
and I think it probable that it was—then the artist did not intend to
represent the betrayal of the peasants. On the contrary, we may say
that the monument actually participates in that betrayal. The bitter
irony we initially perceived was constituted less by concrete evidence
of Dürer's subverisveness than by our own sympathy for the peasants,
sympathy conditioned by our century's ideology, by recent historical
scholarship, and, no doubt above all, by our safe distance from the
fear and loathing of 1525. But this acknowledgment, though necessary, seems inadequate, for our solidarity with early sixteenth-century
German peasants is of interest only insofar as it seems to have been
called forth by Dürer's monument and not simply read into it. The
question then is how Dürer could have created a brilliant, detailed,
and coherent design that could lend itself to a strong interpretation
so much at odds with his own probable intentions, a design that has
become in effect two quite different monuments.

Our interpretive strategy here must not be to disclaim our response as anachronistic: there were those in 1525 who could have seen in Dürer's design precisely what we initially saw in it. Still less should we attempt, in the name of a "correct" response, to put aside sympathy for the peasants and recreate in ourselves the murderous loathing that probably inspired the monument. Rather we should try to understand more fully the historical and aesthetic contingencies that led to the making of this odd and disturbing design. Here we must return not to Dürer's own feelings but to the resources and the pressures of genre. The generic situation will lead us to the elements in Dürer's work that occasion both its radical discontinuity in relation to ourselves—and hence make possible the transvaluation of interpretation—and its continuity. If the latter is less striking than the former—if indeed it seems all but invisible—it nonetheless makes possible the sense of strangeness, even exhilaration, that arises from our recognition of the reversal of meaning. For it is the survival into the late twentieth century of the commemorative mode—our continued need to represent "historic" events, to construct monuments in public spaces, to attach plaques to buildings and erect markers by the roadside—that makes the vicissitudes of Dürer's design available at all as a significant subject.[14]

Let us recall that in the *Painter's Manual* the monument we have been considering is situated between the high heroic tribute to military victory and the mock-heroic celebration of the drunkard, the former suited to tragedy and the latter to comedy. What does the intermediate position signify? I suggest that a monument to celebrate a victory over rebellious peasants created a genre problem, a problem to which Dürer was particularly sensitive since he had already, as we have seen, entertained playful doubts about the more conventional victory monument. Indeed Dürer may have thought up the problem as well as undertaken a solution to it because his was a book about problem-solving: the design takes its place alongside such questions as how to interlace two solids of the same size so that in each case one point pierces the corresponding surface of the second solid.[15]

A victory over rebellious peasants calls for a commemorative column—after all, the fate of worldly rule, that is human civilization itself, depends upon this struggle—and yet the enemy is an object of contempt and derision. The princes and nobles for whom such monuments were built could derive no dignity from the triumph, any more than they could derive dignity from killing a mad dog. A heroic encounter is a struggle for honor and must conform to the code which requires that the combatants be of roughly equal station. This requirement does not originate in some rudimentary sense of "fair play" but rather in the symbolic economics of appropriation suggested by the Church of England hymn: "Conquering Kings their titles take / From the foes they captive make."[16] "I better brook the loss of brittle life," gasps the defeated Hotspur to Hal, "than those proud titles thou hast won of me" (I Henry IV, 5.4.78–79). But the peasants, of course, have no titles to seize, and can yield up no trophies fit to adorn the victor's monument. Indeed, in the economy of honor they are not simply a cipher but a deficit, since even a defeat at the hands of a prince threatens to confer upon them some of the prince's store of honor, while what remains of the victorious prince's store can be tarnished by the unworthy encounter.

Dürer then cannot dignify the peasants in his design by representing them as worthy enemies, nor can he include an image of the triumphant nobleman, for the image could only be tarnished by such a base encounter. He could, I suppose, have chosen more symbolic modes of representation, such as Hercules slaying the Hydra, but by doing so he would have robbed his design of its wit, its sense of problem-solving. Dürer had in the surrounding monuments committed himself to a kind of commemorative realism: the victory column composed of cannons, the drunkard's of food and drink. To have abandoned the mode in the peasant's column would, in effect, have signalled the defeat of his art at the hands of history itself.

Instead Dürer depicts a peasant, but one utterly without signs of honor; he has been killed in battle perhaps, but it may as well have been in an abattoir. The victor is spared representation, and even his sword is untainted, for it has not *encountered* a base adversary (which would imply face-to-face combat) but has *overtaken* him from behind. In a culture sensitive to the semiotics of execution, the weapon's position would not have gone unnoticed.[17]

So extreme a humiliation of a single, unarmed man is difficult to represent, however, without evoking Christ and hence risking semiotic contamination of the entire commemorative exercise. Dürer heightens this risk, as we have seen, by directly modelling his defeated peasant on the iconographic type of Christ in Distress. This aesthetic decision may signal a deep ambivalence on Dürer's part, a secret, subversive sympathy with the vanquished encoded at the very pinnacle of the victor's monument. I do not think we can rule out this possibility, one that satisfies a perennial longing since Romanticism to discover that all great artists have allied themselves, if only indirectly or unconsciously, with the oppressed and revolutionary masses.[18] What is poignant and powerful about Dürer's design is that the identical signs can be interpreted as signifying both the radical irony of personal dissent and the harsh celebration of official order. This uncanny convergence is not, I would suggest, the theoretical condition of *all* signs, but the contingent condition of certain signs as particular historical moments, moments in which the ruling elite, deeply threatened, conjure up images of repression so harsh that they can double as images of protest.

It is all too easy for us to perceive the possibility of ironic dissent in Dürer's sketch; the difficult task is to perceive the celebration of order. Thus the allusion to Christ in Distress at first seems unambiguously sympathetic to the peasants, but Dürer may have chosen the iconographic type because it conveyed more powerfully than any other image of the body available in his culture a mood of utter forsakenness, desolation, and helplessness. He may have expected his audience to register this mood without concluding that the peasants were Christlike in innocence or ultimately destined to triumph over their tormentors. More precisely, he may have felt that the manifest purpose of the monument itself, the peasant dress, and above all the sword in the back would abruptly check any drift toward a perception of the vanquished as the scourged Christ and would leave the viewer with only the potent representation of defeat.

This strategy depends, to be sure, upon the drastic splitting of a traditional representation—the leaching-out of the sublime innocence of Christ from the imagery of battered, weary mourning. But it is by comparable strategies that the whole design is governed: thus, as we have seen, Dürer sustains the honor code paradoxically by reversing or cancelling its principal elements. Here too there is a risk: the reversal or cancellation of the monument's genre. Far from avoiding this consequence, Dürer's strategy is to embrace it: insofar as the victory monument suggests epic and tragedy, he endows it, by composing the column of livestock, farm produce, and tools, with the signs of pastoral and georgic and the implications of comedy. The compositional elements have in addition a probable topical reference, for the peasant's labor was a principal issue in the revolt. With the dead rebel at the top of the column, the grain may suggest the violent reaffirmation of the *corvée* system, while the cattle at the base may imply something akin to Luther's observation that instead of rising up in revolt, the peasants hereafter should thank God if they have to give up only one cow to enjoy the other cow in peace.[19]

The broader generic implications here are as important as any topical reference. The pastoral and georgic elements from which the column is composed function as signs of the pacification of the peasants, a pacification whose principal means is graphically depicted at the top, and of their vulnerability and lowliness, their social distance from the armed defenders of order. (I am reminded of the Fascist inscription still—or once again—visible beneath the whitewash in Italian villages: "The plough furrows the land, but the sword defends it.") The comic implications arise from the incongruous inclusion of pastoral and georgic elements on a victory column, just as the humor of the drunkard's memorial consists in the solemn public representation of the board game, drinking bowls, and bread basket. The lard tub, butter churn, chicken basket and the like do not in this context suggest the centrality and importance of agricultural production but rather the producer's outlandishness, a marginality that insures that no honor will accrue to the defeated peasant.

If pastoral, georgic, and comedy are both the logical outcome and the cancellation of the monument's heroic and tragic codes when they are applied to rebellious peasants, Dürer's design provokes a reciprocal cancellation: neither the celebration of leisure nor the celebration of labor survives the sword thrust in the peasant's back, and the laughter that the monument generates is baffled in the instant it bursts forth. For, even as the occasion banishes the normal symbolism of heroic commemoration, the very form of the monument precludes genuinely comic treatment by continuing to insist upon the tragic and epic dimensions of the victory.

Such then are the interlocking pressures of history on genre and of generic conventions on historical representation: a victory thought to be of world-historical importance is commemorated in a column in which the enemy is reduced to impotent absurdity, while the victor is entirely effaced. Dürer cleverly solves the generic problems posed by the historical circumstances of the representation only by creating a design that risks collapse into its own antithesis. That collapse has, in fact, by now fully occurred, so that we can recover Dürer's probable intentions only by setting aside the manifest and "self-evident" imagery of betrayal. That imagery does not vanish altogether; instead, it is self-consciously repressed, in an interpretive strategy comparable to the repression for which Luther called, when he advised his readers to set aside all sympathy for the peasants: "There is no place for patience or mercy. This is the time of the sword, not the day of grace."[20] Given the peculiarities of Dürer's surrounding designs—a victory column that unsettles the ethos of the victory column itself and a commemorative pillar that humorously mocks the man it professors to honor—it may be that Dürer was wittily conscious of the need for this reinterpretation. The risk would have seemed less grave in a country still in the grip of intense fear and class hatred; readers would be inclined to interpret the monument correctly, and the stifling of sympathy would be a small, aestheticized model of the larger and more compelling historical task. The symbolism of betrayal, generated by the historical pressures on the generic codes, could be recuperated ideologically as a type of "false consciousness," a sentimental attitudinizing that must be overcome if the rebellious peasants are to be defeated and if that defeat is to be properly celebrated.

We have constructed then a reading of Dürer's design based upon the complex interplay of three forces: the artist's intention, genre, and the historical situation. By the latter I mean both the particular objects of representation and the specific structure of ideology and event that renders something—person, place, institution, thing, idea, or action—sufficiently notable to be represented. Neither intention nor genre can be reduced to this historical situation: a given genre, as Dürer's design powerfully demonstrates, may have great difficulty accommodating a particular representational object, and artistic intention has an arsenal of strategies—including irony, laughter, open revolt, and subversive submission, to name but a few—designed to differentiate it from the surrounding world. But this differentiation is not the same as autonomy, and the most important lesson to be learned from our discussion of Dürer's design is that intention and genre are as social, contingent, and ideological, as the historical situation they combine to represent. The genre of the monument is no more neutral and timeless than the Peasants' War, and Dürer's artistic intentions, as we have been able to reconstruct them, express a specific mode of engagement with the people and events to which his design refers.

If intention, genre, and historical situation are all equally social and ideological, they by no means constitute a single socio-ideological "language." On the contrary, as Dürer's design suggests, they are, in effect, separate forces that may jostle, enter into alliance, or struggle fiercely with one another.[21] What they cannot do, once they are engaged in a living work of art, is to be neutral—"pure," free-floating signifiers—for they are already, by their very existence, specific points of view on the world. As such they make demands upon us, as we do upon them: hence the possibility we have already encountered in response to the peasant monument that our own intentions may appropriate the work and transform its meaning. Dürer's design helps us see that what is at stake in interpretation is never simply a passive submission to the pure and unitary original meaning of a work of art. The production and consumption of such works are not unitary to begin with; they always involve a multiplicity of interests, however well organized, for the crucial reason that art is social and hence presumes more than one consciousness. And in response to the art of the past, we inevitably register, whether we wish to or not, the shifts in value and interest that are produced in the struggles of social and political life.

I want to turn now from early sixteenth-century Germany to late sixteenth-century England and look briefly at several different artists encountering a genre problem closely comparable to Dürer's, for concentration on a single artist tends to conceal the range of "solutions" generated in response to historical pressures on generic codes. The pressure in this case was not a Peasants' War but the unrest and class hostility that afflicted England sporadically throughout Elizabeth's reign. Inflation, unemployment, and periodic bad harvests, along with continuing religious and political differences, led to a series of disturbances that alarmed the propertied class. The depth of this alarm has been somewhat obscured by the fact that there was no major conflagration, nothing comparable to the Armada, the conspiracies surrounding Mary Queen of Scots, or Essex's abortive rebellion, and hence little that could leave a mark upon the great chronicles of the realm. But the patient work of local historians has revealed an official concern sufficiently intense and wide-spread as to constitute something like a national preoccupation.

For Essex alone, Emmison has culled a substantial number of cases of alleged sedition that came before the Quarter Sessions and Assizes. When the accused appeared to have been idly boasting or ranting in his cups, the judges could be relatively lenient, though it is noteworthy that even in such cases charges were actually brought and investigated. Thus in 1591 John Feltwell, a laborer of Great Wenden, was pilloried for having declared that "The Queen is but a woman and ruled by noblemen, and the noblemen and gentlemen are all one, and the gentlemen and farmers will hold together so that the poor can get nothing."[22] Feltwerll's dark talk of a rising to make the world "merry" again was clearly regarded as so much wind, noxious but not a serious threat to anyone. When, however, the talk was not isolated, when, in a season of discontent, there were signs of collaboration, the official response was ferocious. "We can get no work," Edward White, woolen-weaver, was alleged to have said in 1566, "nor we have no money, and if we should steal we should be hanged, and if we should ask, no man would give us, but we will have a remedy one of these days, or else we will lose all, for the commons will rise, we know not how soon, for we look for it every hour. Then will up two or three thousand in Colchester and about Colchester, and we look for it every day, for there is no more to do but one to ride on a horse with a clap and cry, 'They are up, they are up!', and another to ring 'Awake,' for ye shall see the hottest harvest that ever was in England."[23] White and three fellow workers who had spoken similarly were hanged.

"The poor hate the rich," wrote Deloney in 1597, "because they will not set them on work; and the rich hate the poor, because they seem burdensome."[24] It is in the context of this hatred, and of its ally, fear, that we must attempt to understand the frequent representations in Elizabethan literature of the victory of the forces of property, order, and true religion over the many-headed monster. These representations rarely depict the actual method most often used to punish those whom the magistrates deemed serious threats: the thousands of hangings carried out locally throughout Tudor and Stuart England. Instead of depicting the ordinary operation of the law, functioning to defend property, English artists most often narrate events at once more menacing and more socially prestigious, events colored by the feudal fantasies in which the sixteenth-century gentry dressed their craving for honor.[25] Thus instead of the assizes and a hempen rope, we have tales of mass rebellion and knightly victories. But the victories are not commemorated with the heroic solemnity normally associated with the Indian summer of English chivalry; they echo instead with a strange laughter—not belly laughter, not even the laughter that accompanies a sudden release from menace, but a taut, cruel laughter that is at once perfectly calculated and, as in a nightmare, out of control. A passage from Sidney's "New" *Arcadia*, the version revised in the early 1580s, will serve as an example. Disguised as the Amazon Zelmane and the shepherd Dorus, the two young princes, Pyrocles and Mucidorus, are fighting against "an unruly sort of clowns and other rebels" who have risen up against foolish, ineffectual, but legitimate King Basilius. The "mad multitude" forces the royal party to retreat, in the course of which the heroes deftly dispatch a number of the churls. A sample of Sidney's manner follows:

> "O," said a miller that was half drunk, "see the luck of a good-fellow" and with that word ran with a pitchfork at Dorus; but the nimbleness of the wine carried his head so fast that it made it over-run his feet, so that he fell withal just between the legs of Dorus, who, setting his foot on his neck (though he offered two milch kine and four fat hogs for his life) thrust his sword quite through from one ear to the other, which took it very unkindly, to feel such news before they heard of them, instead of hearing, to be put to such feeling. But Dorus, leaving the miller to vomit his soul out in wine and blood, with his two-hand sword strake off another quite by the waist who the night before had dreamed he was grown a couple, and, interpreting it that he should be married, had bragged of his dream that morning among his neighbours. But that blow astonished quite a poor painter who stood by with a pike in his hands. This painter was to counterfeit the skirmish between the Centaurs and Lapithes, and had been very desirous to see some notable wounds, to be able the more lively to express them; and this morning, being carried by the stream of this company, the foolish fellow was even delighted to see the effect of blows. But this

last, happening near him, so amazed him that he stood stock still, while Dorus, with a turn of his sword, strake off both his hands. And so the painter returned well skilled in wounds, but with never a hand to perform his skill.[26]

Hatred and fear of rebellion from below have many voices; why should they adopt this particular tone in this particular work? Why should Sidney, sensitive, generous, and idealistic, choose to depict the heroes of his romance in this grotesque and lurid light? In part the explanation lies in certain recurrent features of Sidney's style and in his personal circumstances: the aggression that frequently makes itself felt in his writing, the impression of anxiety masquerading as forced high spirits, the frustrations in his political career and his longing for decisive action, even the fact that Penshurst, where Sidney was raised, was itself the result of early sixteenth-century enclosures bitterly resisted and resented by the poor.[27] These factors are important in any attempt to understand Sidney's tone, but they are insufficiently *conscious* to account by themselves for his intentions and insufficiently *public* to account for the broad appeal of his work.

Though it was not published during his lifetime, shortly after Sidney's death *Arcadia* became one of the most celebrated literary achievements of the age, the work that expressed more than any other the whole ethos of the English aristocracy and of those—and they were a great part of the entire propertied class—who fashioned themselves after that ethos.

What then is the public basis of a passage such as the one I have just quoted? What social and aesthetic problems does Sidney's grotesque comedy attempt to solve? The answer, I suggest, lies in the aesthetically codified stock of social knowledge, that is, in genre, and we may begin by noting certain similarities between Sidney's account of his heroes' victory over the "mad multitude" and Dürer's plan for a monument to commemorate a victory over rebellious peasants. In both there is a conspicuous insistence upon objects that would normally have no place in a battle; and in both an exaggerated representation of the vulnerability of the social inferiors. Dürer's monument protects the social status of the victors by effacing them entirely, leaving only the avenging sword; Sidney cannot, of course, similarly protect his heroes whose presence is essential to the narrative, but the romance tradition provides the means for a partial effacement through disguise. As the shepherd Dorus and the Amazon Zelmane—disguises conspicuously marginal in class and gender—Musidorus and Pyrocles do not have their princely honor compromised by a skirmish with unruly clowns. We may, of course, observe that their honor was already compromised by the disguise itself—and elsewhere in his work Sidney makes much of the potential stain of a masquerade brought about by the power of love—but paradoxically the heroes' victory over the peasants at least partially restores the honor tarnished by their disguise, while their disguise protects the honor that would otherwise have been tarnished by such a victory.

Like the anonymous sword in Dürer's design, the heroes' disguise in *Arcadia* also functions to deprive the defeated peasants of any honor that might accrue to them from the social distinction of the victors. And like Dürer, Sidney carefully reinforces the boundaries of the honor code by means of cruel laughter: the livestock at the base of the victory column and the lard tub at its top find their narrative equivalent in the miller's offer of "two milch kine and four fat hogs for his life" and in the grotesquely comic appropriateness of each act of violence. Peasants are, of course, a staple of laughter in Renaissance art, but it is important to distinguish between a laughter that levels— that draws lord and clown together in the shared condition of the flesh—and a laughter that attempts to inscribe ineradicable differences.[28] Laughter in an artist like Rabelais affirms the oneness of the body with the earth and celebrates the crossing or destruction of boundaries; Sidneian laughter, by contrast, draws sharp distinctions: only the others, the defeated boors, are returned to the earth, while the noble victors soar above it: "Zelmane made them perceive the odds between an eagle and a kite, with such a nimble steadiness and such an assured nimbleness that while one was running back for fear, his fellow had her sword in his guts"(379). In the context of a battle, the rebels' occupations are for Sidney inherently ridiculous, and their fates are made to match not their misdeeds so much as their social absurdity. A "dapper fellow, a tailor by occupation" and "suitor to a seamster's daughter," has his nose struck off and stoops down "because he had heard that if it were fresh put to, it would cleave on again. But as his hand was on the ground to bring his nose to his head, Zelmane with a blow sent his head to his nose" (380). If we recall that the handsome princes are suitors to the king's daughters, we can savor to the full the social differentiation charted by such comic violence.

The climax of this episode, and of Sidney's strategy of marking status boundaries, is the mutilation of the "poor painter," and it is here that we can most clearly observe Sidney, like Dürer, confronting the principal danger of this particular representational enterprise: the inadvertent staining of the noble victors and the ennobling of the base vanquished. The danger then is the effacement or, alternatively, the redrawing of boundaries, so that we perceive resemblance instead of difference or betrayal instead of victory. The safest way to avoid this unsettling of the fixed ratios of praise and blame is literally to dehumanize the rebels, thereby allowing them no hint of a resemblance to either the victors or the artist himself. But Dürer, let us recall, did not turn away from the sympathetic rendering of the peasant that threatened to invalidate the purpose of his monument. Rather, in an act of aesthetic bravado, he embraced the threat, facing it down by representing it. Here, similarly, in the midst of his depiction of the skirmish, Sidney introduces an artist on the side of—or at least in the orbit of—the rebels, a lower-class artist then who is setting about to depict just such a skirmish. The resemblance between Sidney and the poor painter would seem to be heightened by the painter's theme—the battle between the Centaurs and the Lapiths—since this favorite subject of Renaissance iconography is used by several of the *Arcadia*'s literary sources to describe exactly the type of disorder that Sidney himself is depicting.[29]

But what threat would such an imaged resemblance represent? The threat of a status loss to Sidney himself equivalent to that which threatens his disguised heroes. The fear of such a loss haunts many of Sidney's literary works, never more so perhaps than in the rhetorical urgencies and ironies of the *Defense of Poetry*. Here in *Arcadia*, a work composed in the enforced idleness of a humiliating rustication at the hands of the displeased Queen, Sidney mirrors himself as a useless idler on the field of battle, one who has fallen from the high heroic vocation to which he was born to the marginal status of a foolish artisan,[30] and then having let the image stand for a moment, he mutilates it: "Dorus, with a turn of his sword, strake off both his hands. And so the painter returned well skilled in wounds, but with never a hand to perform his skill." In the grim, tight-lipped laughter that such a passage seeks to provoke, Sidney reaffirms the social and aesthetic differences that the representation itself would seem to call into question: in effect, he attacks the professional as opposed to the amateur, cutting the hands off the artist who would allow himself to drift toward solidarity with the rebels—the painter stood by "with a pike in his hands"—and blocking an art that might, through this solidarity, compromise the comic mode in which the killing of tailors, millers, butchers, and poor painters should be represented.[31]

Having thus by means of violence reestablished threatened boundaries, the *Arcadia* goes on to attribute the defeat of the uprising not to the power of the sword but to the power of the word. The sword is inadequate because of the size of the multitude: the "very killing," Sidney writes, begins to weary the princes who fear "lest in long fight they should be conquered with conquering" (380). Sidney then acknowledges the inability of superior force alone to protect rulers against a popular rebellion; the heroes' military prowess suffices only to enable them and the royal party to withdraw from the open country, where they are fully exposed to rebel attack, to the slightly greater security of the princely lodge. This withdrawal quite literally images the reaffirmation of status boundaries—the royal party is now walled off from the surrounding populace—but the boundaries are vulnerable to attack: the rebels "went about with pickaxe to the wall and fire to the gate to get themselves entrance" (381).

Faced with the limitations of both offensive and defensive military strategy, Sidney's heroes turn to what for Renaissance humanists was the original and ultimate prop of the social order: rhetoric.[32] Pyrocles, in his disguise as Zelmane, bravely issues forth from the lodge, quickly ascends to the nearby judgment-seat of the prince, and signals that he wishes to make a speech. The multitude, at first unwilling to listen, is quieted by one of the rebel leaders, a young farmer who "was caught in a little affection towards Zelmane" (382). Unlike the more sanguine humanists, Sidney does not pretend that, through the magical power of its tropes, Zelmane's speech is able to pacify the crowd; rather its cunning rhetoric, piercing "the rugged wilderness of their imaginations" (386), reawakens the rebels' dormant divisions of economic, political, and social interest:

> For the artisans, they would have corn and wine set at a lower price, and bound to be kept so still; the ploughmen, vine-labourers and farmers would none of that. The countrymen demanded that every man might be free in the chief towns: that could not the burgesses like of. The peasants would have all the gentlemen destroyed; the citizens (especially such as cooks, barbers, and those other that lived most on gentlemen) would but have them reformed. (383)

Before long the crowd falls apart, "each one killing him that was next for fear he should do as much to him" (388), and with only a small additional intervention by the royal party, the rebellion is crushed. The young farmer, we might add, is killed in a final, parenthetical touch of the comic violence that secures status boundaries and drives the rebels to the "frontiers":

> But then came down Zelmane, and Basilius with Dorus issued; and . . . made such havoc (among the rest Zelmane striking the farmer to the heart with her sword, as before she had done with her eyes) that in a while they of the contrary side were put to fight and fled to certain woods upon the frontiers, where feeding wildly and drinking only water, they were disciplined for their drunken riots. (389)

Sidney's solution to the problem of representing a victory over a popular rebellion is a brilliant one, but it depends, as we have seen, upon the disguise of the aristocratic heroes, a disguise whose stain to their princely honor is only partially washed away by the rebels' blood. If we turn from *Arcadia* to the other massive achievement of late sixteenth-century English literature, *The Faerie Queene*, we encounter an alternative solution that manages, unlike Dürer, to represent the victor and, unlike Sidney, to represent him *in propria persona*. In Canto 2 of Book 5—printed in 1596, three years after the posthumous publication of Sidney's work—Spenser's hero Artegall, the champion of Justice, and his companion, the iron man Talus, come upon an immense crowd assembled to listen to a "mighty Gyant." The giant—"admired much of fooles, women, and boys"—stands on a rock overlooking the sea and boasts that with a "huge great paire of ballance in his hand," he will weigh all the world and reduce everything to its original state of equality. The vulgar flock about him "like foolish flies about an hony crocke," in hopes of obtaining "vncontrolled freedome":

> All which when *Artegall* did see, and heare,
> How he mis-led the simple peoples traine,
> In sdeignfull wize he drew unto him neare.[33]

Spenser's hero thus retains his proper shape and name, as he advances to confront the nameless giant. By representing the radical leader as literally monstrous—for in faery land, of course, such grotesqueries need not appear merely the figurative excesses of political rhetoric—Spenser greatly reduces the threat of an inadvertent ennobling of rebellion in the commemoration of its defeat. The giant bears in the form of his body the ineradicable sign of his disobedience, a sign that links him to the primal disobedience of the giants who rebelled against Jove and hence, by traditional mythographic analogy, to the rebel angels of the Christian story. These associations would seem to call for the hero to attack, just as, earlier in the same Canto, he had destroyed the mighty Saracen *Pollente* and as, at the book's close, he beheads the giant Grantorto. Such warfare is a crucial and recurrent structural principle in Spenser's epic which rests on the chivalric conviction, congenial to militant Protestantism, that acts of violence against evil oppressors are necessary, inevitable, and redemptive. But the Giant in Canto 2 is not an extorter or oppressor; rather he bears, in the huge balances and in his project of restoring all things to their just and ancient proportions, signs that link him to Artegall himself and to Astraea who taught the knight, as Spenser writes, "to weigh both right and wrong / In equall ballance" (V. i.7). And just at the point when the hero seems to be girding himself for battle—"In sdeignfull wize he drew vnto him neare"—he turns instead to rhetoric: "And thus vnto him spake, without regard or fear" (V.ii.33).

Artegall's purpose in the debate that follows is clearly to discredit the Giant, to expose the fraudulence of his claims, and hence to distinguish firmly between the demonic parody of social justice and the true exercise of justice embodied in Artegall's own knightly vocation. But the distinction is achieved paradoxically by the poem's insistence now not on the uncanny resemblance between the Giant's iconographic sign and Artegall's, but on the still more uncanny resemblance between the Giant's rhetoric and Spenser's own. Artegall declares that the egalitarian social project is belied by the absolute stability of the geocentric cosmos:

> The earth was in the middle centre pight,
> In which it doth immoueable abide,
> Hemd in with waters like a wall in sight;
> And they with aire, that not a drop can slide:
> Al which the heauens containe, and in their courses guide.
>
> Such heauenly iustice doth among them raine,
> That euery one doe know their certaine bound,
> In which they doe these many yeares remaine,
> And mongst them al no change hath yet beene found.
>
> (35–36)

This stability—the perfection of objects "hemd in" and "bound"—is decisive evidence of God's absolute power and hence of the need for all creatures, men as well as planets, to submit passively to the divine will: "He maketh Kings to sit in souerainty; He maketh subjects to their powre obay" (41). The Giant indignantly appeals to the signs of vast observable change both in the physical universe and in the social order—

> Seest not, how badly all things present bee,
> And each estate quite out of order, goth?—
>
> (37)

to which Artegall replies with a blend of challenges reminiscent of the Book of Job and arguments for the transcendent orderliness and ultimate self-cancellation of all change. But these arguments, though fully sanctioned by the outcome of the episode, are curiously at odds

with the poet's own perceptions, in the proem to Book 5, which seem
to accord far more with the Giant's:

> Me seemes the world is runne quite out of square,
> From the first point of his appointed sourse,
> And being once amisse growes daily wourse and wourse.
>
> (V.Pr.1)

How are we to account for this likeness and how then are we to
explain the contradiction between the positive value attached to the
poet's own account of disorder and the negative value attached to the
Giant's quite similar account? The likeness, we may suggest, derives
from the critical, even apocalyptic, strain that is recurrent in Spenser's work, from his awareness of deep disorder in the human and
natural realms, from his nagging sense of social marginality, whether
in relation to the Spencers of Althorpe or to the court, and from
his powerful conception of himself as a prophetic moralist. These
elements do not, of course, ever lead Spenser to a call for rebellion or
the redistribution of wealth, but they do lead to the strong expression
of arguments upon which such a call could be based. For as the
German peasant rebellion of 1525 suggests, radical protest in the early
modern period appealed not to perceptions utterly alien to those
expressed in official circles but rather drew unacceptable conclusions
from those same perceptions.[34]

Yet in Book 5, Artegall does not only object to the Giant's conclusions; he objects as strenuously to the arguments on which the Giant
professes to base his program, arguments that, as we have seen, closely
resemble the poet's own. To explain this apparent inconsistency, we
may argue, following Paul Alpers' sensitive account of Spenser's poetic practice, that the rhetorical nature of *The Faerie Queene* obviates
the necessity of strict narrative consistency and appeals instead to the
reader's "trust in the poem," that is, to his acceptance of the meanings
made apparent in any particular episode.[35] But given the close proximity of Spenser's Proem and Artegall's encounter with the Giant, we
should add that his trust depends upon the drawing of a firm boundary
between acceptable and subversive versions of the same perceptions
and that this boundary is affirmed, as in Sidney and Dürer, by the
representation of violence:

> Whom when so lewdly minded *Talus* found,
> Approching nigh vnto him cheeke by cheeke,
> He shouldered him from off the higher ground,
> And down the rock him throwing, in the sea him dround.

Like as a ship, whom cruell tempest driues
Vpon a rocke with horrible dismay,
Her shattered ribs in thousand peeces riues,
And spoyling all her geares and goodly ray,
Does make her selfe misfortunes piteous pray.
So downe the cliffe the wretched Gyant tumbled;
His battred ballances in peeces lay,
His timbered bones all broken rudely rumbled,
So was the high aspyring with huge ruine humbled. (49–50)

Talus's violence, in destroying the Giant, exorcises the potentially dangerous social consequences—the praxis—that might follow from Spenser's own eloquent social criticism. The cosmological vision and the moral outrage remain, but the "great expectations" of a radical reordering of wealth and power are shattered. Indeed, from this perspective, the proximity of the Proem and the episode is not an embarrassment but a positive achievement, for Spenser's narrative can function as a kind of training in the rejection of subversive conclusions drawn from licensed moral outrage.

This outrage, to be sure, is not licensed insofar as it is voiced by the Giant; rather it is answered by Artegall's arguments for perfectly secure cosmological and social boundaries. But as a further aspect of the reader's training, Artegall's rhetoric is not allowed to undermine the Proem's perception of injustice in the world; otherwise, the knight of justice would be completely immobilized: in a divinely ordered universe in which "no change hath yet been found" from the original state of perfection, there would be nothing for him to do. Instead the arguments are understood to be true, but *only* in relation to the Giant who is not himself persuaded by them and impiously refuses the boundaries proposed by Artegall.[36] Hence the necessity for pushing the Giant out of bounds and hence, too, the necessity for the push to come, unasked for, from Talus, agent of the inflexible execution of the strict letter of the law. In the special context of this episode, Artegall must be freed from the necessity of direct action, for his refutation of the Giant suggests that active intervention in the universe is not justified.

What we are given then is a more rigorous and explicit version than in Sidney of the separation of rhetoric and violence, a separation here sufficiently strong to save the noble hero entirely from the threat of the strain that would attend a base encounter. That threat is directly acknowledged when, in the wake of the Giant's destruction, "the people" rise up for revenge; seeing the "lawlesse multitude" coming toward him, Artegall "much was troubled," we are told, "ne wist what to doo":

For loth he was his noble hands t'embrew
In the base blood of such a rascall crew;
And otherwise, if that he should retire,
He fear'd least they with shame would him pursew.
Therefore he Talus to them sent, i'inquire
The cause of their array, and truce for to desire.

But soone as they him nigh approaching spide,
They gan with all their weapons him assay,
And rudely stroke at him one euery side:
Yet nought they could him hurt, ne ought dismay.
But when at them he with his flaile gan lay,
He like a swarme of flyes them ouerthrew;
Ne any of them durst come in his way,
But here and there before his presence flew,
And his themselues in holes and bushes from his vew.

(52–53)

Artegall takes the nobler course which is to persuade and to negotiate; the violence—characteristically unleashed on those who are represented as pathetically vulnerable—is the prerogative of Talus who can no more receive dishonor than can a Cruise missile.

Spenser's solution to the representational problem posed by a victory over popular rebellion hinges then upon Talus, that is, upon the allegorical separation of rhetoric and violence. In consequence, however, direct action remains a problem for Spenser's hero through the rest of Book 5 which ends, significantly, not with Artegall's glorious victory over the tyrant Grantorto, but with the slanders heaped on the victor by Envy, Detraction, and the Blatant Beast. Like Dürer and Sidney, Spenser saves the heroic as genre but at a high cost to the hero himself: in Dürer the victor is absent, in Sidney disguised, in Spenser split off from heroic actions imputed now to a mechanical monster. If we turn now to our final example of a late sixteenth-century artist grappling with this problem, we encounter a solution that reconstitutes the social status of the hero and in so doing fundamentally alters the heroic genre.

The artist is Shakespeare; the problem is the representation of Jack Cade's rebellion in *2 Henry VI*, a play probably first performed in 1590. Shakespeare depicts Cade's rebellion as a grotesque and sinister farce, the archetypal lower class revolt both in its motives and in its ludicrousness.[37] Like Dürer and Sidney, Shakespeare calls attention to the comic humbleness of the rebels' social origins—"There's Best's son, the tanner of Wingham, . . . And Dick the butcher, . . . And Smith the weaver" (4.2.21ff)—and like Spenser, he wryly depicts their "great expectations":

> There shall be in England seven half-penny loaves
> sold for a penny; the three-hoop'd pot shall have ten
> hoops; and I will make it felony to drink small beer.
> (4.2.62–5)

How can such buffoons be put down without embarrassment to the victors? In part the answer lies, as for Spenser, in the separation of rhetoric and violence. Cade and his "rabblement" reach London—"Up Fish Street! down Saint Magnus' Corner! kill and knock down! throw them into Thames!" (4.8.1–2)—but are brought up short by the appearance of the Duke of Buckingham and Lord Clifford. These noblemen come, as they say, as "ambassadors from the King / Unto the commons" and pronounce "free pardon" to all who will go home in peace. A few rousing speeches from the aristocrats, with the invocation of the name of Henry V and the threat of a French invasion, suffice; the rebellion instantly collapses, the state triumphs, and Cade flees. But if the rebels can be easily reabsorbed into the ranks of loyal Englishmen, only momentarily misled by a demagogue, the rebel leader must still be destroyed, and the history play will not accommodate a mechanical man to do the killing.

Shakespeare's solution is simple, effective, and, in its way, elegant. Cade escapes to the country only to be threatened with starvation, "Wherefore," he conveniently tells us, "on a brick wall have I climb'd into this garden, to see if I can eat grass, or pick a sallet" (4.10.6–8) The owner of the garden enters, voicing to himself the familiar sentiments of retirement poetry:

> Lord! who would live turmoiled in the court,
> And may enjoy such quiet walks as these?
> This small inheritance my father left me
> Contenteth me, and worth a monarchy.
> (4.10.16–19)

Beyond the familiar contrast of court and country, Shakespeare is careful to note in these lines that the speaker is the garden's actual owner, that the property is a modest inheritance, and that he is thus to be distinguished from a tenant, on the one hand, and a great lord, on the other. This care in placing the speaker in relation to property is underscored by Cade's immediate response: "Here's the lord of the soil come to seize me for a stray, for entering his fee-simple without leave" (4.10.24–25). This aside, which rests on the legal right of a property owner with absolute title to his land to impound stray animals that wander onto estate, makes it clear that the garden is *enclosed private property*, not in any sense, then, a public or common domain. And the owner's reply to Cade's grotesquely aggressive challenge— "I'll make thee eat iron like an ostrich, and swallow my sword like a great pin"—reiterates again the property rights that are at stake here:

> Why, rude companion, whatso'er thou be,
> I know thee not . . .
> Is't not enough to break into my garden,
> And like a thief to come to rob my grounds,
> Climbing my walls in spite of me the owner,
> But thou wilt brave me with these saucy terms?
> (4.10.30–35)

What is happening, I suggest, is that status relations—"I say it was never merry world in England since gentlemen came up" (4.2.7–9)— are being transformed before our eyes into property relations, and the concern, as in Sidney and Spenser, for maintaining social and even cosmic boundaries is reconceived as a concern for maintaining free-hold boundaries. Symbolic estate gives way to real estate. And in this revised context, the context of property rather than rank, the fear of stain in the representation of an unequal encounter vanishes altogether. The owner of the garden does not hide his name, nor does he look for someone else to do the killing. Quite the contrary, he proudly names himself, as he prepares, with unembarrassed complacency, for the unequal encounter:

> Nay, it shall ne'er be said, while England stands,
> That Alexander Iden, esquire of Kent,
> Took odds to combat a poor famish'd man.
> Oppose thy steadfast-gazing eyes to mine,
> See if thou canst outface me with thy looks:
> Set limb to limb, and thou art far the lesser;
> Thy hand is but a finger to my fist;
> Thy leg a stick compared with this truncheon.
> (4.10.41–48)

Iden perceives Cade not as a social rebel but as a belligerent thief who has tried to steal a salad; theirs is a contest not between an aristocrat and a churl but between a well-fed owner of property and "a poor famished man." Only from Cade's dying words does Iden learn whom he has slain, and his reaction enables us to gauge the extraordinary distance between Shakespeare's representation of this victory and the others at which we have looked:

> Is't Cade that I have slain, that monstrous traitor?
> Sword, I will hallow thee for this thy deed,
> And hang thee o'er my tomb when I am dead:
> Ne'er shall this blood be wiped from thy point,
> But thou shalt wear it as a herald's coat,
> To emblaze the honour that thy master got.
>
> (2.10.65–70)

The sword that Dürer had to depict without anyone to wield it becomes Iden's proudest possession; the deed that Sidney's heroes had to perform in disguise becomes a claim to distinction; and the blood that Spenser's knight did not wish to get on his hands becomes a badge of honor. The aristocrat has given way to the man of property, and heroic commemoration has been absorbed into a new genre, the history play.

## Notes

1. Albrecht Dürer, *The Painter's Manual* [*Unterweisung der Messung*, 1525], translated by Walter L. Strauss (New York: Abaris, 1977), p. 227.

2. Sebastiano Serlio, "*Scena tragica*," in *Architettura* (1551) [*The Book of Architecture* (London, 1611), Fol. 25ᵛ].

3. *Orlando Furioso*, Canto 9: 88–91; also Canto 11: 21–28. See Edgar Wind, *Pagan Mysteries in the Renaissance* (Harmondsworth: Penguin, 1967), pp. 108–109.

4. *Painter's Manual*, p. 233. The mock encomium recalls Erasmus's *Praise of Folly*.

5. This mode of depicting Christ seems to date from the late fourteenth century and probably derives from a traditional representation of Job: the mourning figure would then suggest perfect patience in humiliation as well as perfect innocence. See G. von der Osten, "Job and Christ," *Journal of the Warburg and Courtauld Institute* 16 (1953), 153–58; Hans Kauffmann, "Albrecht Dürers Dreikönigs-Altar," *Wallraf-Richartz-Jahrbuch (Westdeutsches Jahrbuch für Kunstgeschichte)* 10 (1938), 166–78; Michael Baxandall, *The Limewood Sculptors of Renaissance Germany* (New Haven: Yale University Press, 1980), p. 314. I am indebted to Professor Baxandall for suggesting to me the connection between Dürer's peasant and the figure of Christ in Distress.

6. On the Peasants' War, see especially Peter Blickle, *The Revolution of 1525*, translated by Thomas A. Brady, Jr. and H. C. Erik Midelfort (Baltimore: Johns Hopkins University Press, 1981 [original edition 1977]).

7. "Admonition to Peace, A Reply to the Twelve Articles of the Peasants in Swabia [1525]," translated by Charles M. Jacobs, revised by Robert C. Schultz, in *Luther's Works*, ed. Helmut T. Lehmann, 55 vols. (Philadelphia: Fortress Press, 1967), vol. 46, p. 39. See Hubert Kirchner, *Luther and the Peasants' War*, translated by Darrell Jodock (Philadelphia: Fortress Press, 1972); Mark U. Edwards, Jr., *Luther and the False Brethren* (Stanford: Stanford University Press, 1975), pp. 60–81; Hans Althaus, *Luthers Haltung im Bauernkrieg* (Darmstadt, 1969 [1st ed., Tubingen, 1952]; Robert N. Crossley, *Luther and the Peasants' War* (New York: Exposition Press, 1972).

8. "Against the Robbing and Murdering Hordes of Peasants [1525]," in *Luther's Works*, vol. 46, p. 50. On Luther's apocalyptic expectations at this time, see M. Greschat, "Luthers Haltung im Bauernkrieg," *Archiv für Reformationsgeschichte* 56 (1965), 31–47. For a dissenting view, see Hartmut Lehmann, "Luther und der Bauernkrieg," in *Geschichte in Wissenschaft und Unterricht* 20 (1969), 129–39.

9. "Against the Robbing . . . ," *Luther's Works*, vol. 46, pp. 53–54. See also "Whether Soldiers, Too, Can Be Saved [1526]," in *Luther's Works*, vol. 46, pp. 89–137.

10. Thus in January, 1525, three young painters, all of whom had studied with Dürer, were called before the Nuremberg City Council to answer charges of radicalism. One of them, Barthel Beham, was reported to have declared that people should stop working until all property was divided equally, and he reputedly told the City Council that he recognized no authority other than God's. Later in 1525 Hieronymus Andreae Formschneyder, who had cut many of Dürer's designs into wood, was ostracized for openly supporting the rebellious peasants. See Walter L. Strauss, *The Complete Drawings of Albrecht Dürer* (New York: Abaris Books, 1974), vol. 4, pp. 2269. Sebald Beham seems, however, to have subsequently attacked the rebellious peasants in woodcuts executed in 1535; I have profited from an unpublished paper by Keith P. F. Moxey, "Sebald Beham's 'Church Anniversary Holidays': Festive Peasants as Instruments of Repressive Humour."

11. Erwin Panofsky, *Albrecht Dürer*, 2 vols. (Princeton: Princeton University Press, 1943), vol. 1, p. 233. On Dürer's admiration for Luther in the early 1520s, see Strauss, *Complete Drawings*, vol. 4, pp. 1903–1907. Dürer's admiration for Luther may not necessarily have extended to his social views at the time of the Peasants' War.

12. Quoted in Marcel Brion, *Albrecht Dürer: His Life and Work*, trans. James Cleugh (London: Thames & Hudson, 1960), p. 269; see also Strauss, *Complete Drawings*, vol. 4, pp. 2280–81. Dürer's exquisite watercolor is the record of a private experience that requires elaborate and careful notation, as opposed to the public monument which is conceived as an object whose symbolism is readily decipherable. Dürer had earlier recorded his vision of the Apocalypse in his immensely powerful illustrations to the book of Revelations.

13. "An Open Letter on the Harsh Book Against the Peasants [1525]," in *Luther's Works*, vol. 46, p. 70.

14. We seem to be in a period in which public commemorative monuments, though continually erected, are extremely difficult to design successfully. Consider the national debate over the recently dedicated monument to the Vietnam War dead or the controversy over Robert Arneson's bust of the slain San Francisco mayor, George Moscone (particularly over the inclusion, on the pedestal, of a hyper-realistic representation of the murder weapon). Dürer's monument is inadvertently recalled and transformed in a Salvadorean poster, currently circulating in Berkeley, that depicts a peasant crucified on farm implements.

15. The Renaissance displays a markedly increased sensitivity, nourished by classicism, to the theoretical implications of genre differentiation. Dürer's designs imply, if only as a nostalgic and shadowy recollection, the existence of a form of heroic commemoration in which there is a full sympathetic relationship between the object that is represented and the representation itself. This form is at once recalled and ironically (or at least playfully) represented in the design for a victory monument made out of the objects that have given the victory: a monument that collapses the distance of representation, but at the expense of the human victor. Set against this heroic commemoration, there is the comic monument which depends upon the continued force of the old heroic values, now deliberately violated for amusement's sake. And in the middle, there is what we may call, following Joel Fineman, the monument of praise paradox: at once an acknowledgment of the distance between the monument and the original heroic values and an attempt to preserve those values precisely through such an acknowledgment.

    This praise paradox is in the middle in another sense: it is located between the symbolic and the narrative modes. In the symbolic mode the elements are organized according to a conceptual schema that provides a syntax; in the narrative mode the elements are organized to tell a story, and this story too provides a syntax. But in the Dürer monument there is no syntax; the elements in the monument are paratactic. Parataxis—the refusal of both paradigmatic organization according to a schema of conceptual values and a syntagmatic organization according to a schema of narrative values—is the perfect expression of the monument's intermediate, paradoxical position.

16. Quoted by Julian Pitt-Rivers, "Honour and Social Status," in J. G. Peristiany, ed., *Honour and Shame: The Values of Mediterranean Society* (Chicago: University of Chicago Press, 1966), p. 24.

17. On the semiotics of execution, see Samuel Y. Edgerton, Jr., "*Maniera* and the *Mannaia:* Decorum and Decapitation in the Sixteenth Century," in *The Meaning of Mannerism*, edited by Franklin W. Robinson and Stephen G. Nichols, Jr. (Hanover, N.H.: University Press of New England, 1972), pp. 67–103.

18. Even were scholars to discover a letter against the peasants written in Dürer's own hand, someone could argue that in the wake of the public attacks upon his radical students and associates, he was being ironic or self-protective. I should add that a radical letter would be subject to comparable qualifications and doubts. We must understand that what is at stake is more than Dürer's personal orientation, and the path to such an understanding is the study of the genre problem.

19. "Open Letter," *Luther's Works*, vol. 46, p. 75.

20. "Against The Robbing. . . . ," *op. cit.*, p. 53.

21. See Mikhail Bakhtin's important concept of "heteroglossia," in *The Dialogic Imagination*, ed Michael Holquist, translated by Caryl Emerson and Michael Holquist (Austin: University of Texas Press, 1981), pp. 288ff.

22. F. G. Emmison, *Elizabethan Life: Disorder (Mainly from Essex Sessions and Assize Records)* (Chelmsford: Essex County Council, 1970), p. 57.

23. Emmison, *op. cit.*, pp. 63–64.

24. Thomas Deloney, *Jack of Newberrie*, quoted in Christopher Hill, "The Many-Headed Monster in Late Tudor and Early Stuart Political Thinking," in *From the Renaissance to the Counter-Reformation: Essays in Honor of Garrett Mattingly*, edited by Charles H. Carter (New York: Random House, 1965), p. 302.

25. See Arthur B. Ferguson, *The Indian Summer of English Chivalry* (Durham, N.C.: Duke University Press, 1960); Frances A. Yates, "Elizabethan Chivalry: The Romance of the Accession Day Tilts," in *Astraea: The Imperial Theme in the Sixteenth Century* (London: Routledge, 1975), pp. 88—111; and Roy Strong, *The Cult of Elizabeth: Elizabethan Portraiture and Pagentry* (London: Thames and Hudson, 1977).

26. Sir Philip Sidney, *The Countess of Pembroke's Arcadia*, edited by Maurice Evans (New York: Penguin, 1977), pp. 380–81.

27. See Don Wayne, *Penshurst: The Semiotics of Place and the Poetics of History* (Madison: University of Wisconsin, 1984). On Sidney's social attitudes, see Richard McCoy, *Sir Philip Sidney: Rebellion in Arcadia* (New Brunswick, N.J.: Rutgers University Press, 1979).

28. On carnivalesque laughter, see Mikhail Bakhtin, *Rabelais and His World*, translated by Helene Iswolsky (Cambridge, Mass.: MIT Press, 1968); on peasants and laughter, see Svetlana Alpers, "Bruegel's Festive Peasants," in *Simiolus: Netherlands Quarterly for the History of Art* 6. (1972/73), 163–76).

29. Jack Winkler, "Lollianos and the Desperadoes," in *Journal of Hellenic Studies* 100 (1980), 155–81.

30. Nashe cunningly replicates and parodies this imagined threat in his comical, sadistic account of the slaughter of the Anabaptists: "This tale must at one time or other give up the ghost, and as good now as stay longer. I would gladly rid my hands of it cleanly if I could tell how, for

what with talking of cobblers and tinkers and ropemakers and butchers and dirt daubers, the mark is clean gone out of my muse's mouth" *(The Unfortunate Traveler,* in *Elizabethan Prose Fiction,* edited by Meritt Lawlis [New York: Odyssey, 1967], p. 474).

31. For an illuminating account of the difference between the professional and amateur writers, see Richard Helgerson, *The Laureate in His Generation: Self-Presentation and the Renaissance Literary System* (forthcoming, U.C. Press). I am grateful to Professor Jonathan Goldberg for valuable suggestions about the "poor painter."

32. On rhetoric as social discipline, see for example Thomas Wilson, *The Arte of Rhetorique* [1560]: "Neither can I see that men could haue beene brought by any other meanes, to liue together in fellowship of life, to maintaine Cities, to deale truely, and willingly obeye one an other, if men at the first had not by art and eloquence, perswaded that which they full ofte found out by reason. For what man I pray you, beeing better able to maintaine himself by valiaunt courage, then by liuing in base subiection, would not rather looke to rule like a Lord, then to live like an vnderling: if by reason he were not perswaded, that it behoueth euery man to liue in his owne vocation," in *English Literary Criticism: The Renaissance,* ed. O. B. Hardison, Jr. (New York: Appleton-Century-Crofts, 1963), pp. 27–28.

33. Citations of the *Faerie Queene* are to *The Works of Edmund Spenser: A Variorum Edition,* edited by Edwin Greenlaw et al. (Baltimore: Johns Hopkins University Press, 1932–57). There is a brilliant account of Book 5 in Angus Fletcher, *The Prophetic Moment: An Essay on Spenser* (Chicago: University of Chicago Press, 1971). See also the valuable commentary in Jane Aptekar, *Icons of Justice: Iconography and Thematic Imagery in Book V of "The Faerie Queene"* (New York: Columbia University Press, 1969); T. K. Dunseath, *Spenser's Allegory of Justice in Book Five of "The Faerie Queene"* (Princeton: Princeton University Press, 1976).

34. See my "Invisible Bullets: Renaissance Authority and Its Subversion," in *Glyph* 8 (1981), 40–61.

35. Paul J. Alpers, "How to Read *The Faerie Queene,*" in *Essays in Criticism* 18 (1968), 440. Alpers would not necessarily discount contradictions in passages so close together; moreover, he finds Book V of *The Faerie Queene* the inferior work of an exhausted and demoralized poet.

36. The paradox is defused but not altogether resolved by the mythic stature of Spenser's narrative: Book V is an account of the *origin* of disorder, and Artegall, who had been trained by Astraea, may well have believed that no substantial change, physical or moral, had yet afflicted the universe.

37. All citations of *2 Henry VI* are form the Arden edition of the play, edited by Andrew S. Cairncross (London: Methuen, 1957). Shakespeare bases his depiction of Cade's rebellion less upon accounts of the actual rising in 1449–1450 than upon accounts of the Peasants' Revolt of 1381.

# 7

# Psychoanalysis and Renaissance Culture

An experience recurs in the study of Renaissance literature and culture: an image or text seems to invite, even to demand, a psychoanalytic approach and yet turns out to baffle or elude that approach. The bafflement may only reflect the interpreter's limitations, the melancholy consequence of ignorance or resistance or both. But I will argue here that the mingled invitation and denial has a more historical dimension; the bafflement of psychoanalytic interpretation by Renaissance culture is evident as early as Freud's own suggestive but deeply inadequate attempts to explicate the art of Leonardo, Michelangelo, and Shakespeare. The problem, I suggest, is that psychoanalysis is at once the fulfillment and effacement of specifically Renaissance insights: psychoanalysis is, in more than one sense, the end of the Renaissance.

Let me sketch what I mean by turning not to a literary text but to a series of documents that constitute the historical record of the case of Martin Guerre. This record, part of which formed the basis of a fine historical novel by Janet Lewis, *The Wife of Martin Guerre*, has recently been amplified and analyzed with great power by the historian Natalie Zemon Davis in a short book called *The Return of Martin Guerre* and dramatized in a French film of the same title.[1]

The story is this: Martin Guerre was the only son of a prosperous French peasant who owned and farmed a property near the village of Artigat, in southwestern France. In 1538, at the tender age of 14, Martin was betrothed to Bertrande de Rols—a fine match for the Guerre family—but the marriage was not consummated: Martin was thought to be the victim of sorcery, and his humiliating impotence continued for eight years until the charm was finally lifted by a series of religious rituals. Bertrande became pregnant and gave birth to a son who was given Martin's father's Basque name, Sanxi.

Martin's problems were far from over. In 1548 he seems to have had a terrible quarrel with his father, a quarrel that was almost certainly over the control and management of the family property. Accused by his father of a theft of grain, the troubled young man turned his back on parents, wife, son, and patrimony and disappeared without a trace.

Years passed. Martin's mother and father died, and in the absence of the heir the property was managed by his paternal uncle. Unable to remarry, Bertrande raised her son and waited. Then, in the summer of 1556, Martin Guerre returned. He had wandered across the Pyrenees, become a servant, then enlisted as a soldier and fought in the Spanish wars in the Netherlands. Now he seemed a changed man, kinder and less troubled. There is evidence that his resumed marriage was more loving—recorded gestures of tenderness and concern—and in the three years that followed Bertrande gave birth to two daughters. But there were also signs of strain between himself and his uncle, once again over the family property, and in 1559 this strain erupted into a series of court battles that culminated in the accusation that this was not in fact Martin Guerre but an imposter.

The extraordinary trial that followed had as its purpose the determination of the identity of the man who claimed to be Martin Guerre. Most of the inhabitants of Artigat and many from the surrounding villages were called as witnesses—from Martin's four sisters who testified that the man on trial was in fact their brother, to neighbors and friends who were divided: some upholding his claim, others swearing that he was an imposter, still others refusing to identify the prisoner one way or another. There were rumors, eagerly backed by the uncle's party, that the real Martin Guerre had lost a leg while serving as a soldier. Bertrande officially joined in the uncle's complaint, but in court she refused to swear that the defendant was not Martin Guerre, and she was seen during the period of the trial ministering to her husband, even washing his feet. It appeared either that she had been forced to become a plaintiff against her will or that she hoped that this trial would settle once and for all the question of identity, and hence authority, in her husband's favor. Her husband himself took the stand and recalled in great detail events from his childhood and adolescence that only the real Martin Guerre could have known.

The case dragged on through this trial, at the end of which the prisoner was found guilty, and then through an appeal before the Parlement of Toulouse. Finally, all the evidence had been sifted, and the court prepared its verdict, which seemed likely to be in favor of the accused and against the uncle. At this point, and without warning, a man with a wooden leg appeared in the courtroom. Bitterly upbraided Bertrande for having dishonored him, the man declared that he was the real Martin Guerre. The accused insisted that this was someone hired by the desperate uncle, but virtually all the witnesses now agreed that the one-legged man was in fact Martin Guerre. After the court found for the uncle, the accused man finally confessed that he was an impostor, one Arnaud du Tilh, alias Pansette. At first, it seems, he had merely intended to take advantage of his striking resemblance to Martin Guerre in order to rob the gullible household, but he had fallen in love with Bertrande and decided to assume forever the missing man's identity. Bertrande herself denied any complicity, but it is difficult to know where else Arnaud would have gone for the intimate family history, and though in Janet Lewis's novel Bertrande only senses gradually and very belatedly that her returned husband is an impostor, Natalie Davis suggests, with considerable plausibility, that the wife would have known almost at once. This certainly seems to have been Martin Guerre's own bitter conclusion.

On September 16, 1560, Arnaud du Tilh knelt barefoot in a white shirt before the church in Artigat, formally repented of his crime, and asked the forgiveness of all whom he had offended. This ritual of penitence completed, he was led to the Guerre house in front of which a gibbet had been erected. Mounting the ladder, he asked Martin Guerre to be kind to Bertrande who had been, he declared, entirely innocent. He asked Bertrande's pardon. Arnaud du Tilh, alias Pansette, was then hanged and his corpse burned.

This case, which interested Montaigne, among others, seems to solicit psychoanalytic interpretation. Surrounded by his four sisters, his nurse, and his mother, betrothed at an unusually early age, and thrust, with the familiar rowdy folk rituals, toward adult sexuality, Martin had great difficulty establishing himself in his masculine identity. He was only able to consummate the marriage after he had radically externalized the psychic threat by imagining that he had been bewitched and by undergoing a ritual cure. And when his masculinity was finally confirmed by the birth of the son to whom he gave his father's name, Martin evidently felt compelled to try to displace his father altogether—with a theft, significantly, of his father's grain, his seed. But the attempt was a disastrous failure: his father responded violently, and Martin faced an assault not merely upon his fragile masculinity, but upon his entire identity, an identity from which in effect he fled.

Not only are Martin's impotence, oedipal transgression, and flight the classic materials of Freudian speculation, but the subsequent trial seems to confirm a principle essential to the constitution of the Freudian subject: the real Martin Guerre cannot be definitively robbed of his identity, even when he has apparently abandoned it and even when its superficial signs have been successfully mimicked by a cunning impostor. To be sure, this principle of inalienable self-possession would appear far indeed from Freud's characteristic concerns: the subject of Freud is most often encountered in states of extreme alienation. Driven by compulsions over which it has little or no control, haunted by repressed desires, shaped by traumatic experiences that it can neither fully recall nor clearly articulate, the self as Freud depicts it is bound up not with secure possession but with instability and loss. Such articulation of identity as exists occurs in states of self-abandonment—in dreams and parapraxes—and the self seems lost not only to others but to the cunning representations of others within the self. No mere judicial procedure, no simple execution of the impostor, could suffice to make restitution for this theft of identity, for the criminal is already ensconced within the psyche of the victim.

Yet the intensity of Freud's vision of alienation would seem, in much of his writing, to depend upon the dream of authentic possession, even if that possession is never realized and has never been securely established. There is nothing radically new about an anthropology based upon the desire for the recovery of what was lost and yet was never actually possessed: it is already subtly articulated in Augustine for whom fallenness is defined in terms of an innocence from which all existing humans, including infants, are by definition excluded. What needs to be posited is not an actual, historical moment of possession, but a virtual possession, a possession that constitutes a structurally determinative pre-history. The hysteric in Freud may be alienated from her own body—earlier centuries would postulate a demonic agent to account for comparable symptoms—but the alienation implies at least a theoretically prior stage of nonalienation. There are in fact moments in Freud in which he appears to glimpse such a stage actually embodied in the regal figure of His Majesty the Infant. And if the historical impact of Freud is bound up with a sustained lese majesty, that is, with an assault on the optimistic assumption of a centered, imperial self, the network of psychoanalytic scandals—the unconscious, repression, infantile sexuality, primary process—nevertheless confirms at least the romantic assumption behind that discredited optimism: the faith that the child is the father of the man and that one's days are bound each to each in biological necessity.

This necessity secures the continuity of the subject, no matter how self-divided or dispersed, so that the Rat Man, for example, is still himself when he is acting under compulsions he does not comprehend. Identity in Freud does not depend upon existential autonomy; it is far more often realized precisely at moments in which the executive agency of the will has been relinquished. Freud's tormented subjects may lose everything, but, as Freud's narrative case studies eloquently attest, they do not and cannot lose a primal, creatural individuation. This irreducible identity is not necessarily a blessing; on the contrary, it most often figures as a burden. Along with the secret of incestuous fantasy, the Oedipus myth discloses the tragic inescapability of continuous selfhood.

We may propose then that in Freud individuation characteristically emerges at moments of risk or alienation and hence that those moments do not so much disrupt as secure authentic identity. And with this perception we may return to Martin Guerre, for the consequence of his self-loss was to trigger a communal inquiry into the authentic Martin Guerre. This inquiry was based upon—or helped to fashion— a communal conviction that there was an authentic Martin Guerre, authentic even (or perhaps especially) in his moments of flight and eclipse. Had the one-legged man never returned, the impostor would nevertheless have remained an actor, forever at one remove from his role. Arnaud du Tilh can manipulate appearances, he can draw the surrounding world into complicity with a strategy of deception, he can improvise the mannerisms and insinuate himself into the complex social network of Martin Guerre, but he cannot seize the other man's inner life. The testimony of the community is important—in the court of law, indispensable—but the roots of Martin's identity lie deeper than society; they reach down, as psychoanalysis would assure us, through the frail, outward memories of his sisters and friends to the psychic experience of his infancy—the infancy only he can possess and that even the most skillful impostor cannot appropriate—and beneath infancy to his biological individuality.

It is here in the body's uniqueness and irreducibility, and in the psychic structures that follow from this primary individuation, that the impostor's project must come to grief. Two bodies cannot occupy the same space at the same time; my body is mine until I die, and no improvisation, however cunning, can ever overturn that elementary possession. The mind can play strange tricks, but the body will not be mocked. Martin's identity is guaranteed by the same bodily principle that guarantees the identity of Freud's patients, twisting away from themselves in a thousand tormenting ways, alienated and abused more cunningly by their own inward ruses than ever Martin was abused by Arnaud, and yet permanently anchored, even in their own horror, in the lived experience of their unique bodily being.

But these latter conclusions, though they are ones with which I myself feel quite comfortable, are not ones drawn either explicitly or implicitly by anyone in the sixteenth century. They are irrelevant to the point of being unthinkable: no one bothers to invoke Martin's biological individuality or even his soul, let alone an infancy that would have seemed almost comically beside the point.[2] This irrelevance need not in itself discourage us—the universalist claims of psychoanalysis are unruffled by the indifference of the past to its categories. It may in any case be argued that we are encountering not indifference but either a technical exclusion of certain postulates from a legal proceeding where they have no standing or a self-evidence so deep and assured that the postulates quite literally go without saying. But I think it is worth noting that the canniest Renaissance observer of the case, Montaigne—also the canniest Renaissance observer of the self—draws conclusions that are quite the opposite to those we have drawn. Far from concluding that the trial vindicates or rests upon Martin Guerre's ultimate and inalienable possession of his own identity—a possession intensified in the experience of self-loss—Montaigne writes that the condemnation of the alleged impostor seemed to him reckless. He would have preferred a still franker version of the verdict that the Areopagites were said to have handed down in perplexing cases: "Come back in a hundred years." For, writes Montaigne, if you are going to execute people, you must have luminously clear evidence—"A tuer les gens, il faut une clarté lumineuse et nette"—and there was no such clarity in the trial of Martin Guerre.[3]

I do not mean to suggest that psychoanalysis by contrast would have supported the execution of Arnaud; on the contrary, by complicating and limiting society's conception of responsibility, psychoanalysis would seem to have made it more difficult to execute convicted murderers, let alone nonviolent impostors. But diminished responsibility is not diminished selfhood; indeed for psychoanalysis the self is at its most visible, most expressive, perhaps most interesting at moments in which the moral will has ceded place to the desires that constitute the deepest stratum of psychic experience. The crucial historical point is that for Montaigne, as for the judge at the trial, Jean de Coras, what is at stake in this case is not psychic experience at all but rather a communal judgment that must, in extraordinary cases, be clarified and secured by legal authority. Martin's body figured prominently in the trial, but not as the inalienable phenomenological base of his psychic history; it figured rather as a collection of attributes—lines, curves, volumes (that is, scars, features, clothing, shoe size, and so on)—that could be held up against anyone who claimed the name and property of Martin Guerre. The move is not from distinct physical traits to the complex life experience generated within, but outward to the community's determination that this particular body possesses by right a particular identity and hence a particular set of possessions. At issue is not Martin Guerre as subject but Martin Guerre as object, the placeholder in a complex system of possessions, kinship bonds, contractual relationships, customary rights, and ethical obligations. Arnaud, the court ruled, had no right to that place, and the state had the obligation to destroy him for trying to seize it. Martin's subjectivity—or, for that matter, Arnaud's or Bertrande's—does not any the less exist, but it seems peripheral, or rather, it seems to be the *product* of the relations, material objects, and judgments exposed in the case rather than the *producer* of these relations, objects, and judgments. If we may glimpse analyzable services—identities that invite deep psychological speculation—these selves seem brought into being by the institutional processes set in motion by Arnaud's imposture. Psychoanalysis is, from this perspective, less the privileged explanatory key than the distant and distorted consequence of this cultural nexus.

In a remarkable essay Leo Spitzer observed years ago that medieval writers seem to have had little or no "concept of intellectual property" and consequently no respect for the integrity or propriety of the first-person pronoun.[4] A medieval writer would incorporate without any apparent concern the experiences of another into his own first-person account; indeed he would assume the "I" of another. In such a discursive system, psychoanalytic interpretation seems to me crippled: it is only when proprietary rights to the self have been secured—rights made most visible, we may add, in moments of self-estrangement or external threat—that the subject of psychoanalysis, both its method and the materials upon which it operates, is made possible. The case of Martin Guerre is, to be sure, a remarkable oddity, and I could scarcely claim that by itself it secured much beyond the early death of a gifted impostor. But I suggest that the accumulation of institutional decisions and communal pressures of the kind revealed there did help to fashion the historical mode of selfhood that psychoanalysis has tried to universalize into the very form of the human condition.

This attempted universalization is not the result of a mere blunder or of overwhelming hermeneutic ambition, for there exist, after all, complex forms of self-consciousness and highly discursive personhood in the West long before the sixteenth century. The sense of identity secured in the trial of Arnaud du Tilh has its roots in an exceedingly rich and ancient tradition, a tradition so dense and multifaceted that it provokes simultaneously an historiographical paralysis and an interpretive license. The judicial decision to terminate the life of a man who has tried to assume the identity of another is a tiny episode in a vast history, a history without convenient narrative lines, with too many precedents, with a bewildering network of contributing and limiting factors: theology, philosophy, law, social ritual, family customs. It is deeply tempting in the face of such a history to assume that it is, in effect, no history at all, that the self is at its core a stable point of reference, a given upon which to construct interpretations, psychoanalytic or other. Such interpretations based upon a fixed value of identity offer the intellectual gratification—consoling in the face of a frightening accumulation of traces from the past or from other societies or from the dark corners of our own lands—of a totalizing comprehension, a harmonious vision of the whole.

But this unitary vision is achieved, as Natalie Davis's book makes clear, only by repressing history, or, more accurately, by repressing *histories*—multiple, complex, refractory stories. Such stories become, in effect, decorative incidents, filigrees enchased on the surface of a solid and single truth, or (in subtler versions) interesting variants on the central and irreducible universal narrative, the timeless master myth.

But what if we refuse the lure of a totalizing vision? The alternative frequently proposed is a relativism that refuses to privilege one narrative over another, that celebrates the uniqueness of each cultural moment. But this stance—akin to congratulating both the real and the pretended Martin Guerre for their superb performances—is not, I think, either promising or realistic. For thorough-going relativism has a curious resemblance to the universalizing that it proposes to displace: both are uncomfortable with histories. Histories threaten relativism, though they seem superficially allied, because the connections and ruptures with which historians are concerned sort ill with the unorganized, value-neutral equivalences that would allow each moment a perfect independence and autonomy. The power of the story of Martin Guerre, as Natalie Davis helps us understand, lies not in an absolute otherness that compels us to suspend all our values in the face of an entirely different system of consciousness, but rather in the intimations of an obscure link between those distant events and the way we are. The actual effect of relativism is not to achieve a perfect ethical neutrality—as if we could cleanly bracket all our beliefs and lift ourselves off our moral world—but to block a disconcerting recognition: that our identity may not originate in (or be guaranteed by) the fixity, the certainty, of our own body.

But if we reject both the totalizing of a universal mythology and the radical particularizing of relativism, what are we left with? We are left with a network of lived and narrated stories, practices, strategies, representations, fantasies, negotiations, and exchanges that, along with the surviving aural, tactile, and visual traces, fashion our experience of the past, of others, and of ourselves. The case of Martin Guerre offers, in this context, neither a universal myth nor a perfectly unique and autonomous event; it is a peculiarly *Renaissance* story, the kind of story that the age told itself in a thousand variations over and over again. The point of this telling is not to confirm a truth always and already known, nor—as the fate of Arnaud poignantly exemplifies— is the telling without consequences: in the judicial murder of the impostor we witness in tiny compass part of the process that secures our concept of individual existence. That existence depends upon institutions that limit and, when necessary, exterminate a threatening mobility; the secure possession of one's body is not the *origin* of identity but one of the consequences of the compulsive cultural stabilizing unusually visible in this story.

It is important to characterize the case of Martin Guerre as a *story* not only in order to acknowledge the way that a record of these particular lives, out of so many millions lost to our view, managed to survive in the sixteenth-century narratives of Jean de Coras and Montaigne and the twentieth-century narratives of Janet Lewis, Natalie Davis, Jean-Claude Carrière, and Daniel Vigne, but also in order to make the crucial connection between this relatively obscure, local series of events and the larger historical process in which they participate. For it is in stories—above all, literary fantasies— produced and consumed by those who had never heard of Martin Guerre, that the issues raised by his case escape their immediate territorial and cultural boundaries and receive their fullest rehearsal, elaboration, and exploration. And conversely, the trial and execution of Arnaud du Tilh enables us to understand aspects of the social significance of these literary fantasies that would otherwise remain obscure.

Jean de Coras's account of the Guerre case was not translated into English nor did Montaigne's brief recounting have substantial impact, but sixteenth- and seventeenth-century English writers invented, in effect, dozens of versions of this story. The drama is particularly rich in such versions, from the larcenous impersonation of the missing husband in John Marston's play, *What You Will*, to the romantic impersonations in Beaumont and Fletcher's tragicomedies, from Perkin Warbeck's regal pretentions in John Ford's play of that name to the sleazy tricks of Ben Jonson's rogues. ("But were they gulled / With a belief that I was Scoto?" asks Volpone. "Sir," replies the parasite Mosca, "Scoto himself could hardly have distinguished.") Above all, there are the instances of imposture and loss of personal moorings in Shakespeare: the buffoonery of the false Vincentio in *The Taming of the Shrew*, the geometry of the paired twins in *The Comedy of Errors*, the more impassioned geometry of *Twelfth Night*. Even when there is no malicious, accidental, or natural double, Shakespeare's characters are frequently haunted by the sense that their identity has been lost or stolen: "Who is it that can tell me who I am?" cries the anguished Lear. And in the most famous of the tragedies, the ghost of Old Hamlet—"Of life, of crown, of queen at once dispatched"—returns to his land to demand that his son take the life of the impostor who has seized his identity.

Not by accident is it in the drama that this exploration of the issue at stake in the trial of Arnaud du Tilh is most intense, for the form of the drama itself invites reflection upon the extent to which it is possible for one man to assume the identity of another. Every theatrical performance at once confirms and denies this possibility: confirms it with varying degrees of success depending upon the skill of the actor and denies it because that skill is itself perceived by virtue of the small but unbridgeable distance between the actor's real and fictive identity. All Renaissance drama is in this sense a playful enactment of the case of Martin Guerre: a convincing impersonation before a large audience that is complicit with the deception only to bear witness at the close to the imposture's end. In some instances the impersonation seemed less playful, more dangerous than others: powerful noblemen complained that they were themselves being represented on stage, and they successfully sought a legal prohibition of the miming of living notables. But even with fictive or long-dead characters, the drama continually celebrates the mystery of Arnaud's art: the successful insertion of one individual into the identity of another. And inevitably this celebration is at the same time an anatomy, an exposing to view of the mechanisms of imposture. What is entirely unacceptable—indeed punishable by death in the everyday world— is both instructive and delightful in spaces specially marked off for the exercise of impersonation. For in these spaces, and only in these spaces, there is by a widely shared social agreement no imposture.

It is no accident too that in virtually all of these plays—and there are other instances in Shakespeare's work and the work of his contemporaries—the intrigue that arises from the willed or accidental mistaking of one person for another centers on property and proper names: purse and person are here inseparably linked as they were in the parish records that began to be kept systematically in England only in the sixteenth century. Henry VIII's insatiable craving for money to finance his military adventures abroad and his extravagances at home led him to exact the so-called Loan of 1522, which was based upon a survey undertaken at royal command earlier that year. The survey, whose financial objectives were kept secret, required authorities in the land to certify in writing the names of all the men above the age of sixteen and "whom they belong to." They were to record as well "who is the lord of every town and hamlet . . . who be parsons of the same towns, and what the benefices be worth by the year . . . also who be the owners of every parcel of land within any town, hamlet, parish, or village . . . with the year value of every man's land within the same."[5] The secrecy built into the survey—for were its purpose known, there would have been widespread evasion and concealment—had the effect of naturalizing the relationship between name and wealth. A man's goods were to be recorded not for the specific purpose of taxation but for the general purpose of identification: to enable the kingdom to know itself and hence to know its resources and its strength.

To the momentous survey of 1522 must be added an innovation less immediately spectacular but in the long run more important: the parish records that Cromwell instituted in 1538.[6] The parish chest, which is for demography what the Renaissance English theater is for literary history, signals, along with other innovative forms of Tudor record-keeping, a powerful official interest in identity and property, and identity *as* property. Precisely this interest is voiced, tested, and deepened throughout Shakespeare's career. It is often said, with a sense of irony and resignation, that though we possess a surprising amount of documentary evidence about Shakespeare's life, virtually none of it is of real significance for an understanding of his plays, for most of the surviving documents are notarial records of real estate transactions. I think property may be closer to the wellsprings of the Shakespearean conception of identity than we imagine.

Shakespeare and his contemporaries, to be sure, knew the difference between a complex individual and what the Norwegian captain in *Hamlet* calls "a little patch of ground / That hath in it no profit but the name." Yet I think that in all the literary instances I have cited, identity is conceived in a way that renders psychoanalytic interpretations marginal or belated. For what most matters in the literary texts, as in the documents that record the case of Martin Guerre, are communally secured proprietary rights to a name and a place in an increasingly mobile social world, and these rights seem more an historical condition that enables the development of psychoanalysis than a psychic condition that psychoanalysis itself can adequately explain.

In Renaissance drama, as in the case of Martin Guerre, the traditional linkages between body, property, and name are called into question; looking back upon the theatrical and judicial spectacle, one can glimpse the early stages of the slow, momentous transformation of the middle term from "property" to "psyche."[7] But that transformation had by no means already occurred; it was on the contrary the result (not yet perfectly realized in our own time) of a prolonged series of actions and transactions. The consequence, I think, is that psychoanalytic interpretation seems to follow upon rather than to explain Renaissance texts. If psychoanalysis was, in effect, made possible by (among other things) the legal and literary proceedings of the sixteenth and seventeenth centuries, then its interpretive practice is not irrelevant to those proceedings, nor is it exactly an anachronism. But psychoanalytic interpretation is causally belated, even as it is causally linked: hence the curious effect of a discourse that functions *as if* the psychological categories it invokes were not only simultaneous with but even prior to and themselves causes of the very phenomena of which in actual fact they were the results. I do not propose that we abandon the attempts at psychologically deep readings of Renaissance texts; rather, in the company of literary criticism and history, psychoanalysis can redeem its belatedness only when it historicizes its own procedures.

There are interesting signs of this historicizing—perhaps most radically in the school of Hegelian psychoanalysis associated with the work of Jacques Lacan, where identity is always revealed to be the identity of another, always registered (as in those parish registers) in language. But I want to end with a glance at a much earlier and still powerful attempt to formulate an historical conception of the self, an attempt that significantly locates the origins of this conception in language and more specifically in literary practice.

"A PERSON," writes Hobbes,

> is he whose words or actions are considered, either as his own, or as representing the words or actions of an other man, or of any other thing to whom they are attributed, whether Truly or by Fiction. When they are considered as his owne, then is he called a Naturall Person: And when they are considered as representing the words and actions of another, then is he a Feigned or Artificiall person. The word Person is latine . . . as *Persona* in latine signifies the *disguise,* or *outward appearance* of a man, counterfeited on the stage; and sometimes more particularly that part of it, which disguiseth the face, as a Mask or Visard: And from the Stage, hath been translated to any Representer of speech and action, as well in Tribunalls, as Theaters. So that a *Person* is the same that an *Actor* is, both on the Stage and in common Conversation.[8]

Psychoanalysis will in effect seize upon the concept of a "natural person" and will develop that concept into a brilliant hermeneutical system centered upon stripping away layers of strategic displacement that obscure the self's underlying drives. But in Hobbes the "natural person" originates in the "artificial person"—the mask, the character on a stage "translated" from the theater to the tribunal. There is no layer deeper, more authentic, than theatrical self-representation. This conception of the self does not deny the importance of the body—all consciousness for Hobbes derives from the body's responses to external pressure—but it does not anchor personal identity in an inalienable biological continuity. The crucial consideration is ownership: what distinguishes a "natural" person from an "artificial" person is that the former is considered to *own* his words and actions. Considered by whom? By authority. But is authority itself then natural or artificial? In a move that is one of the cornerstones of Hobbes's absolutist political philosophy, authority is vested in an artificial person who represents the words and actions of the entire nation. All men therefore are impersonators of themselves, but impersonators whose clear title to identity is secured by an authority irrevocably deeded to an artificial person. A great mask allows one to own as one's own face another mask.

If we conceive of a mask (as psychoanalysis has, in effect, taught us) as a defensive strategy, a veneer hiding the authentic self beneath, then Hobbes's conception must seem brittle and inadequate. But for Hobbes there is no person, no coherent, enduring identity, beneath the mask; strip away the theatrical role and you reach either a chaos of unformed desire that must be tamed to ensure survival or a dangerous assembly of free thoughts ("because thought is free," 3.37.478) that must—again to ensure survival—remain unspoken. Identity is only possible as a mask, something constructed and assumed, but this need not imply that identity so conceived is a sorry business. In our culture masks are trivial objects for children to play with and discard, and theatrical roles have the same air of pasteboard insubstantiality. But this is not always and everywhere the case; a man who lived in the shadow of Shakespeare might have had a deeper sense of what could be counterfeited on the stage or represented before a tribunal. In his conception of a person as a theatrical mask secured by authority, Hobbes seems far closer than Freud to the world of Shakespeare and, of course, Arnaud du Tilh.

## Appendix

The social fabrication of identity is, I have argued, particularly marked in the drama where, after all, identity is fashioned out of public discourse, and even soliloquies tend to take the form of rhetorical declamations. But nondramatic literature is, in its own way, deeply involved in the prepsychoanalytic fashioning of the proprietary rights of selfhood. Thus even in *The Faerie Queene*, where property seems to be absorbed altogether into the landscape of the mind, Spenser's concern with psychic experience is not manifested in the representation of a particular individual's inner life but rather in the representation of the hero's externalized struggle to secure clear title to his allegorical attributes and hence to his name. If that struggle is itself a vision of the inner life, it is one that suggests that for Spenser the psyche can only be conceived as a dangerous, factionalized social world, a world of vigilance, intrigue, extreme violence, and brief, fragile moments of intense beauty—just such a world as Spenser the colonial administrator inhabited in Ireland.

What does it mean that Spenser looks deep within himself and imagines that realm as eerily like the outward realm in which he bustled? It means that for him the noblest representation of the inner life is not lyric but epic—hence the compulsion of Spenserean characters to secure their identity by force of arms. And it means too that even the most well-defended existence is extremely vulnerable to fraud—identity may be imitated, misused, falsely appropriated, as Arnaud du Tilh appropriated the name and property and wife of Martin Guerre.

Evil in *The Faerie Queene* has its large-boned, athletic champions, but its most dangerous agents are the impostors, those who have the power to assume with uncanny accuracy all the signs of virtue. Thus when the subtle Archimago wishes to divide the Red Cross Knight from his beloved Una, truth's allegorical embodiment, he contrives "the person to put on / Of that good knight." "And when he sate vpon his courser free," Spenser concludes, "*Saint George* himself ye would haue deemed him to be." The disguise is sufficiently effective to take in Una herself—even truth cannot unmask a perfect falsehood— and the impostor's identity is only revealed after he is half-killed by the pagan Sansloy. Conversely, Red Cross's own identity—his name—is only revealed to him when he too has undergone the trials that belong to the signs he wears. And that name, first disclosed to the reader as the identity that Archimago falsely assumed, is paradoxically disclosed late in the poem to Red Cross as his true origin, an origin he can only possess at the *end* of his quest.

With the idea of an origin that is only conferred upon one at the end of a series of actions and transactions, I return to the notion that psychoanalysis is the historical outcome of certain characteristic Renaissance strategies.

### Notes

1. Natalie Zemon Davis, *The Return of Martin Guerre* (Cambridge: Harvard University Press, 1983). Davis's text was originally published in French,

together with a "recit romanesque" written by the film's screenwriter and director, Jean-Claude Carrière and Daniel Vigne (*Le Retour de Martin Guerre* [Paris: Robert Laffont, 1982]).

2. The only conspicuous religious element in the story is at best equivocal: Bertrande and the false Martin Guerre apparently frequented a Protestant conventicle. Natalie Davis speculates that the couple may have been seeking, in the Protestant ethos of the companionate marriage, a kind of ethical validation of their deception.

3. Montaigne, "Des boyteux" [Of Cripples], in *Essais*, ed. Maurice Rat, 2 vols. (Paris: Garnier, 1962), 2:478–79.

4. Leo Spitzer, "Notes on the Empirical and Poetic 'I' in Medieval Authors," *Traditio* 4 (1946): 414–22.

5. Quoted in W.G. Hoskins, *The Age of Plunder: King Henry's England, 1500–1547* (London: Longman, 1976), 20–21.

6. See William E. Tate, *The Parish Chest: A Study of the Records of Parochial Administration in England* (Cambridge: Cambridge University Press, 1946).

7. It is important to grasp that this transformation is at once a revolution and a continuation; "psyche" is neither a mere mystification for "property" nor a radical alternative to it.

8. Thomas Hobbes, *Leviathan*, ed. C.B. Macpherson (New York: Penguin, 1968), 1.16.217.

# 8

# Towards a
# Poetics of Culture

I feel in a somewhat false position, which is not a particularly promising way to begin, and I might as well explain why.[1] My own work has always been done with a sense of just having to go about and do it, without establishing first exactly what my theoretical position is. A few years ago I was asked by *Genre* to edit a selection of Renaissance essays, and I said OK. I collected a bunch of essays and then, out of a kind of desperation to get the introduction done, I wrote that the essays represented something I called a "new historicism." I've never been very good at making up advertising phrases of this kind; for reasons that I would be quite interested in exploring at some point, the name stuck much more than other names I'd very carefully tried to invent over the years. In fact I have heard—in the last year or so—quite a lot of talk about the "new historicism" (which for some reason in Australia is called Neohistoricism); there are articles about it, attacks on it, references to it in dissertations: the whole thing makes me quite giddy with amazement. In any case, as part of this peculiar phenomenon I have been asked to say something of a theoretical kind about the work I'm doing. So I shall try if not to define the new historicism, at least to situate it as a practice—a practice rather than a doctrine, since as far as I can tell (and I should be the one to know) it's no doctrine at all.

One of the peculiar characteristics of the "new historicism" in literary studies is precisely how unresolved and in some ways disingenuous it has been—I have been—about the relation to literary theory. On the one hand it seems to me that an openness to the theoretical ferment of the last few years is precisely what distinguishes the new historicism from the positivist historical scholarship of the early twentieth century. Certainly, the presence of Michel Foucault on the Berkeley campus for extended visits during the last five or six years of his life, and more generally the influence in America of European (and especially French) anthropological and social theorists, has helped to shape my own literary critical practice. On the other hand the historicist critics have on the whole been unwilling to enrol themselves in one or the other of the dominant theoretical camps.

I want to speculate on why this should be so by trying to situate myself in relation to Marxism on the one hand, and poststructuralism on the other. In the 1970s I used to teach courses with names like "Marxist Aesthetics" on the Berkeley campus. This came to an inglorious end when I was giving such a course—it must have been the mid-1970s—and I remember a student getting very angry with me. Now it's true that I tended to like those Marxist figures who were troubled in relation to Marxism—Walter Benjamin, the early rather than the later Lukács, and so forth—and I remember someone finally got up and screamed out in class "You're either a Bolshevik or a Menshevik— make up your fucking mind," and then slammed the door. It was a little unsettling, but I thought about it afterwards and realized that I wasn't sure whether I was a Menshevik, but I certainly wasn't a Bolshevik. After that I started to teach courses with names like "Cultural Poetics." It's true that I'm still more uneasy with a politics and a literary perspective that is untouched by Marxist thought, but that doesn't lead me to endorse propositions or embrace a particular philosophy, politics or rhetoric, *faute de mieux*.

Thus the crucial identifying gestures made by the most distinguished American Marxist aesthetic theorist, Fredric Jameson, seem to me highly problematic. Let us take, for example, the following eloquent passage from *The Political Unconscious:*

> the convenient working distinction between cultural texts that are social and political and those that are not becomes something worse than an error: namely, a symptom and a reinforcement of the reification and privatization of contemporary life. Such a distinction reconfirms that structural, experiential, and conceptual gap between the public and the private, between the social and the psychological, or the political and the poetic, between history or society and the 'individual,' which—the tendential law of social life under capitalism—maims our existence as individual subjects and paralyzes our thinking about time and change just as surely as it alienates us from our speech itself.[2]

A working distinction between cultural texts that are social and political and those that are not—that is, an aesthetic domain that is in some way marked off from the discursive institutions that are operative elsewhere in a culture—becomes for Jameson a malignant symptom of "privatization." Why should the "private" immediately enter into this distinction at all? Does the term refer to private property, that is, to the ownership of the means of production and the regulation of the mode of consumption? If so, what is the historical relation between this mode of economic organization and a working distinction between the political and the poetic? It would seem that in print, let alone in the electronic media, private ownership has led not to "privatization" but to the drastic communalization of all discourse, the constitution of an ever larger mass audience, the organization of a commercial sphere unimagined and certainly unattained by the comparatively modest attempts in pre-capitalist societies to organize public discourse. Moreover, is it not possible to have a communal sphere of art that is distinct from other communal spheres? Is this communal differentiation, sanctioned by the laws of property, not the dominant practice in capitalist society, manifestly in the film and television industries, but also, since the invention of movable type, in the production of poems and novels as well? Would we really find it less alienating to have no distinction at all between the political and the poetic—the situation, let us say, during China's Cultural Revolution? Or, for that matter, do we find it notably liberating to have our own country governed by a film actor who is either cunningly or pathologically indifferent to the traditional differentiation between fantasy and reality?

For *The Political Unconscious* any demarcation of the aesthetic must be aligned with the private which is in turn aligned with the psychological, the poetic, and the individual, as distinct from the public, the social, and the political. All of these interlocking distinctions, none of which seems to me philosophically or even historically bound up with the original "working distinction," are then laid at the door of capitalism with its power to "maim" and "paralyze" us as "individual subjects." Though we may find a differentiation between cultural discourses that are artistic and cultural discourses that are social or political well before the European seventeenth century, and in cultures that seem far removed from the capitalist mode of production, Jameson insists that somehow the perpetrator and agent of the alleged maiming is capitalism. A shadowy opposition is assumed between the "individual" (bad) and the "individual subject" (good); indeed the maiming of the latter creates the former.

The whole passage has the resonance of an allegory of the fall of man: once we were whole, agile, integrated; we were individual subjects but not individuals, we had no psychology distinct from the shared life of the society; politics and poetry were one. Then capitalism arose and shattered this luminous, benign totality. The myth echoes throughout Jameson's book, though by the close it has been eschatologically reoriented so that the totality lies not in a past revealed to have always already fallen but in the classless future. A philosophical claim then appeals to an absent empirical event. And literature is invoked at once as the dark token of fallenness and the shimmering emblem of the absent transfiguration.

But, of course, poststructuralism has raised serious questions about such a vision, challenging both its underlying oppositions and the primal organic unity that it posits as either paradisal origin or utopian, eschatological end.[3] This challenge has already greatly modified, though by no means simply displaced, Marxist discourse. I could exemplify this complex interaction between Marxism and poststructuralism by discussing Jameson's own most recent work in which he finds himself, from the perspective of postmodernism, deploring the loss of those "working distinctions" that at least enabled the left to identify its enemies and articulate a radical program.[4] But to avoid confusions, I want to focus instead on the work of Jean-François Lyotard. Here, as in *The Political Unconscious*, the distinction between discursive fields is once again at stake: for Lyotard the existence of proper names makes possible

> the co-existence of those worlds that Kant calls fields, territories, and domains—those worlds which of course present the same object, but which also make that object the stakes of heterogenous (or incommensurable) expectations in universes of phrases, none of which can be transformed into any other.[5]

Lyotard's model for these differentiated discourses is the existence of proper names. But now it is the role of capitalism not to demarcate discursive domains but, quite the opposite, to make such domains untenable. "Capital is that which wants a single language and a single network, and it never stops trying to present them" (p. 55). Lyotard's principal exhibit of this attempt by capital to institute a single language—what Bakhtin would call monologism—is Faurisson's denial of the Holocaust, and behind this denial, the Nazis' attempt to obliterate the existence of millions of Jews and other undesirables, an attempt Lyotard characterizes as the will "to strike from history and from the map entire worlds of names."

The immediate problem with this account is that the Nazis did not seem particularly interested in exterminating names along with the persons who possessed those names; on the contrary, they kept, in so far as was compatible with a campaign of mass murder, remarkably full records, and they looked forward to a time in which they could share their accomplishment with a grateful world by establishing a museum dedicated to the culture of the wretches they had destroyed. The Faurisson affair is at bottom not an epistemological dilemma, as Lyotard claims, but an attempt to wish away evidence that is both substantial and verifiable. The issue is not an Epicurean paradox— "if death is there, you are not there; if you are there, death is not there; hence it is impossible for you to prove that death is there"—but a historical problem: what is the evidence of mass murder? How reliable is this evidence? Are there convincing grounds for denying or doubting the documented events? And if there are not such grounds, how may we interpret the motives of those who seek to cast doubt upon the historical record?

There is a further problem in Lyotard's use of the Faurisson affair as an instance of capitalist hostility to names: the conflation of Fascist apologetics and capitalism would seem to be itself an instance of monologism, since it suppresses all the aspects of capitalism that are wedded to the generation and inscription of individual identities and to the demarcation of boundaries separating those identities. We may argue, of course, that the capitalist insistence upon individuality is fraudulent, but it is difficult, I think, to keep the principle of endlessly proliferated, irreducible individuality separate from the market place version against which it is set. For it is capitalism, as Marx suggested, that mounts the West's most powerful and sustained assault upon collective, communal values and identities. And it is in the market place and in the state apparatus linked to the circulation and accumulation of capital that names themselves are forged. Proper names, as distinct from common names, seem less the victims than the products of property—they are bound up not only with the property one has in oneself, that is, with the theory of possessive individualism, but quite literally with the property one possesses, for proper names are insisted upon in the early modern period precisely in order to register them in the official documents that enable the state to calculate and tax personal property.[6]

The difference between Jameson's capitalism, the perpetrator of separate discursive domains, the agent of privacy, psychology, and the individual, and Lyotard's capitalism, the enemy of such domains and the destroyer of privacy, psychology, and the individual, may in part be traced to a difference between the Marxist and poststructuralist projects. Jameson, seeking to expose the fallaciousness of a separate artistic sphere and to celebrate the materialist integration of all discourses, finds capitalism at the root of the false differentiation; Lyotard, seeking to celebrate the differentiation of all discourses and to expose the fallaciousness of monological unity, finds capitalism at the root of the false integration. History functions in both cases as a convenient anecdotal ornament upon a theoretical structure, and capitalism appears not as a complex social and economic development in the West but as a malign philosophical principle.[7]

I propose that the general question addressed by Jameson and Lyotard—what is the historical relation between art and society or between one institutionally demarcated discursive practice and another?—does not lend itself to a single, theoretically satisfactory answer of the kind that Jameson and Lyotard are trying to provide. Or rather theoretical satisfaction here seems to depend upon a utopian vision that collapses the contradictions of history into a moral imperative. The problem is not simply the incompatibility of two theories—Marxist and poststructuralist—with one another, but the inability of either of the theories to come to terms with the apparently contradictory historical effects of capitalism. In principle, of course, both Marxism and poststructuralism seize upon contradictions: for the former they are signs of repressed class conflicts, for the latter they disclose hidden cracks in the spurious certainties of logocentrism. But in practice Jameson treats capitalism as the agent of repressive differentiation, while Lyotard treats it as the agent of monological totalization. And this effacement of contradiction is not the consequence of an accidental lapse but rather the logical outcome of theory's search for the obstacle that blocks the realization of its eschatological vision.

If capitalism is invoked not as a unitary demonic principle, but as a complex historical movement in a world without paradisal origins or chiliastic expectations, then an inquiry into the relation between art and society in capitalist cultures must address both the formation of the working distinction upon which Jameson remarks and the totalizing impulse upon which Lyotard remarks. For capitalism has characteristically generated neither regimes in which all discourses seem coordinated, nor regimes in which they seem radically isolated or discontinuous, but regimes in which the drive towards differentiation and the drive towards monological organization operate simultaneously, or at least oscillate so rapidly as to create the impression of simultaneity.

In a brilliant paper that received unusual attention, elicited a response from a White House speech-writer, and most recently generated a segment on CBS's "Sixty Minutes," the political scientist and historian Michael Rogin recently observed the number of times President Reagan has, at critical moments in his career, quoted lines from his own or other popular films. The President is a man, Rogin remarks, "whose most spontaneous moments—('Where do we find such men?' about the American D-Day dead; 'I am paying for this microphone,

Mr. Green,' during the 1980 New Hampshire primary debate)—are not only preserved and projected on film, but also turn out to be lines from old movies."[8] To a remarkable extent, Ronald Reagan, who made his final Hollywood film, *Hellcats of the Navy*, in 1957, continues to live within the movies; he has been shaped by them, draws much of his cold war rhetoric from them, and cannot or will not distinguish between them and an external reality. Indeed his political career has depended upon an ability to project himself and his mass audience into a realm in which there is no distinction between simulation and reality.

The response from Anthony Dolan, a White House speech-writer who was asked to comment on Rogin's paper, was highly revealing. "What he's really saying," Dolan suggested, "is that all of us are deeply affected by a uniquely American art form: the movies."[9] Rogin had in fact argued that the presidential character "was produced from the convergence of two sets of substitutions which generated Cold War countersubversion in the 1940s and underlie its 1980s revival—the political replacement of Nazism by Communism, from which the national security state was born; and the psychological shift from an embodied self to its simulacrum on film." Both the political and the psychological substitution were intimately bound up with Ronald Reagan's career in the movies. Dolan in response rewrites Rogin's thesis into a celebration of the power of "a uniquely American art form" to shape "all of us." Movies, Dolan told the *New York Times* reporter, "heighten reality rather than lessen it."

Such a statement appears to welcome the collapse of the working distinction between the aesthetic and the real; the aesthetic is not an alternative realm but a way of intensifying the single realm we all inhabit. But then the spokesman went on to assert that the President "usually credits the films whose lines he uses." That is, at the moment of appropriation, the President acknowledges that he is borrowing from the aesthetic and hence acknowledges the existence of a working distinction. In so doing he respects and even calls attention to the difference between his own presidential discourse and the fictions in which he himself at one time took part; they are differences upon which his own transition from actor to politician in part depends, and they are the signs of the legal and economic system that he represents. For the capitalist aesthetic demands acknowledgments—hence the various marks of property rights that are flashed on the screen or inscribed in a text—and the political arena insists that it is not a fiction. That without acknowledgment the President delivers speeches written by Anthony Dolan or others does not appear to concern any-one; this has long been the standard operating procedure of American politicians. But it would concern people if the President recited speeches that were lifted without acknowledgment from old movies. He would then seem not to know the difference between fantasy and reality. And that might be alarming.

The White House, of course, was not responding to a theoretical problem, but to the implication that somehow the President did not fully recognize that he was quoting, or alternatively that he did realize it and chose to repress the fact in order to make a more powerful impression. In one version he is a kind of sleepwalker, in the other a plagiarist. To avoid these implications the White House spokesman needed in effect to invoke a difference that he had himself a moment before undermined.

The spokesman's remarks were hasty and *ad hoc*, but it did not take reflection to reproduce the complex dialectic of differentiation and identity that those remarks articulate. That dialectic is powerful precisely because it is by now virtually thoughtless; it takes a substantial intellectual effort to *separate* the boundaries of art from the subversion of those boundaries, an effort such as that exemplified in the work of Jameson or Lyotard. But the effect of such an effort is to remove itself from the very phenomenon it had proposed to analyze, namely, the relation between art and surrounding discourses in capitalist culture. For the effortless invocation of two apparently contradictory accounts of art is characteristic of American capitalism in the late twentieth century and an outcome of long-term tendencies in the relationship of art and capital: in the same moment a working distinction between the aesthetic and the real is established and abrogated.

We could argue, following Jameson, that the establishment of the distinction is the principal effect, with a view towards alienating us from our own imaginations by isolating fantasies in a private, apolitical realm. Or we could argue, following Lyotard, that the abrogation of the distinction is the principal effect, with a view towards effacing or evading differences by establishing a single, monolithic ideological structure. But if we are asked to choose between these alternatives, we will be drawn away from an analysis of the relation between capitalism and aesthetic production. For from the sixteenth century, when the effects for art of joint-stock company organization first began to be felt, to the present, capitalism has produced a powerful and effective oscillation between the establishment of distinct discursive domains and the collapse of those domains into one another. It is this restless oscillation rather than the securing of a particular fixed position that constitutes the distinct power of capitalism. The individual elements—a range of discontinuous discourses on the one hand, the monological unification of all discourses on the other—may be found fully articulated in other economic and social systems; only capitalism has managed to generate a dizzying, seemingly inexhaustible circulation between the two.

My use of the term *circulation* here is influenced by the work of Derrida, but sensitivity to the practical strategies of negotiation and exchange depends less upon poststructuralist theory than upon the circulatory rhythms of American politics. And the crucial point is that it is not politics alone but the whole structure of production and consumption—the systematic organization of ordinary life and consciousness—that generates the pattern of boundary making and breaking, the oscillation between demarcated objects and monological totality, that I have sketched. If we restrict our focus to the zone of political institutions, we can easily fall into the illusion that everything depends upon the unique talents—if that is the word—of Ronald Reagan, that he alone has managed to generate the enormously effective shuttling between massive, universalizing fantasies and centerlessness that characterizes his administration. This illusion leads in turn to what John Carlos Rowe has called the humanist trivialization of power, a trivialization that finds its local political expression in the belief that the fantasmatics of current American politics are the product of a single man and will pass with him. On the contrary, Ronald Reagan is manifestly the product of a larger and more durable American structure—not only a structure of power, ideological extremism and militarism, but of pleasure, recreation, and interest, a structure that shapes the spaces we construct for ourselves, the way we present "the news," the fantasies we daily consume on television or in the movies, the entertainments that we characteristically make and take.

I am suggesting then that the oscillation between totalization and difference, uniformity and the diversity of names, unitary truth and a proliferation of distinct entities—in short between Lyotard's capitalism and Jameson's—is built into the poetics of everyday behavior in America.[10] Let us consider, for example, not the President's Hollywood career but a far more innocent California pastime, a trip to Yosemite National Park. One of the most popular walks at Yosemite is the Nevada Falls Trail. So popular, indeed, is this walk that the Park Service has had to pave the first miles of the trail in order to keep them from being dug into trenches by the heavy traffic. At a certain point the asphalt stops, and you encounter a sign that tells you that you are entering the wilderness. You have passed then from the National Forests that surround the park—forests that serve principally as state-subsidized nurseries for large timber companies and hence are not visibly distinguishable from the tracts of privately-owned forest with which they are contiguous—to the park itself, marked by the payment of admission to the uniformed ranger at the entrance kiosk, and finally to a third and privileged zone of publicly demarcated Nature. This zone, called the wilderness, is marked by the abrupt termination of the asphalt and by a sign that lists the rules of behavior that you must now observe: no dogs, no littering, no fires, no camping without a permit, and so forth. The wilderness then is signalled by an intensification of the rules, an intensification that serves as the condition of an escape from the asphalt.

You can continue on this trail then until you reach a steep cliff onto which the guardians of the wilderness have thoughtfully bolted a cast-iron stairway. The stairway leads to a bridge that spans a rushing torrent, and from the middle of the bridge you are rewarded with a splendid view of Nevada Falls. On the railing that keeps you from falling to your death as you enjoy your vision of the wilderness there are signs—information about the dimensions of the falls, warnings against attempting to climb the treacherous, mist-slickened rocks, trail markers for those who wish to walk further—and an anodyzed aluminum plaque on which are inscribed inspirational, vaguely Wordsworthian sentiments by the California environmentist John Muir. The passage, as best I can recall, assures you that in years to come you will treasure the image you have before you. And next to these words, also etched into the aluminum, is precisely an image: a photograph of Nevada Falls taken from the very spot on which you stand.

The pleasure of this moment—beyond the pleasure of the mountain air and the waterfall and the great boulders and the deep forests of Lodgepole and Jeffrey pine—arises from the unusually candid glimpse of the process of circulation that shapes the whole experience of the park. The wilderness is at once secured and obliterated by the official gestures that establish its boundaries; the natural is set over against the artificial through means that render such an opposition meaningless. The eye passes from the "natural" image of the waterfall to the aluminum image, as if to secure a difference (for why else bother to go to the park at all? Why not simply look at a book of pictures?), even as that difference is effaced. The effacement is by no means complete—on the contrary, parks like Yosemite are one of the ways in which the distinction between nature and artifice is constituted in our society—and yet the Park Service's plaque on the Nevada Falls bridge conveniently calls attention to the interpenetration of nature and artifice that makes the distinction possible.

What is missing from this exemplary fable of capitalist aesthetics is the question of property relations, since the National Parks exist precisely to suspend or marginalize that question through the ideology of protected public space. Everyone owns the parks. That ideology is somewhat bruised by the actual development of a park like Yosemite, with its expensive hotel, a restaurant that has a dress code, fancy gift shops and the like, but it is not entirely emptied out: even the administration of the right-wing Secretary of the Interior James Watt stopped short of permitting a private golf course to be constructed on park grounds, and there was public outrage when a television production company that had contracted to film a series in Yosemite decided to paint the rocks to make them look more realistic. What we need is an example that combines recreation or entertainment, aesthetics, the public sphere, and private property. The example most compelling to a literary critic like myself is not a political career or a national park but a novel.

In 1976, a convict named Gary Gilmore was released from a federal penitentiary and moved to Provo, Utah. Several months later, he robbed and killed two men, was arrested for the crimes, and convicted of murder. The case became famous when Gilmore demanded that he be executed—a punishment that had not been inflicted in America for some years, due to legal protections—and, over the strenuous objections of the American Civil Liberties Union and the National Association for the Advancement of Colored People, had his way. The legal maneuvers and the eventual firing-squad execution became national media events. Well before the denouement the proceedings had come to the attention of Norman Mailer and his publisher Warner Books which is, as it announces on its title pages, "a Warner Communications Company." Mailer's research assistant, Jere Herzenberg, and a hack writer and interviewer, Lawrence Schiller, conducted extensive interviews and acquired documents, records of court proceedings, and personal papers such as the intimate letters between Gilmore and his girlfriend. Some of these materials were in the public domain but many of them were not; they were purchased, and the details of the purchases themselves become part of the materials that were reworked by Mailer into *The Executioner's Song*,[11] a "true life novel" as it is called, that brilliantly combines documentary realism with Mailer's characteristic romance themes. The novel was a critical and popular success—a success signalled not only by the sheaves of admiring reviews but by the Universal Product Code printed on its paperback cover. It was subsequently made into an NBC-TV mini-series where on successive evenings it helped to sell cars, soap powder, and deodorant.

Mailer's book had further, and less predictable, ramifications. While he was working on *The Executioner's Song*, there was an article on Mailer in *People* magazine. The article caught the attention of a convict named Jack H. Abbott who wrote to offer him first-hand instruction on the conditions of prison life. An exchange of letters began, and Mailer grew increasingly impressed not only with their detailed information but with what he calls their "literary measure." The letters were cut and arranged by a Random House editor, Erroll McDonald, and appeared as a book called *In the Belly of the Beast*. This book too was widely acclaimed and contributed, with Mailer's help, to win a parole for its author.

"As I am writing these words," Mailer wrote in the Introduction to Abbott's book, "it looks like Abbott will be released on parole this summer. It is certainly the time for him to get out."[12] "I have never come into bodily contact with another human being in almost twenty years," wrote Abbott in his book, "except in combat; in acts of struggle, of violence" (63). Shortly after his release, Abbott, now a celebrity, approached a waiter in an all-night restaurant and asked to use the men's room. The waiter—Richard Adan, an aspiring actor and playwright—told Abbott that the restaurant had no men's room and asked him to step outside. When Adan followed him on to the sidewalk, Abbott, apparently thinking that he was being challenged, stabbed Adan in the heart with a kitchen knife. Abbott was arrested and convicted once again of murder. The events have themselves been made into a play, also called *In the Belly of the Beast*, that recently opened to very favorable reviews.

Literary criticism has a familiar set of terms for the relationship between a work of art and the historical events to which it refers: we speak of allusion, symbolization, allegorization, representation, and above all mimesis. Each of these terms has a rich history and is virtually indispensable, and yet they all seem curiously inadequate to the cultural phenomenon which Mailer's book and Abbott's and the television series and the play constitute. And their inadequacy extends to aspects not only of contemporary culture but of the culture of the past. We need to develop terms to describe the ways in which material—here official documents, private papers, newspaper clippings, and so forth—is transferred from one discursive sphere to another and becomes aesthetic property. It would, I think, be a mistake to regard this process as uni-directional—from social discourse to aesthetic discourse—not only because the aesthetic discourse in this case is so entirely bound up with capitalist venture but because the social discourse is already charged with aesthetic energies. Not only was Gilmore explicitly and powerfully moved by the film version of *One Flew Over the Cuckoo's Nest*, but his entire pattern of behavior seems to have been shaped by the characteristic representations of American popular fiction, including Mailer's own.

Michael Baxandall has argued recently that "art and society are analytical concepts from two different kinds of categorization of human experience. . . .unhomologous systematic constructions put upon interpenetrating subject-matters." In consequence, he suggests, any attempt to relate the two must first "modify one of the terms till it matches the other, but keeping note of what modification has been necessary since this is a necessary part of one's information."[13] It is imperative that we acknowledge the modification and find a way to measure its degree, for it is only in such measurements that we can hope to chart the relationship between art and society. Such an admonition is important—methodological self-consciousness is one of the distinguishing marks of the new historicism in cultural studies as opposed to a historicism based upon faith in the transparency of signs and interpretive procedures—but it must be supplemented by an understanding that the work of art is not itself a pure flame that lies at the source of our speculations. Rather the work of art is itself the product of a set of manipulations, some of them our own (most striking in the case of works that were not originally conceived as "art" at all but rather as something else—votive objects, propaganda, prayer, and so on), many others undertaken in the construction of the original work. That is, the work of art is the product of a negotiation between a creator or class of creators, equipped with a complex, communally shared repertoire of conventions, and the institutions and practices of society. In order to achieve the negotiation, artists need to create a currency that is valid for a meaningful, mutually profitable exchange. It is important to emphasize that the process involves not simply appropriation but exchange, since the existence of art always implies a return, a return normally measured in pleasure and interest. I should add that the society's dominant currencies, money, and prestige, are invariably involved, but I am here using the term "currency" metaphorically to designate the systematic adjustments, symbolizations and lines of credit necessary to enable an exchange to take place. The terms "currency" and "negotiation" are the signs of our manipulation and adjustment of the relative systems.

Much recent theoretical work must, I think, be understood in the context of a search for a new set of terms to understand the cultural phenomenon that I have tried to describe. Hence, for example, Wolfgang Iser writes of the creation of the aesthetic dimension through the "dynamic oscillation" between two discourses; the East German Marxist Robert Weimann argues that

> the process of making certain things one's own becomes inseparable
> from making other things (and persons) alien, so that the act of
> appropriation must be seen always already to involve not only self-

projection and assimilation but alienation through reification and expropriation . . .

Anthony Giddens proposes that we substitute a concept of textual distanciation for that of the autonomy of the text, so that we can fruitfully grasp the "recursive character" of social life and of language.[14] Each of these formulations—and, of course, there are significant differences among them—pulls away from a stable, mimetic theory of art and attempts to construct in its stead an interpretive model that will more adequately account for the unsettling circulation of materials and discourses that is, I have argued, the heart of modern aesthetic practice. It is in response to this practice that contemporary theory must situate itself: not outside interpretation, but in the hidden places of negotiation and exchange.

## Notes

1. This is the text of a lecture given at the University of Western Australia on 4 September 1986. A slightly different version appeared in Murray Krieger, ed., *The Aims of Representation: Subject/Text/History* (New York: Columbia University Press, 1987), pp. 257–73.

2. Fredric Jameson, *The Political Unconscious: Narrative as a Socially Symbolic Act* (Ithaca: Cornell University Press, 1981), p. 20.

3. See Mark Poster, "Foucault, Poststructuralism, and the Mode of Information," in *The Aims of Representation*.

4. Jameson himself does not directly account for the sudden reversal in his thinking; he suggests rather that it is not his thinking that has changed but capitalism itself. Following Ernest Mandel, he suggests that we have moved into late capitalism, and in this state cultural production and consumption operate by wholly different rules. In the cultural logic of postmodernism, the working distinctions Jameson earlier found paralyzing and malignant have in fact vanished, giving way to an organization of discourse and perception that is at once dreadful and visionary. Dreadful because the new postmodern condition has obliterated all the place markers—inside and outside, culture and society, orthodoxy and subversion—that made it possible to map the world and hence mount a critique of its power structures. Visionary because this new multi-national world, a world with intensities rather than emotions, elaborated surfaces rather than hidden depths, random, unreadable signs rather than signifiers, intimates a utopian release from the traditional nightmare of traditional history. The doubleness of the postmodern is perfectly figured for Jameson by contemporary architecture, most perfectly by the Bonaventura Hotel in Los Angeles.
   The rapidity of the shift between modern and postmodern charted in Jameson's shift from *The Political Unconscious* (1981) to "Postmodern-

ism, or The Cultural Logic of Late Capitalism," *New Left Review*, No. 146 (July–August 1984), 53–93, is, to say the least, startling.

5. J.-F. Lyotard, "Judiciousness in Dispute or, Kant after Marx," in *The Aims of Representation*, p. 37.

6. See, for example, William E. Tate, *The Parish Chest: A Study in the Records of Parochial Administration in England* (Cambridge: Cambridge University Press, 1946).

7. Alternatively, of course, we can argue, as Jameson in effect does, that there are two capitalisms. The older, industrial capitalism was the agent of distinctions; the new, late capitalism is the effacer of distinctions. The detection of one tendency or the other in the phase of capitalism where it does not theoretically belong can be explained by invoking the distinction between residual and emergent. I find this scholastic saving of the theory infinitely depressing.

8. Michael Rogin, "'Ronald Reagan': The Movie" and other Episodes in Political Demonology* (Berkeley: University of California Press, 1987).

9. Quoted by reporter Michael Tolchin in the *New York Times* account of Rogin's paper, headlined "How Reagan Always Gets the Best Lines," *New York Times*, 9 September 1985, p. 10.

10. I borrow the phrase "the poetics of everyday behavior" from Iurii M. Lotman. See his essay in *The Semiotics of Russian Cultural History*, ed. A.D. Nakhimovsky and A.S. Nakhimovsky (Cornell: Cornell University Press, 1985).

11. N. Mailer, *The Executioner's Song* (New York: Warner Books, 1979).

12. Introduction to Jack Henry Abbott, *In the Belly of the Beast: Letters from Prison* (New York: Random House, 1981), p. xviii.

13. Michael Baxandall, "Art, Society, and the Bouger Principle," *Representations*, 12 (1985), 40–41.

14. All in *The Aims of Representation*.

# 9

# Resonance and Wonder

In a small glass case in the library of Christ Church, Oxford, there is a round, broad-brimmed cardinal's hat; a note card identifies it as having belonged to Cardinal Wolsey. It is altogether appropriate that this hat should have wound up at Christ Church, for the college owed its existence to Wolsey, who had decided at the height of his power to found in his own honor a magnificent new Oxford college. But the hat was not a direct bequest; historical forces, as we sometimes say—in this case, taking the ominous form of Henry VIII—intervened, and Christ Church, like Hampton Court Palace, was cut off from its original benefactor. Instead, as the note informs us, after it had passed through the hands of various owners—including Bishop Burnet, Burnet's son, Burnet's son's housekeeper, the Dowager Countess of Albemarle's butler, the countess herself, and Horace Walpole—the hat was acquired for Christ Church in the nineteenth century, purchased, we are told, for the sum of sixty-three pounds, from the daughter of the actor Charles Kean. Kean is said to have worn the hat when he played Wolsey in Shakespeare's *Henry VIII*. If this miniature history of an artifact is too slight to be of much consequence, it nonetheless evokes a vision of cultural production that I find compelling. The peregrinations of Wolsey's hat suggest that cultural artifacts do not stay still, that they exist in time, and that they are bound up with personal and institutional conflict, negotiations, and appropriations.

The term culture has, in the case of the hat, a convenient material referent—a bit of red cloth stitched together—but that referent is only a tiny element in a complex symbolic construction that originally marked the transformation of Wolsey from a butcher's son to a prince of the church. Wolsey's gentleman usher, George Cavendish, has left a remarkably circumstantial contemporary account of that construction, an account that enables us even to glimpse the hat in its place among all the other ceremonial regalia:

And after Mass he would return in his privy chamber again and, being advertized of the furniture of his chamber without with noblemen and gentlemen . . . , would issue out into them apparelled all in red in the habit of a Cardinal; which was either of fine scarlet or else of crimson satin, taffeta, damask, or caffa [a rich silk cloth], the best that he could get for money; and upon his head a round pillion with a neck of black velvet, set to the same in the inner side. . . . There was also borne before him first the Great Seal of England, and then his Cardinal's hat by a nobleman or some worthy gentleman right solemnly, bareheaded. And as soon as he was entered into his chamber of presence where was attending his coming to await upon him to Westminster Hall, as well noblemen and other worthy gentlemen as noblemen and gentlemen of his own family; thus passing forth with two great crosses of silver borne before him, with also two great pillars of silver, and his sergeant at arms with a great mace of silver gilt. Then his gentlemen ushers cried and said, 'On my lords and masters, make way for my lord's grace!'"[1]

The extraordinary theatricality of this manifestation of clerical power did not escape the notice of the Protestant reformers who called the Catholic church "the Pope's playhouse." When the Reformation in England dismantled the histrionic apparatus of Catholicism, they sold some of its gorgeous properties to the professional players—not only a mark of thrift but a polemical gesture, signifying that the sanctified vestments were in reality mere trumpery whose proper place was a disreputable world of illusion-mongering. In exchange for this polemical service, the theatrical joint-stock companies received more than an attractive, cut-rate wardrobe; they acquired the tarnished but still potent charisma that clung to the old vestments, charisma that in paradoxical fashion the players at once emptied out and heightened. By the time Wolsey's hat reached the library at Christ Church, its charisma must have been largely exhausted, but the college could confer upon it the prestige of an historical curiosity, as a trophy of the distant founder. And in its glass case it still radiates a tiny quantum of cultural energy.

Tiny indeed—I may already have seemed to make much more of this trivial relic than it deserves. But I am fascinated by transmigrations of the kind I have just sketched here—from theatricalized rituals to the stage to the university library or museum—because they seem to reveal something critically important about the *textual* relics with which my profession is obsessed. They enable us to glimpse the social process through which objects, gestures, rituals, and phrases are fashioned and moved from one zone of display to another. The display cases with which I am most involved—books—characteristically conceal this process, so that we have a misleading impression of fixity and little sense of the historical transactions through which the great texts we study have been fashioned. Let me give a literary example, an appropriately tiny textual equivalent of Wolsey's hat. At the close of Shakespeare's *Midsummer Night's Dream*, the Fairy King Oberon declares that he and his attendants are going to bless the beds of the three couples who have just been married. This ritual of blessing will ensure the happiness of the newlyweds and ward off moles, harelips, and other prodigious marks that would disfigure their offspring. "With this field-dew consecrate," the Fairy King concludes,

> Every fairy take his gait,
> And each several chamber bless,
> Through this palace, with sweet peace,
> And the owner of it blest
> Ever shall in safety rest.
>
> (5.1.415–20)

Oberon himself, we are told, will conduct the blessing upon the "best bride-bed," that of the ruler Theseus and his Amazon queen Hippolyta.

The ceremony—manifestly the sanctification of ownership and caste, as well as marriage—is a witty allusion to the traditional Catholic blessing of the bride-bed with holy water, a ceremony vehemently attacked as pagan superstition and banned by English Protestants. But the conventional critical term "allusion" seems inadequate, for the term usually implies a bloodless, bodiless thing, while even the tiny, incidental detail of the field dew bears a more active charge. Here, as with Wolsey's hat, I want to ask what is at stake in the shift from one zone of social practice to another, from the old religion to public theater, from priests to fairies, from holy water to field dew, or rather to theatrical fairies and theatrical field dew on the London stage. When the Catholic ritual is made into theatrical representation, the transposition at once naturalizes, denaturalizes, mocks, and celebrates. It naturalizes the ritual by transforming the specially sanctified water into ordinary dew; it denaturalizes the ritual by removing it from human agents and attributing it to the fairies; it mocks Catholic practice by associating it with notorious superstition and then by enacting it on the stage where it is revealed as a histrionic illusion; and it celebrates such practice by reinvesting it with the charismatic magic of the theater.

Several years ago, intending to signal a turn away from the formal, decontextualized analysis that dominates new criticism, I used the term "new historicism" to describe an interest in the kinds of issues I have been raising—in the embeddedness of cultural objects in the contingencies of history—and the term has achieved a certain currency. But like most labels, this one is misleading. The new historicism, like the Holy Roman Empire, constantly belies its own name. *The American Heritage Dictionary* gives three meanings for the term "historicism":

1. The belief that processes are at work in history that man can do little to alter.
2. The theory that the historian must avoid all value judgments in his study of past periods or former cultures.
3. Veneration of the past or of tradition.

Most of the writing labelled new historicist, and certainly my own work, has set itself resolutely against each of these positions.

1. *The belief that processes are at work in history that man can do little to alter.* This formulation rests upon a simultaneous abstraction and evacuation of human agency. The men and women who find themselves making concrete choices in given circumstances at particular times are transformed into something called "man." And this colorless, nameless collective being cannot significantly intervene in the "processes . . . at work in history," processes that are thus mysteriously alienated from all of those who enact them.

New historicism, by contrast, eschews the use of the term "man"; interest lies not in the abstract universal but in particular, contingent cases, the selves fashioned and acting according to the generative rules and conflicts of a given culture. And these selves, conditioned by the expectations of their class, gender, religion, race and national identity, are constantly effecting changes in the course of history. Indeed if there is any inevitability in the new historicism's vision of history it is this insistence on agency, for even inaction or extreme marginality is understood to possess meaning and therefore to imply intention. Every form of behavior, in this view, is a strategy: taking up arms or taking flight is a significant social action, but so is staying put, minding one's business, turning one's face to the wall. Agency is virtually inescapable.

Inescapable but not simple: new historicism, as I understand it, does not posit historical processes as unalterable and inexorable, but it does tend to discover limits or constraints upon individual intervention. Actions that appear to be single are disclosed as multiple; the apparently isolated power of the individual genius turns out to be bound up with collective, social energy; a gesture of dissent may be an element in a larger legitimation process, while an attempt to stabilize the order of things may turn out to subvert it. And political valences may change, sometimes abruptly: there are no guarantees, no absolute, formal assurances that what seems progressive in one set of contingent circumstances will not come to seem reactionary in another.

The new historicism's insistence on the pervasiveness of agency has apparently led some of its critics to find in it a Nietzschean celebration of the ruthless will to power, while its ironic and skeptical reappraisal of the cult of heroic individualism has led others to find in it a pessimistic doctrine of human helplessness. Hence, for example, from a Marxist perspective one critic characterizes the new historicism as a "liberal disillusionment" that finds that "any apparent site of resistance ultimately serves the interests of power" (33), while from a liberal humanist perspective, another critic proclaims that "anyone who, like me, is reluctant to accept the will to power as the defining human essence will probably have trouble with the critical procedures of the new historicists and with their interpretive conclusions."[2] But the very idea of a "defining human essence" is precisely what new historicists find vacuous and untenable, as I do the counter-claim that love rather than power makes the world go round. The Marxist critique is more plausible, but it rests upon an assertion that new historicism argues that "*any* apparent site of resistance" is ultimately coopted. Some are, some aren't.

I argued in an essay published some years ago that the sites of resistance in Shakespeare's second tetralogy are coopted in the plays' ironic, complex, but finally celebratory affirmation of charismatic kingship. That is, the formal structure and rhetorical strategy of the plays make it difficult for audiences to withhold their consent from the triumph of Prince Hal. Shakespeare shows that the triumph rests upon a claustrophobic narrowing of pleasure, a hypocritical manipulation of appearances, and a systematic betrayal of friendship, and yet these manifestations of bad faith only contrive to heighten the spectators' knowing pleasure and the ratification of applause. The subversive perceptions do not disappear, but insofar as they remain within the structure of the play, they are contained and indeed serve to heighten a power they would appear to question.

I did not propose that all manifestation of resistance in all literature (or even in all plays by Shakespeare) were coopted—one can readily think of plays where the forces of ideological containment break down. And yet characterizations of this essay in particular, and new historicism in general, repeatedly refer to a supposed argument that any resistance is impossible.[3] A particularizing argument about the subject position projected by a set of plays is at once simplified and turned into a universal principle from which contingency and hence history itself is erased.

Moreover, even my argument about Shakespeare's second tetralogy is misunderstood if it is thought to foreclose the possibility of dissent or change or the radical alteration of the processes of history. The point is that certain aesthetic and political structures work to contain the subversion perceptions they generate, not that those perceptions simply wither away. On the contrary, they may be pried loose from the order with which they were bound up and may serve to fashion a new and radically different set of structures. How else could change ever come about? No one is forced—except perhaps in school—to take aesthetic or political wholes as sacrosanct. The order of things is never simply a given: it takes labor to produce, sustain, reproduce, and transmit the way things are, and this labor may be withheld or transformed. Structures may be broken in pieces, the pieces altered, inverted, rearranged. Everything can be different than it is; everything could have been different than it was. But it will not do to imagine that this alteration is easy, automatic, without cost or obligation. My objection was to the notion that the rich ironies in the history plays were themselves inherently liberating, that to savor the tetralogy's skeptical cunning was to participate in an act of political resistance. In general I find dubious the assertion that certain rhetorical features in much-loved literary works constitute authentic acts of political liberation; the fact that this assertion is now heard from the left, where in my college days it was more often heard from the right, does not make it in most instances any less fatuous and presumptuous. I wished to show, at least in the case of Shakespeare's histories and in several analogous discourses, how a set of representational and political practices in the late sixteenth century could produce and even batten upon what appeared to be their own subversion.

To show this is not to give up on the possibility of altering historical processes—if this is historicism I want no part of it—but rather to eschew an aestheticized and idealized politics of the imagination.

2. *The theory that the historian must avoid all value judgments in his study of past periods or former cultures.* Once again, if this is an essential tenet of historicism, then the new historicism belies its name. My own critical practice and that of many others associated with new historicism was decisively shaped by the American 1960s and early

70s, and especially by the opposition to the Viet Nam War. Writing that was not engaged, that withheld judgments, that failed to connect the present with the past seemed worthless. Such connection could be made either by analogy or causality; that is, a particular set of historical circumstances could be represented in such a way as to bring out homologies with aspects of the present or, alternatively, those circumstances could be analyzed as the generative forces that led to the modern condition. In either mode, value judgments were implicated, because a neutral or indifferent relation to the present seemed impossible. Or rather it seemed overwhelmingly clear that neutrality was itself a political position, a decision to support the official policies in both the state and the academy.

To study the culture of sixteenth-century England did not present itself as an escape from the turmoil of the present; it seemed rather an intervention, a mode of relation. The fascination for me of the Renaissance was that it seemed to be powerfully linked to the present both analogically and causally. This doubled link at once called forth and qualified my value judgments: called them forth because my response to the past was inextricably bound up with my response to the present; qualified them because the analysis of the past revealed the complex, unsettling historical genealogy of the very judgments I was making. To study Renaissance culture then was simultaneously to feel more rooted and more estranged in my own values.[4]

Other critics associated with the new historicism have written directly and forcefully about their own subject position and have made more explicit than I the nature of this engagement.[5] If I have not done so to the same extent, it is not because I believe that my values are somehow suspended in my study of the past but because I believe they are pervasive: in the textual and visual traces I choose to analyze, in the stories I choose to tell, in the cultural conjunctions I attempt to make, in my syntax, adjectives, pronouns. "The new historicism," someone has written in a lively critique, "needs at every point to be more overtly self-conscious of its methods and its theoretical assumptions, since what one discovers about the historical place and function of literary texts is in large measure a function of the angle from which one looks and the assumptions that enable the investigation."[6] I am certainly not opposed to methodological self-consciousness, but I am less inclined to see overtness—an explicit articulation of one's values and methods—as inherently necessary or virtuous. Nor, though I believe that my values are everywhere engaged in my work, do I think that there need be a perfect integration of those values and the objects I am studying. On the contrary, some of the most interesting and powerful ideas in cultural criticism occur precisely at moments of disjunction, disintegration, unevenness. A criticism that never en-counters obstacles, that celebrates predictable heroines and rounds up the usual suspects, that finds confirmation of its values everywhere it turns, is quite simply boring.[7]

3. *Veneration of the past or of tradition.* The third definition of histori-cism obviously sits in a strange relation to the second, but they are not simply alternatives. The apparent eschewing of value judgments was often accompanied by a still more apparent admiration, however cloaked as objective description, of the past. One of the more irritating qualities of my own literary training had been its relentlessly celebra-tory character: literary criticism was and largely remains a kind of secular theodicy. Every decision made by a great artist could be shown to be a brilliant one; works that had seemed flawed and uneven to an earlier generation of critics bent on displaying discriminations in taste were now revealed to be organic masterpieces. A standard criti-cal assignment in my student years was to show how a text that seemed to break in parts was really a complex whole: thousands of pages were dutifully churned out to prove that the bizarre subplot of *The Changeling* was cunningly integrated into the tragic mainplot or that every tedious bit of clowning in *Doctor Faustus* was richly significant. Behind these exercises was the assumption that great works of art were triumphs of resolution, that they were, in Bakhtin's term, monological—the mature expression of a single artistic inten-tion. When this formalism was combined, as it often was, with both ego psychology and historicism, it posited aesthetic integration as the reflection of the artist's psychic integration and posited that psychic integration as the triumphant expression of a healthy, integrated community. Accounts of Shakespeare's relation to Elizabethan cul-ture were particularly prone to this air of veneration, since the Ro-mantic cult of poetic genius could be conjoined with the still older political cult that had been created around the figure of the Virgin Queen.

Here again new historicist critics have swerved in a different direc-tion. They have been more interested in unresolved conflict and con-tradiction than in integration; they are as concerned with the margins as with the center; and they have turned from a celebration of achieved aesthetic order to an exploration of the ideological and mate-rial bases for the production of this order. Traditional formalism and historicism, twin legacies of early nineteenth-century Germany, shared a vision of high culture as a harmonizing domain of reconcilia-tion based upon an aesthetic labor that transcends specific economic or political determinants. What is missing is psychic, social, and material resistance, a stubborn, unassimilable otherness, a sense of distance and difference. New historicism has attempted to restore this distance; hence its characteristic concerns have seemed to some critics off-center or strange. "New historicists," writes a Marxist observer, "are likely to seize upon something out of the way, obscure, even bizarre: dreams, popular or aristocratic festivals, denunciations of witchcraft, sexual treatises, diaries and autobiographies, descriptions of clothing, reports on disease, birth and death records, accounts of insanity."[8] What is fascinating to me is that concerns like these should have come to seem bizarre, especially to a critic who is committed to the historical understanding of culture. That they have done so indicates how narrow the boundaries of historical understanding had become, how much these boundaries needed to be broken.

For none of the cultural practices on this list (and one could extend it considerably) is or should be "out of the way" in a study of Renaissance literature or art; on the contrary, each is directly in the way of coming to terms with the period's methods of regulating the body, its conscious and unconscious psychic strategies, its ways of defining and dealing with marginals and deviants, its mechanisms for the display of power and the expression of discontent, its treatment of women. If such concerns have been rendered "obscure," it is because of a disabling idea of causality that confines the legitimate field of historical agency within absurdly restrictive boundaries. The world is parcelled out between a predictable group of stereotypical causes and a large, dimly lit mass of raw materials that the artist chooses to fashion.

The new historicist critics are interested in such cultural expressions as witchcraft accusations, medical manuals, or clothing not as raw materials but as "cooked"—complex symbolic and material articulations of the imaginative and ideological structures of the society that produced them. Consequently, there is a tendency in at least some new historicist writings (certainly in my own) for the focus to be partially displaced from the work of art that is their formal occasion onto the related practices that had been adduced ostensibly in order to illuminate that work. It is difficult to keep those practices in the background if the very concept of historical background has been called into question.

I have tried to deal with the problem of focus by developing a notion of cultural negotiation and exchange, that is, by examining the points at which one cultural practice intersects with another, borrowing its forms and intensities or attempting to ward off unwelcome appropriations or moving texts and artifacts from one place to another. But it would be misleading to imagine that there is a complete homogenization of interest; my own concern remains centrally with imaginative literature, and not only because other cultural structures resonate powerfully within it. If I do not approach works of art in a spirit of veneration, I do approach them in a spirit that is best described as wonder. Wonder has not been alien to literary criticism, but it has been associated (if only implicitly) with formalism rather than historicism. I wish to extend this wonder beyond the formal boundaries of works of art, just as I wish to intensify resonance within those boundaries.

It will be easier to grasp the concepts of resonance and wonder if we think of the way in which our culture presents to itself not the textual traces of its past but the surviving visual traces, for the latter are put on display in galleries and museums specially designed for the purpose. By resonance I mean the power of the object displayed to reach out beyond its formal boundaries to a larger world, to evoke in the viewer the complex, dynamic cultural forces from which it has emerged and for which as metaphor or more simply as metonymy it may be taken by a viewer to stand. By wonder I mean the power of the object displayed to stop the viewer in his tracks, to convey an arresting sense of uniqueness, to evoke an exalted attention.

The new historicism obviously has distinct affinities with resonance; that is, its concern with literary texts has been to recover as far as possible the historical circumstances of their original production and consumption and to analyze the relationship between these circumstances and our own. New historicist critics have tried to understand the intersecting circumstances not as a stable, prefabricated background against which the literary texts can be placed, but as a dense network of evolving and often contradictory social forces. The idea is not to find outside the work of art some rock onto which literary interpretation can be securely chained but rather to situate the work in relation to other representational practices operative in the culture at a given moment in both its history and our own. In Louis Montrose's convenient formulation, the goal has been to grasp simultaneously the historicity of texts and the textuality of history.

Insofar as this approach, developed for literary interpretation, is at all applicable to visual traces, it would call for an attempt to reduce the isolation of individual "masterpieces," to illuminate the conditions of their making, to disclose the history of their appropriation and the circumstances in which they come to be displayed, to restore the tangibility, the openness, the permeability of boundaries that enabled the objects to come into being in the first place. An actual restoration of tangibility is obviously in most cases impossible, and the frames that enclose pictures are only the ultimate formal confirmation of the closing of the borders that marks the finishing of a work of art. But we need not take that finishing so entirely for granted; museums can and on occasion do make it easier imaginatively to recreate the work in its moment of openness.

That openness is linked to a quality of artifacts that museums obviously dread, their precariousness. But though it is perfectly reasonable for museums to protect their objects—I would not wish it any other way—precariousness is a rich source of resonance. Thomas Greene, who has written a sensitive book on what he calls the "vulnerable text," suggests that the symbolic wounding to which literature is prone may confer upon it power and fecundity. "The vulnerability of poetry," Greene argues, "stems from four basic conditions of language: its historicity, its dialogic function, its referential function, and its dependence on figuration."[9] Three of these conditions are different for the visual arts, in ways that would seem to reduce vulnerability: painting and sculpture may be detached more readily than language from both referentiality and figuration, and the pressures of contextual dialogue are diminished by the absence of an inherent *logos*, a constitutive word. But the fourth condition—historicity—is in the case of material artifacts vastly increased, indeed virtually literalized. Museums function, partly by design and partly in spite of themselves, as monuments to the fragility of cultures, to the fall of sustaining institutions and noble houses, the collapse of rituals, the evacuation of myths, the destructive effects of warfare, neglect, and corrosive doubt.

I am fascinated by the signs of alteration, tampering, even destructiveness which many museums try simply to efface: first and most obviously, the act of displacement that is essential for the collection of virtually all older artifacts and most modern ones—pulled out of chapels, peeled off church walls, removed from decaying houses, seized as spoils of war, stolen, "purchased" more or less fairly by the economically ascendent from the economically naive, the poor, the hard-pressed heirs of fallen dynasties and impoverished religious orders. Then too there are the marks on the artifacts themselves: the attempt to scratch out or deface the image of the devil in numerous late-medieval and Renaissance paintings, the concealing of the genitals in sculptured and painted figures, the iconoclastic smashing of human or divine representations, the evidence of cutting or reshaping to fit a new frame or purpose, the cracks or scorch marks or broken-off noses that indifferently record the grand disasters of history and the random accidents of trivial incompetence. Even these accidents—

the marks of a literal fragility— can have their resonance: the climax of an absurdly hagiographical Proust exhibition several years ago was a display case holding a small, patched, modest vase with a notice, "This vase broken by Marcel Proust."

As this comical example suggests, wounded artifacts may be compelling not only as witnesses to the violence of history but as signs of use, marks of the human touch, and hence links with the openness to touch that was the condition of their creation. The most familiar way to recreate the openness of aesthetic artifacts without simply renewing their vulnerability is through a skillful deployment of explanatory texts in the catalogue, on the walls of the exhibit, or on cassettes. The texts so deployed introduce and in effect stand in for the context that has been effaced in the process of moving the object into the museum. But insofar as that context is partially, often primarily, visual as well as verbal, textual contextualism has its limits. Hence the mute eloquence of the display of the palette, brushes, and other implements that an artist of a given period would have employed or of objects that are represented in the exhibited paintings or of materials and images that in some way parallel or intersect with the formal works of art.

Among the most resonant moments are those in which the supposedly contextual objects take on a life of their own, make a claim that rivals that of the object that is formally privileged. A table, a chair, a map, often seemingly placed only to provide a decorative setting for a grand work, become oddly expressive, significant not as "background" but as compelling representational practices in themselves. These practices may in turn impinge upon the grand work, so that we begin to glimpse a kind of circulation: the cultural practice and social energy implicit in map-making drawn into the aesthetic orbit of a painting which has itself enabled us to register some of the representational significance of the map. Or again the threadbare fabric on the old chair or the gouges in the wood of a cabinet juxtapose the privileged painting or sculpture with marks not only of time but of use, the imprint of the human body on the artifact, and call attention to the deliberate removal of certain exalted aesthetic objects from the threat of that imprint.

For the effect of resonance does not necessarily depend upon a collapse of the distinction between art and non-art; it can be achieved by awakening in the viewer a sense of the cultural and historically contingent construction of art objects, the negotiations, exchanges, swerves, exclusions by which certain representational practices come to be set apart from other representational practices that they partially resemble. A resonant exhibition often pulls the viewer away from the celebration of isolated objects and toward a series of implied, only half-visible relationships and questions. How have the objects come to be displayed? What is at stake in categorizing them as of "museum-quality"? How were they originally used? What cultural and material conditions made possible their production? What were the feelings of those who originally held these objects, cherished them, collected them, possessed them? What is the meaning of my relationship to these same objects now that they are displayed here, in this museum, on this day?

It is time to give a more sustained example. Perhaps the most purely resonant museum I have ever seen is the State Jewish Museum in Prague. This is housed not in a single building but in a cluster of old synagogues scattered through the city's former Jewish Town. The oldest of these—known as the Old-New Synagogue—is a twin-nave medieval structure dating to the last third of the 13th century; the others are mostly Renaissance and Baroque. In these synagogues are displayed Judaica from 153 Jewish communities throughout Bohemia and Moravia. In one there is a permanent exhibition of synagogue silverworks, in another there are synagogue textiles, in a third there are Torah scrolls, ritual objects, manuscripts and prints illustrative of Jewish beliefs, traditions, and customs. One of the synagogues shows the work of the physician and artist Karel Fleischmann, principally drawings done in the Terezin concentration camp during his months of imprisonment prior to his deportation to Auschwitz. Next door in the Ceremonial Hall of the Prague Burial Society there is a wrenching exhibition of children's drawings from Terezin. Finally, one synagogue, closed at the time of my visit to Prague, has simply a wall of names—thousands of them—to commemorate the Jewish victims of Nazi persecution in Czechoslovakia.

"The Museum's rich collections of synagogue art and the historic synagogue buildings of Prague's Jewish town," says the catalogue of the State Jewish Museum, "form a memorial complex that has not been preserved to the same extent anywhere else in Europe." "A memorial complex"—this museum is not so much about artifacts as about memory, and the form the memory takes is a secularized kaddish, a commemorative prayer for the dead. The atmosphere has a peculiar effect on the act of viewing. It is mildly interesting to note the differences between the mordant Grosz-like lithographs of Karel Fleischmann in the pre-war years and the tormented style, at once detached and anguished, of the drawings in the camps, but aesthetic discriminations feel weird, out-of-place. And it seems wholly absurd, even indecent, to worry about the relative artistic merits of the drawings that survive by children who did not survive.

The discordance between viewing and remembering is greatly reduced with the older, less emotionally charged artifacts, but even here the ritual objects in their glass cases convey an odd and desolate impression. The oddity, I suppose, should be no greater than in seeing a Mayan god or, for that matter, a pyx or a ciborium, but we have become so familiarized to the display of such objects, so accustomed to considering them works of art, that even pious Catholics, as far as I know, do not necessarily feel disconcerted by their transformation from ritual function to aesthetic exhibition. And until very recently the voices of the tribal peoples who might have objected to the display of their religious artifacts have not been heard and certainly not attended to.

The Jewish objects are neither sufficiently distant to be absorbed into the detached ethos of anthropological display nor sufficiently familiar to be framed and encased alongside the altarpieces and reliquaries that fill Western museums. And moving as they are as mnemonic devices, most of the ritual objects in the State Jewish Museum are not, by contrast with Christian liturgical art, particularly remarkable either for their antiquity or their extraordinary beauty. They are the products of a people with a resistance to joining figural representation to religious observance, a strong anti-iconic bias. The objects have, as it were, little will to be observed; many of them are artifacts—ark curtains, Torah crowns, breastplates, pointers, and the like—whose purpose was to be drawn back or removed in order to make possible the act that mattered: not vision but reading.

But the inhibition of viewing in the Jewish Museum is paradoxically bound up with its resonance. This resonance depends not upon visual stimulation but upon a felt intensity of names, and behind the names, as the very term resonance suggests, of voices: the voices of those who chanted, studied, muttered their prayers, wept, and then were forever silenced. And mingled with these voices are others—of those Jews in 1389 who were murdered in the Old-New Synagogue where they were seeking refuge; of the great sixteenth-century Kabbalist, Jehuda ben Bezalel, known as Rabbi Loew, who is fabled to have created the Golem; of the twentieth-century's ironic Kabbalist, Franz Kafka.

It is Kafka who would be most likely to grasp imaginatively the State Jewish Museum's ultimate source of resonance: the fact that most of the objects are located in the museum—were displaced, preserved, and transformed categorically into works of art—because the Nazis stored the articles they confiscated in the Prague synagogues that they chose to preserve for this very purpose. In 1941 the Nazi Hochschule in Frankfurt had established an Institute for the Exploration of the Jewish Question which in turn had initiated a massive effort to confiscate Jewish libraries, archives, religious artifacts, and personal property. By the middle of 1942 Heydrich, as Hitler's chief officer within the so-called Protectorate of Bohemia and Moravia, had chosen Prague as the site of the Central Bureau for Dealing with the Jewish Question, and an SS officer, Untersturmführer Karl Rahm, had assumed control of the small existing Jewish museum, founded in 1912, which was renamed the Central Jewish Museum. The new charter of the museum announced that "the numerous, hitherto scattered Jewish possessions of both historical and artistic value, on the territory of the entire Protectorate, must be collected and stored."[10]

During the following months, tens of thousands of confiscated items arrived, the dates of the shipments closely coordinated with the "donors' " deportation to the concentration camps. The experts formally employed by the original Jewish museum were compelled to catalogue the items, and the Nazis compounded this immense task by also ordering the wretched, malnourished curators to prepare a collections guide and organize private exhibitions for SS staff. Between September 1942 and October 1943 four major exhibitions were mounted. Since these required far more space than the existing Jewish Museum's modest location, the great old Prague synagogues—made vacant by the Nazi prohibition of Jewish public worship—were partially refurbished for the occasion. Hence in March 1943, for example, in the seventeenth-century Klaus Synagogue, there was an exhibition of Jewish festival and life-cycle observances; "when Sturmbannführer Günther first toured the collection on April 6, he demanded various changes, including the translation of all Hebrew texts and the addition of an exhibit on kosher butchering" (*Precious Legacy*, p. 36). Plans were drawn up for other exhibitions, but the curators—who had given themselves to the task with a strange blend of selflessness, irony, helplessness, and heroism—were themselves at this point sent to concentration camps and murdered.

After the war, the few survivors of the Czech Jewish community apparently felt they could not sustain the ritual use of the synagogues or maintain the large collections. In 1949 the Jewish Community Council offered as a gift to the Czechoslovak government both the synagogues and their contents. These became the resonant, impure "memorial complex" they are—a cultural machine that generates an uncontrollable oscillation between homage and desecration, longing and hopelessness, the voices of the dead and silence. For resonance, like nostalgia, is impure, a hybrid forged in the barely acknowledged gaps, the cesurae, between words like State, Jewish, and Museum.

I want to avoid the implication that resonance must be necessarily linked to destruction and absence; it can be found as well in unexpected survival. The key is the intimation of a larger community of voices and skills, an imagined ethnographic thickness. Here another example will serve: in the Yucatan there is an extensive, largely unexcavated late-Classic Maya site called Coba, whose principal surviving feature is a high pyramid known as Nahoch Mul. After a day of tramping around the site, I was relaxing in the pool of the nearby Club Med Archaeological Villa in the company of a genial structural engineer from Little Rock. To make conversation, I asked my pool-mate what he as a structural engineer thought of Nahoch Mul. "From an engineer's point of view," he replied, "a pyramid is not very interesting—it's just an enormous gravity structure." "But," he added, "did you notice that Coca Cola stand on the way in? That's the most impressive example of contemporary Maya architecture I've ever seen." I thought it quite possible that my leg was being pulled, but I went back the next day to check—I had, of course, completely blocked out the Coke stand on my first visit. Sure enough, some enterprising Mayan had built a remarkably elegant shelter with a soaring pyramidal roof constructed out of ingeniously intertwining sticks and branches. Places like Coba are thick with what Spenser called the Ruins of Time—with a nostalgia for a lost civilization, in a state of collapse long before Cortés or Montejo cut their paths through the jungle. But, despite frequent colonial attempts to drive them or imagine them out of existence, the Maya have not in fact vanished, and a single entrepreneur's architectural improvisation suddenly had more resonance for me than the mounds of the 'lost' city.

My immediate thought was that the whole Coca Cola stand could be shipped to New York and put on display in the Museum of Modern Art. And that impulse moves us away from resonance and toward wonder. For the MOMA is one of the great contemporary places not for the hearing of intertwining voices, not for historical memory, not for ethnographic thickness, but for intense, indeed enchanting looking. Looking may be called enchanted when the act of attention draws a circle around itself from which everything but the object is excluded, when intensity of regard blocks out all circumambient images, stills all murmuring voices. To be sure, the viewer may have purchased a catalogue, read an inscription on the wall, switched on a cassette, but in the moment of wonder all of this apparatus seems mere static.

The so-called boutique lighting that has become popular in recent years—a pool of light that has the surreal effect of seeming to emerge from within the object rather than to focus upon it from without—is an attempt to provoke or to heighten the experience of wonder, as if modern museum designers feared that wonder was increasingly difficult to arouse or perhaps that it risked displacement entirely onto the windows of designer dress shops and antique stores. The association of that lighting—along with transparent plastic rods and other devices to create the magical illusion of luminous, weightless suspension—with commerce would seem to suggest that wonder is bound up with acquisition and possession, yet the whole experience of most art museums is about *not* touching, *not* carrying home, *not* owning the marvelous objects. Modern museums in effect at once evoke the dream of possession and evacuate it.[11] (Alternatively, we could say that they displace that dream onto the museum gift shop, where the boutique lighting once again serves to heighten acquisition, now of reproductions that stand for the unattainable works of art.)

That evacuation or displacement is an historical rather than structural aspect of the museum's regulation of wonder: that is, collections of objects calculated to arouse wonder arose precisely in the spirit of personal acquisition and were only subsequently detached from it. In the Middle Ages and Renaissance we characteristically hear about wonders in the context of those who possessed them (or who gave them away). Hence, for example, in his *Life of Saint Louis*, Joinville writes that "during the king's stay at Saida someone brought him a stone that split into flakes":

> It was the most marvelous stone in the world, for when you lifted one of the flakes you found the form of a sea-fish between the two pieces of stone. This fish was entirely of stone, but there was nothing lacking in its shape, eyes, bones, or colour to make it seem otherwise than if it had been alive. The king gave me one of these stones. I found a tench inside; it was brown in colour, and in every detail exactly as you would expect a tench to be.[12]

The wonder-cabinets of the Renaissance were at least as much about possession as display. The wonder derived not only from what could be seen but from the sense that the shelves and cases were filled with unseen wonders, all the prestigious property of the collector. In this sense, the cult of wonder originated in close conjunction with a certain type of resonance, a resonance bound up with the evocation not of an absent culture but of the great man's superfluity of rare and precious things. Those things were not necessarily admired for their beauty; the marvelous was bound up with the excessive, the surprising, the literally outlandish, the prodigious. They were not necessarily the manifestations of the artistic skill of human makers: technical virtuosity could indeed arouse admiration, but so could nautilus shells, ostrich eggs, uncannily large (or small) bones, stuffed crocodiles, fossils.

trich eggs, uncannily large (or small) bones, stuffed crocodiles, fossils. And, most importantly, they were not necessarily objects set out for careful viewing.

The experience of wonder was not initially regarded as essentially or even primarily *visual; reports* of marvels had a force equal to the seeing of them. Seeing was important and desirable, of course, but precisely in order to make reports possible, reports which then circulated as virtual equivalents of the marvels themselves. The great medieval collections of marvels are almost entirely textual: Friar Jordanus's *Marvels of the East*, Marco Polo's *Book of Marvels*, Mandeville's *Travels*. Some of the manuscripts, to be sure, were illuminated, but these illuminations were almost always ancillary to the textual record of wonders, just as emblem books were originally textual and only subsequently illustrated. Even in the sixteenth century, when the power of direct visual experience was increasingly valued, the marvelous was principally theorized as a textual phenomenon, as it had been in antiquity. "No one can be called a poet," writes the influential Italian critic Minturno in the 1550s, "who does not excel in the power of arousing wonder."[13] For Aristotle wonder was associated with pleasure as the end of poetry, and in the *Poetics* he examined the strategies by which tragedians and epic poets employ the marvelous to arouse wonder. For the Platonists too wonder was conceived as an essential element in literary art: in the sixteenth century, the Neo-Platonist Francesco Patrizi defined the poet as principal "maker of the marvelous," and the marvelous is found, as he put it, when men "are astounded, ravished in ecstasy." Patrizi goes so far as to posit marvelling as a special faculty of the mind, a faculty which in effect mediates between the capacity to think and the capacity to feel.[14]

Modern art museums reflect a profound transformation of the experience: the collector—a Getty or a Mellon—may still be celebrated, and market value is even more intensely registered, but the heart of the mystery lies with the uniqueness, authenticity, and visual power of the masterpiece, ideally displayed in such a way as to heighten its charisma, to compel and reward the intensity of the viewer's gaze, to manifest artistic genius. Museums display works of art in such a way as to imply that no one, not even the nominal owner or donor, can penetrate the zone of light and actually possess the wonderful object. The object exists not principally to be owned but to be viewed. Even the *fantasy* of possession is no longer central to the museum-gaze, or rather it has been inverted, so that the object in its essence seems not to be a possession but rather to be itself the possessor of what is most valuable and enduring.[15] What the work possesses is the power to arouse wonder, and that power, in the dominant aesthetic ideology of the West, has been infused into it by the creative genius of the artist.

It is beyond the scope of this essay to account for the transformation of the experience of wonder from the spectacle of proprietorship to the mystique of the object—an exceedingly complex, overdetermined history centering on institutional and economic shifts—but I think it is important to say that at least in part this transformation was shaped by the collective project of Western artists and reflects their vision. Already in the early sixteenth century, when the marvelous was still principally associated with the prodigious, Dürer begins, in a famous journal entry describing Mexican objects sent to Charles V by Cortés, to reconceive it:

> I saw the things which have been brought to the King from the new golden land: a sun all of gold a whole fathom broad, and a moon all of silver of the same size, also two rooms full of the armour of the people there, and all manner of wondrous weapons of theirs, harness and darts, wonderful shields, strange clothing, bedspreads, and all kinds of wonderful objects of various uses, much more beautiful to behold than prodigies. These things were all so precious that they have been valued at one hundred thousand gold florins. All the days of my life I have seen nothing that has gladdened my heart so much as these things, for I saw amongst them wonderful works of art, and I marvelled at the subtle *ingenia* of men in foreign lands. Indeed, I cannot express all that I thought there.[16]

Dürer's description is full of the conventional marks of his period's sense of wonder: he finds it important that the artifacts have been brought as a kind of tribute to the king, that large quantities of precious metals have been used, that their market value has been reckoned; he notes the strangeness of them, even as he uncritically assimilates that strangeness to his own culture's repertory of objects (which include harness and bedspreads). But he also notes, in perceptions highly unusual for his own time, that these objects are "much more beautiful to behold than prodigies." Dürer relocates the source of wonder from the outlandish to the aesthetic, and he understands the effect of beauty as a testimony to creative genius: "I saw amongst them wonderful works of art, and I marvelled at the subtle *ingenia* of men in foreign lands."

It would be misleading to strip away the relations of power and wealth that are encoded in the artist's response, but it would be still more misleading, I think, to interpret that response as an unmediated expression of those relations. For Dürer gives voice to an aesthetic understanding—a form of wondering and admiring and knowing—that is at least partly independent of the structures of politics and the marketplace.

This understanding—by no means autonomous and yet not reducible to the institutional and economic forces by which it is shaped—is centered on a certain kind of looking, a looking whose origins lie in the cult of the marvelous and hence in the art work's capacity to generate in the spectator surprise, delight, admiration, and intimations of genius. The knowledge that derives from this kind of looking may not be very useful in the attempt to understand another culture, but it is vitally important in the attempt to understand our own. For it is one of the distinctive achievements of our culture to have fashioned this type of gaze, and one of the most intense pleasures that it has to offer. This pleasure does not have an inherent and necessary politics, either radical or imperialist, but Dürer's remarks suggest that it originates at least in respect and admiration for the *ingenia* of others. This respect is a response worth cherishing and enhancing. Hence, for all of my academic affiliations and interests, I am skeptical about the recent attempt to turn our museums from temples of wonder into temples of resonance.

Perhaps the most startling instance of this attempt is the transfer of the paintings in the Jeu de Paume and the Louvre to the new Musée d'Orsay. The Musée d'Orsay is at once a spectacular manifestation of French cultural *dépense* and a highly self-conscious, exceptionally stylish generator of resonance, including the literal resonance of voices in an enormous vaulted railway station. By moving the Impressionist and Post-Impressionist masterpieces into proximity with the work of far less well-known painters—Jean Béraud, Guillaume Dubuffe, Paul Sérusier, and so forth—and into proximity as well with the period's sculpture and decorative arts, the museum remakes a remarkable group of highly individuated geniuses into engaged participants in a vital, conflict-ridden, immensely productive period in French cultural history. The reimagining is guided by many well-designed informative boards—cue cards, in effect—along, of course, with the extraordinary building itself.

All of this is intelligently conceived and dazzlingly executed—on a cold winter day in Paris, the museum-goer may look down from one of the high balconies by the old railway clocks and savor the swirling pattern formed by the black and gray raincoats of the spectators below, as they pass through the openings in the massive black stone partitions of Gay Aulenti's interior. The pattern seems spontaneously to animate the period's style—if not Manet, then at least Caillebotte; it is as if a painted scene had recovered the power to move and to echo.

But what has been sacrificed on the altar of cultural resonance is visual wonder centered on the aesthetic masterpiece. Attention is dispersed among a wide range of lesser objects that collectively articulate the impressive creative achievement of French culture in the late nineteenth century, but the experience of the old Jeu de Paume— intense looking at Manet, Monet, Cézanne and so forth—has been radically reduced. The paintings are there, but they are mediated by the resonant contextualism of the building itself and its myriad objects and its descriptive and analytical plaques. Moreover, many of the greatest paintings have been demoted, as it were, to small spaces where it is difficult to view them adequately—as if the design of the museum were trying to assure the triumph of resonance over wonder.

But is a triumph of one over the other necessary? I have, for the purposes of this exposition, obviously exaggerated the extent to which these are alternative models for museums (or for the reading of texts): in fact, almost every exhibition worth the viewing has strong elements of both. I think that the impact of most exhibitions is likely to be greater if the initial appeal is wonder, a wonder that then leads to the desire for resonance, for it is easier to pass from wonder to resonance than from resonance to wonder. Why this should be so is suggested by a remarkable passage in his *Commentary on the Metaphysics of Aristotle* by Aquinas's teacher, Albert the Great:

> wonder is defined as a constriction and suspension of the heart caused by amazement at the sensible appearance of something so portentous, great, and unusual, that the heart suffers a systole. Hence wonder is something like fear in its effect on the heart. This effect of wonder, then, this constriction and systole of the heart, spring from an unfulfilled but felt desire to know the cause of that which appears portentous and unusual: so it was in the beginning when men, up to that time unskilled, began to philosophize. . . . Now the man who is puzzled and wonders apparently does not know. Hence wonder is the movement of the man who does not know on his way to finding out, to get at the bottom of that at which he wonders and to determine its cause. . . . Such is the origin of philosophy.[17]

Such too, from the perspective of the new historicism, is the origin of a meaningful desire for cultural resonance. But while philosophy would seek to supplant wonder with secure knowledge, it is the function of the new historicism continually to renew the marvelous at the heart of the resonant.

## Notes

1.  George Cavendish, *The Life and Death of Cardinal Wolsey*, in *Two Early Tudor Lives*, ed. Richard S. Sylvester and Davis P. Harding (New Haven

*Tudor Lives,* ed. Richard S. Sylvester and Davis P. Harding (New Haven and London: Yale University Press, 1962), pp. 24–25. We get another glimpse of the symbolism of hats later in the text, when Wolsey is beginning his precipitous fall from power: "And talking with Master Norris upon his knees in the mire, he would have pulled off his under cap of velvet, but he could not undo the knot under his chin. Wherefore with violence he rent the laces and pulled it from his head and so kneeled bareheaded" (p. 106). I am grateful to Anne Barton for correcting my description of the hat in Christ Church and for transcribing the note card that details its provenance.

2. Walter Cohen, "Political Criticism of Shakespeare," in *Shakespeare Reproduced: The Text in History and Ideology,* ed. Jean E. Howard and Marion F. O'Connor (New York and London: Methuen, 1987), p. 33; Edward Pechter, "The New Historicism and Its Discontents," in *PLMA* 102 (1987), p. 301.

3. "The new historicists and cultural materialists," one typical summary puts it, "represent, and by representing, reproduce in their *new* history of ideas, a world which is hierarchical, authoritarian, hegemonic, unsubvertable. . . . In this world picture, Stephen Greenblatt has poignantly asserted, there can be no subversion—and certainly not for *us!*" Poignantly or otherwise, I asserted no such thing; I argued that the spectator of the history plays was continually tantalized by a resistance simultaneously powerful and deferred.

4. See my *Renaissance Self-Fashioning: from More to Shakespeare* (Chicago: University of Chicago Press, 1980), pp. 174–75: "We are situated at the close of the cultural movement initiated in the Renaissance; the places in which our social and psychological world seems to be cracking apart are those structural joints visible when it was first constructed."

5. Louis Adrian Montrose, "Renaissance Literary Studies and the Subject of History," in *English Literary Renaissance* 16 (1986), pp. 5–12; Don Wayne, "Power, Politics, and the Shakespearean Text: Recent Criticism in England and the United States," in *Shakespeare Reproduced: The Text in History and Ideology,* ed. Howard and O'Connor, pp. 47–67; Catherine Gallagher, "Marxism and the New Historicism," in *The New Historicism,* ed. Harold Veeser (New York and London: Routledge, 1989).

6. Jean E. Howard, "The New Historicism in Renaissance Studies," in *Renaissance Historicism: Selections from "English Literary Renaissance,"* ed. Arthur F. Kinney and Dan S. Collins (Amherst: University of Massachusetts Press, 1987), pp. 32–33.

7. If there is then no suspension of value judgments in the new historicism, there is at the same time a complication of those judgments, what I have called a sense of estrangement. This estrangement is bound up with the abandonment of a belief in historical inevitability, for, with this abandonment, the values of the present could no longer seem the necessary outcome of an irreversible teleological progression, whether of en-

lightenment or decline. An older historicism that proclaimed self-consciously that it had avoided all value judgments in its account of the past—that it had given us historical reality *wie es eigentlich gewesen*—did not thereby avoid all value judgments; it simply provided a misleading account of what it had actually done. In this sense the new historicism, for all its acknowledgment of engagement and partiality, may be slightly less likely than the older historicism to impose its values belligerently on the past, for those values seem historically contingent.

8. Cohen, in *Shakespeare Reproduced*, pp. 33–34.

9. Thomas Greene, *The Vulnerable Text: Essays on Renaissance Literature* (New York: Columbia University Press, 1986), p. 100.

10. Quoted in Linda A. Altshuler and Anna R. Cohn, "The Precious Legacy," in David Altshuler, ed., *The Precious Legacy: Judaic Treasures from the Czechoslovak State Collections* (New York: Summit Books, 1983), p. 24. My sketch of the genesis of the State Jewish Museum is largely paraphrased from this chapter.

11. In effect that dream of possessing wonder is at once aroused and evacuated in commerce as well, since the minute the object—shoe or dress or soup tureen—is removed from its magical pool of light, it loses its wonder and returns to the status of an ordinary purchase.

12. Joinville, *Life of Saint Louis*, in *Chronicles of the Crusades*, trans. M.R.B. Shaw (Harmondsworth: Penguin, 1963), p. 315.

13. Quoted in J.V. Cunningham, *Woe or Wonder: The Emotional Effect of Shakespearean Tragedy* (Denver: Alan Swallow, 1960; orig. ed. 1951), p. 82.

14. Hathaway, pp. 66–69. Hathaway's account of Patrizi is taken largely from Bernard Weinberg, *A History of Literary Criticism in the Italian Renaissance*, 2 vols. (Chicago: University of Chicago Press, 1961).

15. It is a mistake then to associate the gaze of the museum-goer with the appropriative male gaze about which so much has been written recently. But then I think that the discourse of the appropriative male gaze is itself in need of considerable qualification.

16. Quoted in Hugh Honour, *The New Golden Land: European Images of America from the Discoveries to the Present Time* (New York: Pantheon Books, 1975), p. 28.

17. Quoted in Cunningham, pp. 77–78.

184